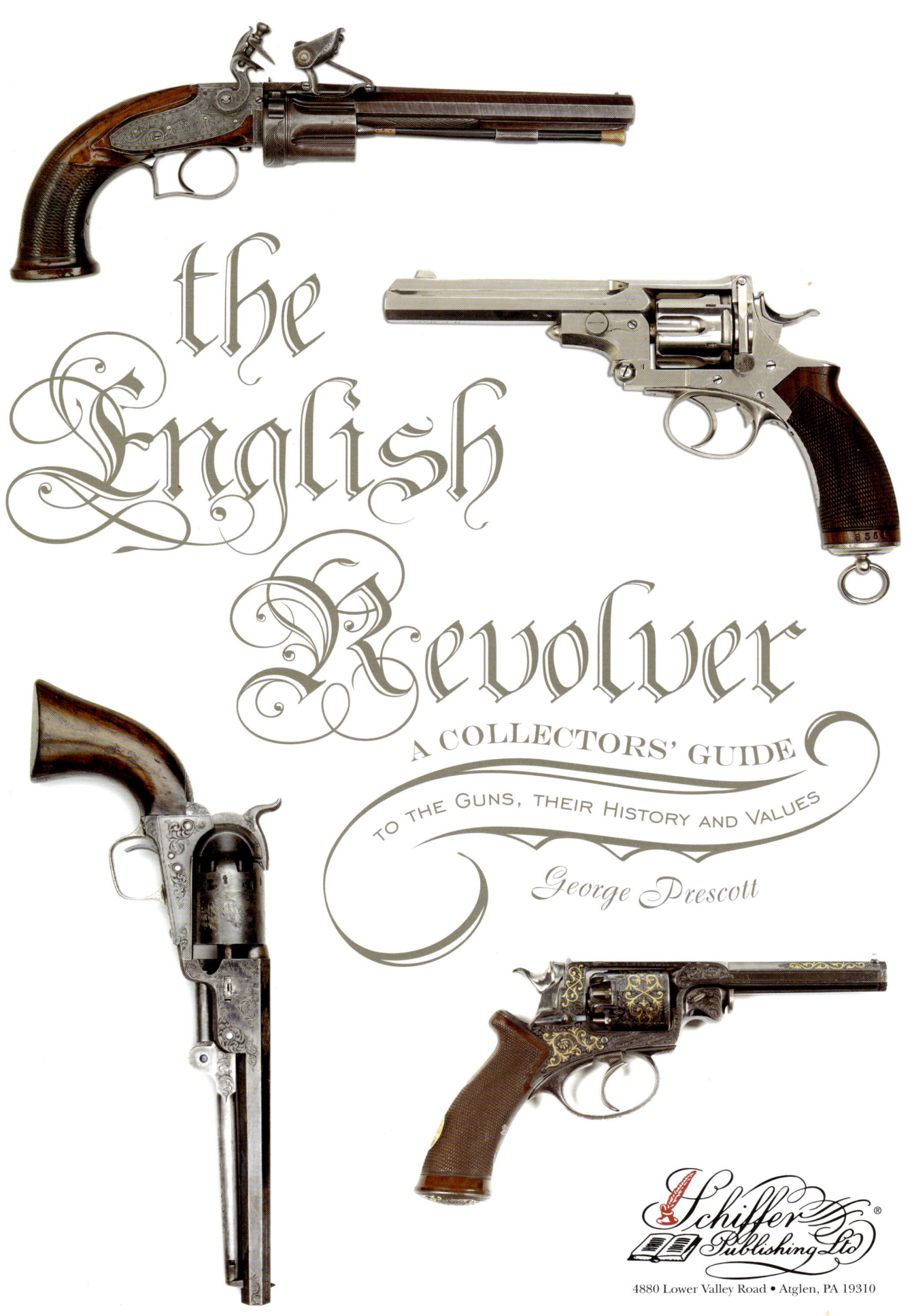

Copyright © 2014 by George Prescott

Library of Congress Control Number: 2014953206

All rights reserved. No part of this work may be reproduced or used in any form or by any means—graphic, electronic, or mechanical, including photocopying or information storage and retrieval systems—without written permission from the publisher.

The scanning, uploading, and distribution of this book or any part thereof via the Internet or via any other means without the permission of the publisher is illegal and punishable by law. Please purchase only authorized editions and do not participate in or encourage the electronic piracy of copyrighted materials.
"Schiffer," "Schiffer Publishing, Ltd. & Design," and the "Design of pen and inkwell" are registered trademarks of Schiffer Publishing, Ltd.

Designed by Justin Watkinson
Type set in Carol Etched/Minion Pro

ISBN: 978-0-7643-4757-3
Printed in China

Published by Schiffer Publishing, Ltd.
4880 Lower Valley Road
Atglen, PA 19310
Phone: (610) 593-1777; Fax: (610) 593-2002
E-mail: Info@schifferbooks.com

For our complete selection of fine books on this and related subjects, please visit our website at www.schifferbooks.com. You may also write for a free catalog.

This book may be purchased from the publisher. Please try your bookstore first.

We are always looking for people to write books on new and related subjects. If you have an idea for a book, please contact us at proposals@schifferbooks.com.

Schiffer Publishing's titles are available at special discounts for bulk purchases for sales promotions or premiums. Special editions, including personalized covers, corporate imprints, and excerpts can be created in large quantities for special needs. For more information, contact the publisher.

Contents

ACKNOWLEDGMENTS 6

INTRODUCTION 7

CHAPTER ONE: ENGLISH REVOLVERS 9
    Revolver characteristics 14
    Glossary 15

CHAPTER TWO: SMALLER ENGLISH REVOLVER MANUFACTURERS 18

CHAPTER THREE: ADAMS AND BEAUMONT-ADAMS REVOLVERS 49
    Robert Adams 49
    The London Armoury Company 49
    The Adams revolver 52
    The Beaumont-Adams revolver 56
    Other makers 60

CHAPTER FOUR: TRANTER REVOLVERS 65
    William Tranter 65
    Tranter Percussion Revolvers 65
    Tranter Cartridge Revolvers 72
    The Kynoch Revolvers 77

CHAPTER FIVE:	WEBLEY REVOLVERS	78
	The Birmingham Gun Trade and the Webley Brothers	78
	Webley Longspur Percussion Revolvers	78
	Webley and Webley-Bentley Self-Cocking Percussion Revolvers	86
	Webley Double-Action Percussion Revolvers	88
	Webley Metal-Cartridge Revolvers	91
	Webley Solid-Frame Cartridge Revolvers	95
	Webley Hinge-Frame Cartridge Revolvers	104
CHAPTER SIX:	ENGLISH MILITARY PISTOLS AND REVOLVERS	119
	Flintlock and Percussion Tower Pistols	119
	Colt and Adams Military Percussion Revolvers	120
	John Adams Military Revolvers	123
	The First Enfield Revolver	126
	Webley Government Issue Revolvers	127
	Enfield Government Issue Revolvers	134
	Government Issue Revolver Cartridges	137
CHAPTER SEVEN:	ACCESSORIES	139
	Revolver Cases	139
	Cartridges and Cartridge Boxes	144

CHAPTER EIGHT:	COLLECTING ANTIQUE REVOLVERS	145
	What is An Antique Firearm ?	145
	What to Look For	145
	NRA Condition Guidelines	146

APPENDIX ONE:	PROOF MARKS	148
	London Gun Maker's Company	148
	Tower Proof marks	149
	Birmingham Proof House	150
	Liege and Other Foreign Marks	151
	Shooting Antique Guns	152

ENDNOTES	153
BIBLIOGRAPHY	156
INDEX	158

Acknowledgments

The author would like to thank the following for granting permission to use many of the pictures included in this book:

- Bonhams (website: www.bonhams.com), for kind permission to use their images.
- Thomas Del Mar Ltd (website: www.thomasdelmar.com)
- James D. Julia Auctioneers, Fairfield, Maine (www.jamesdjulia. com), and most especially their graphic designer, Miss Lisa Oakes, for her invaluable help and unfailing kindness.
- Joel Black, for supplying the images of rare Webley revolvers from his collection.
- Michael Meuwly, for supplying the images of the early Manhattan pepperbox and the .22 caliber revolver.
- Bolk Antiques (website: www.bolk-antiques.nl)
- Horst Held (website: www.horstheld.com)
- Collectible Firearms (website: www.collectiblefirearms.com)
- Peter Finer: Antique Arms and Armour (website:www.peterfiner.com).
- National Firearms Museum (website: www.nramuseum.com)
- Mr. Ronald Birnie
- Mr. Stewart Chamberlain
- Mr. John R. McLean

Special thanks to Kerry Guerin, of the Firearms Technology Museum, who supplied much of the information about and many of the images of Tranter revolvers (www.firearmsmuseum.org.au).

Introduction

The weapons described in this book were manufactured in a period from the beginning of the nineteenth century to 1942, where the book finishes with the Enfield No2, MkI** revolver.

From 1851—when Adams sold his first revolvers—to 1868 and the appearance of the first of Webley's metal cartridge revolvers, the English revolver industry bore little resemblance to its highly mechanized American competitor. With the exception of the three big manufacturers (Adams, Tranter, and Webley), revolvers were usually hand-made by independent gunmakers based in London or Birmingham, in small factories or even smaller workshops. The total number of percussion weapons produced, aside from military sales and excluding Colt's London products, was probably less than 100,000 weapons, perhaps much less. Compare this to the output of the Colt factory, which produced over 300,000 of their Pocket Model alone between 1849 and 1873.

By the latter part of the nineteenth century, metal cartridge weapons were becoming universal, although in Britain by this time the need for firearms designed for personal protection had all but disappeared. Consequently, the English firearms industry, during that latter period, concerned itself mainly with the manufacture of military longarms and sporting weapons, together with some specialist firearms. Revolver manufacture was confined to weapons produced by a few smaller firms, such as Tranter and Webley, for private purchase, export, or military use. Military weapons are encountered both as weapons supplied as part of an Ordnance Department contract and private purchases by officers dissatisfied with issue revolvers.

This book is consequently concerned mainly with early percussion weapons, although the metal cartridge arms of Webley and Tranter are described. The percussion model of LeMat's extraordinary grapeshot revolver is also included here, because there is at least some evidence to suggest that the arm was copied in the Birmingham gun district. Besides, the revolver and its history are exceedingly interesting, which should be sufficient excuse for its inclusion!

Clearly, this is not intended to be a complete discussion of the development of the English revolver during the period covered, because the nature of their early production, at almost the level of a cottage industry, makes a detailed, systematic study difficult. Rather, it is an identification guide that will allow most English revolvers encountered to be correctly identified, although some of the more obscure variations may present difficulties; this being particularly the case in the section dealing with the Webley metal cartridge revolvers. It also provides information of historical interest which may serve as a starting point for further research. Detailed mechanical descriptions of lockwork, for example, have been deliberately excluded, but the bibliography includes texts where such details are available. Pollard and Flayderman's books serve as an excellent starting point for the beginning firearms collector and it would be advisable to buy both before spending money on any sort of firearm.

VALUES

Values quoted in this book are those found for the revolvers sold at UK or U.S. auctions between 2007 and 2012 and are included only as a rough guide. A gun's value is subject to so many conditions that on the day of a sale the prices quoted may vary significantly, in some cases very significantly from those which a seller will actually realize.

In order to obtain a reasonable estimate of the value of any of the revolvers described here, it is best to consult several current websites and/or dealers to determine exactly what price a particular specimen is fetching before buying or selling.

Nock flintlock pepperbox. Hand rotated, each chamber was primed via the pan before it could be fired. *By kind permission of Bonhams.*

CHAPTER ONE

English Revolvers

Repeating or revolving firearms have been manufactured in Britain from about 1770, in the form of both multi-barreled weapons and single-barreled arms equipped with some form of multiple charge carrier. Henry Nock is particularly well known as a maker of this type of weapon, producing a seven-shot "volley gun" which saw use with the Navy, and a sturdy, small-caliber flintlock pepperbox with seven barrels that were turned by hand.

Conventional revolver manufacture really began in 1818, with a flintlock weapon produced by American Elisha Collier. Repeating arms had been seen previously as too unreliable to be seriously considered as a weapon, with mechanisms unsuitable for hard, extended use. Collier's more robust design, with its helical screw turning the cylinder and the positive indexing between barrel and firing chamber, changed this attitude and the gun became very popular with many who tried it. Unfortunately, the mechanism that automatically turned the cylinder when the hammer was cocked gave so much trouble that Collier dispensed with it in later guns and reverted to turning the cylinder by hand.

Sam Colt may have bought one of these revolvers somewhere during his travels and it was claimed that he used some of the features in his early Paterson revolvers. Apart from the use of a revolving cylinder to deliver successive loads to the barrel, however, the mechanism of Colt's revolvers does not share any significant features with Collier's weapon; at least, that was the decision of the U.S courts, when Colt sued the Massachusetts Arms Co. for patent infringement and won.[1]

It was Colt's invention of the linked hammer and cylinder pawl mechanism that was the next major step forward in revolver development. Unfortunately, his "Paterson" Model revolvers proved too complex and prone to stoppages to be reliable military weapons and poor sales put Colt's first revolver company at Paterson out of business. The appearance of the giant "Walker" Colt and its acceptance for use in the Mexican-American war allowed Colt to re-establish himself in a riverside factory at Hartford, Connecticut, and it was from these premises that he launched first the Dragoon, then the hugely successful Pocket and Navy Models. Colt sold well over half a million of these last two revolvers and from then on his success was assured.

He came to England in 1851, to exhibit his revolvers at the Great Exhibition, only to find himself faced with some stiff competition. Robert Adams had designed a robust, solid-framed, self-cocking revolver that he was marketing in opposition to Colt's product. Adams was not averse to learning from his rival, either, and he and his partners, the Deanes, had installed machinery in their factory to improve the speed of production of their revolver.

Proof figures from the London House confirm the revolver's increasing popularity after 1851. Beginning that year, 954 revolvers were submitted for proof, with this figure increasing over six-fold in 1852, to 6,121 weapons. There was a further increase in 1853 to 13,916, clearly showing the sudden rise in their popularity. These figures include Colt and Adams revolvers, as well as pepperbox and transition weapons, so determining what proportion of the year's output was represented by each design is difficult.[2]

EARLY REVOLVER TECHNOLOGY

In the period before 1851, most of the revolving arms produced in Britain were handmade, percussion "pepperbox" revolvers. These weapons consisted of a bar hammer or under hammer lock, usually self-cocking, with an arbor attached, around which a collection of barrels revolved.

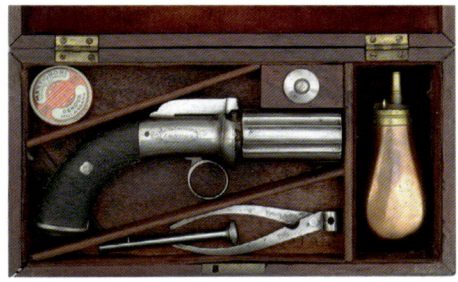

Cased London pepperbox with bullet mold and metal rammer. *By kind permission of Bonhams.*

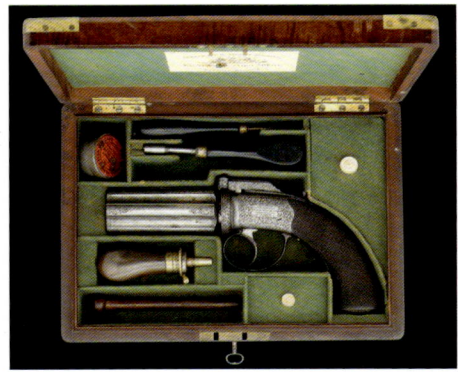

Cased English pepperbox. As with the later revolvers, cased pepperboxes came with a very complete set of accessories, including, in this case, a wooden rammer. *Courtesy of Thomas del Mar Ltd.*

Manhattan 3-barreled pepperbox, from the right. This is a hand-turned American weapon, but its conformation is similar to English guns of the same type. *Courtesy of Mike Meuwly.*

Manhattan 3-barreled pepperbox from the left. *Courtesy of Mike Meuwly.*

Pepperboxes were produced with three, five, and six barrels, with each barrel being loaded, then capped, before the weapon was ready to fire. Makers of such arms were numerous and an extensive list is included in Taylerson.[3] These pepperbox revolvers were the basis for the later "transition" pattern revolver—a development in revolver technology that paralleled Colt and Adam's weapons.

Early examples of this type were open-framed, with a self-cocking bar hammer, the primitive mechanism for which was contained in a lock frame, to which the arbor was attached. A five- or six-chambered cylinder with vertical percussion cones revolved upon this arbor, the barrel locating over the end and secured by a wedge, screws, or a "wing" nut to the single, lower frame bar. A final modification to the lock mechanism, in the form of a "pin stop" fitted to the trigger, crudely indexed the cylinder in line with the barrel, although users may well have felt the need to confirm the indexing of the cylinder by hand. Given the conformation of many transition revolvers, it is tempting to assume that at least some could have been produced by converting pepperbox revolvers. However, this does not appear to be the case, as there has only been one recorded example of such a conversion.[4] The cost and practical problems involved also seem to suggest that converting even a well-made pepperbox would not have been an economic proposition.

These transition revolvers were generally neither robust nor well designed. They were inaccurate, prone to multiple discharges because of the absence of partitions between the percussion cones, and some of the cheaper examples seem also to have allowed excessive quantities of gas to escape from the union between the cylinder and barrel. In truth, their chief attraction lay mainly in their cheapness and simplicity when compared to the weapons of their larger competitors. However, if the number of examples still in collections is any reflection of their popularity, they must have sold remarkably well and such weapons certainly served to fill a gap in the market until Adam's and, particularly, the mass-produced revolvers made at Colt's London factory became so cheap they drove many conventional gunmakers out of business.

From 1856, revolvers produced by Adams, Colt, Tranter, and later Webley came to dominate the percussion revolver market in Britain, although smaller makers, such as Lang and Bentley, did have some early success with their largely hand-made weapons. Rim-fire revolvers were marketed from 1862—when Philip Webley began retailing his excellent copy of Smith & Wesson's rim-fire revolvers—and with the later appearance of Webley and Tranter's well-made, robust, center-fire weapons, percussion revolvers became largely obsolete, although many were converted to accept the new metal cartridges.

An early, crudely made transition revolver by an unknown maker. This weapon is fitted with a bar hammer, reminiscent of pepperbox revolvers from the same period. A butterfly nut secures the breech to the frame.

EARLY PERCUSSION REVOLVER MAKING IN ENGLAND

Revolvers, whether hand-made or produced by machine, were not the usual product of the traditional English gunmaking industry. The demand for such weapons in Britain was never high and the machine-made product in particular necessitated investment in steam engines and associated plant operations that would have made no financial sense to most gunmakers. Even Webley did not start using steam-driven machinery until about 1859,[5] and much of the trade, at least in percussion arms, was carried on by small gunmakers in either London or the Birmingham Gun Quarter. Although these independent gunmakers would have kept a stock of ready-made weapons, a significant portion of their trade was probably from customers placing special orders.

Whether making a revolver for stock or as a special order, the procedure would have been similar. Once the order was placed, the gun maker would have either made or bought components of the required design from a reputable maker who specialized in their production, modifying any standard components to the customer's requirements. Frames and barrels of English revolvers were usually of malleable cast iron, a material which, compared to ordinary cast iron, had increased resistance to the sudden, high stresses occurring in a revolver when it is fired. The process for conversion involved simply packing the cast iron with charcoal, then heating it over a period of several hours, resulting in a material resembling mild steel in many of its properties. This was a relatively simple procedure that could be carried out in an ordinary gun maker's workshop and may have been the reason English gunmakers preferred malleable cast iron to steel when producing their guns. With the various components ready, the gun maker may have sent the frame, with the barrel fitted, for provisional proof, although many makers did not submit their weapons to this initial test.

Regardless of whether or not they had been submitted for this first proof test, all the components then would have been finished, and perhaps polished, by hand, and the frame and cylinder assembled. Many gunsmiths used lockwork and even loading levers patented by another maker; these should have attracted a royalty, payable to the inventor, for every gun produced. Those arms referred to as Webley-Bentley revolvers, in particular, were made under license by a number of gunsmiths, although it is probable that not all were scrupulous about payments and many copies of these revolvers undoubtedly never attracted the patent royalties they should have. Whatever its patent liabilities, when assembled, the cylinder and frame would then have been sent for viewing and definitive proof tests. If it passed, on return to the gunmaker, the revolver would have been given its final polish, before being stocked and engraved. Finally, the action was fitted and properly adjusted before it was supplied to the customer. Philip Webley used a similar system in his early operations, paying piece-workers a set rate for each of the basic components of his revolvers, which were then sent to the factory to be finished, proofed, and assembled into complete weapons.

These production methods mean that the variations observed between certain models of English revolvers are not as significant as they are, for example, amongst the products of the large American companies. Adams, Tranter, and especially Webley made many guns to special order, adapting the barrel/caliber combinations to their customer's requirements. By way of illustration, there is at least one recorded example of a self-cocking Adams with a 20000 "R" serial number and a factory-fitted Adams pattern loading lever—a serial number and configuration usually associated with the later, double-action Beaumont-Adams.

An additional problem in determining the origin of these revolvers involves the fact that many of the products of the Birmingham trade were stamped "LONDON"—a tradition having arisen amongst their customers that quality firearms were only produced by gunmakers in that city, while the Birmingham trade was thought to be solely concerned with crude "trade" or military firearms. Of course, this adds to the difficulty involved in identifying some of these revolvers from the smaller workshops, many of which bear no form of either maker's or retailer's mark.

TRADE GUNS

Many revolvers produced by the Birmingham trade are termed "Trade" guns, sold as cheap alternatives to the more carefully finished revolvers of the big manufacturers, literally "to the trade." Some copies of Adams, Webley, or Tranter revolvers were even stamped with the appropriate trade or patent marks, although the quality of their finish and lockwork show that they never originated from those factories. Other Trade guns, many produced by either Tranter or Webley, were simply cheap alternatives to their usual guns produced in small numbers to take advantage of a section of the public that wanted a small, cheap revolver to keep in their home or pocket, without much expectation that it would see any hard, extended use.

MACHINE-MADE REVOLVERS

Samuel Colt began full-scale, mechanized revolver production at his Hartford factory in 1847, but the idea was quickly accepted in Britain. By the time Colt arrived for the Great Exhibition in 1851, Robert Adams and his partners already had a factory using a wide variety of machines to produce his self-cocking revolver.

ROBERT ADAMS

It is not clear when Robert Adams began his involvement with the gun trade, but an early reference to him in a letter to the *Morning Chronicle* places him as manager for George and John Deane's Gun Manufactory at 46, King William Street, London Bridge, in January 1850. John Deane's original partnership with his brother George was dissolved on 8 July 1851; Deane, Robert Adams, and Deane's son—also John—having earlier formed a new partnership as "Deane, Adams & Deane" around 25 March 1851.

Deane, Adams & Deane made Adams revolvers and some of the early Beaumont-Adams in their factory at 2, Weston Street, in the London borough of Southwark, although the revolvers were sold from their shop on the other side of the river, at 30, King William Street, London Bridge. Adams also licensed a number of Birmingham gunmakers to produce both Adams and Beaumont-Adams revolvers, although details of their manufacturing processes are not known.

In August 1856, Robert Adams ended his partnership with the Deanes and joined the London Armoury Company (L.A.C) as manager, leasing that company his premises on Henry Street, Bermondsey, selling them his equipment, and undertaking to transfer his patents. The L.A.C continued to produce the Beaumont-Adams revolver, although the original company prospectus states that it was established to supply arms on a wholesale basis to the gun trade and would have no retail outlet. This probably explains why the later Beaumont-Adams revolvers have such a wide variety of retailer's inscriptions, although revolvers with the top-strap inscription "Deane & Son" are by far the most common retailer encountered.

Robert Adams's association with the London Armoury Co. ended in 1858, when he resigned as manager and returned to his own business, selling revolvers from his address at 76, King William Street.

DEANE, ADAMS & DEANE'S LONDON FACTORY

Equipment in the Deane, Adams & Deane factory was probably of a very similar pattern to that in the later L.A.C establishment. Raw materials, consisting mainly of iron in the form of flat plates and blocks of walnut, were stored in the basement. From here, the iron was taken to the furnace room—also on one of the lower floors—where the metal was placed in a forge until it had reached red heat, at which time it was withdrawn, then cut and hammered into the required shape by hand. This was a very exacting process and it must have taken considerable skill and experience to cut out a one-piece frame and barrel forging good enough to allow subsequent machining to the limits of accuracy required.

The revolver blanks were then taken into the upper part of the factory, where a machine first bored out the barrel. This device was, effectively, a modified lathe used by all gunsmiths for their barrels, but fitted with a recycling water system that cooled the bit and flushed the residual metal away from the surface of the work—a modification Adams patented in 1854. Barrels were then planed to their final hexagonal configuration and the frames shaped and smoothed. Rifling was carried out on another machine of Adams's design that was protected, along with the boring machine, under British Patent No. 2000/1854.[6]

Cylinders were said to have been bored on a machine that drilled out all five chambers at once, although how the recesses, holes for the percussion cones, and ratchet were cut is not made clear in any account so far published. Frames and cylinders were probably then assembled and sent for proof.

On their return from the Proof house, the revolvers were again disassembled and all the components properly smoothed and finished. The frame and barrel were then inscribed with the appropriate barrel addresses, frame numbers, and Patent information, after which a standard "foliate" pattern was usually engraved on the frame and, occasionally, the barrel. Frames were then blued, which hardened the iron and protected it from rusting, while cylinders and lock parts were color-case hardened, which resulted in a lighter finish that also prevented rusting. After blueing, the revolver was finally reassembled and the mechanism fitted and adjusted to ensure proper operation before it was dispatched to the King William Street retail premises or the L.A.C's London warehouse.[7]

The cases and accessories included with cased revolvers were probably made under contract by a reputable maker, then brought to the factory, where the revolvers and accessories were cased together. Powder flasks made by the firms of Dixon or Hawkesley were certainly contracted for in this manner, as were the oil bottles included in every case. "Eley" percussion caps were also a common addition to many cased English revolvers, including the Adams.

JOHN ADAMS'S LONDON FACTORY

John Adams's first revolver is described in a British Patent of 1857 (British Patent 2824/1857) and was probably made in the L.A.C works while Robert was their manager.[7] To avoid infringing his brother's patent for the one-piece frame while still retaining its advantages, John Adams devised a frame for his revolver made in two pieces. The upper section comprised the barrel, top-strap, and supports for the cylinder arbor, while the lower piece consisted of the butt and lower frame components. Unlike Colt's revolver, in which the frame union could become loosened with time and use, the sections of Adams's frame were securely fixed together and not intended to be separated once they had left the factory. Moreover, the upper section supported the cylinder arbor in a single component, which meant all the firing stresses were confined to this casting, in a manner analogous to Robert Adams's weapon. This was not the younger Adams's only innovation, either. He also claimed to have specifically designed the double-action lock mechanism of his revolver to allow the frame cavity, into which it was fitted, to be machined with circular cutters, thus simplifying and improving production.

In 1864, he formed his own company, "The Adam's Patent Small Arms Co," moving it in 1865 to the premises at 391, The Strand, London, where it was to remain for the rest of its existence. John, incidentally, seems to have had far more interest in breech loading arms than his illustrious brother, having earlier, in 1861, patented both a modification of the French pin-fire cartridge and his Model 1861 breech loading revolver. This revolver was an interesting weapon, incorporating a breech block behind the cylinder, which was pierced at each chamber to allow access to the elongated hammer nose and could be used with either a percussion or center-fire cylinder. It was awkward to load, however, with withdrawal of the cylinder arbor being necessary before access was gained to the chambers in the cylinder. He had another venture in the field of breech loading three years later, in 1864, when he proposed a breech loading rifle with an India-rubber cartridge for purchase by the British Army, although it was the Snider breech-block and Boxer .577 cartridge that were eventually adopted instead of Adams's design.

After his lack of success with the Ordnance Committee, he patented a well designed percussion revolver (his Model 1866), but it only achieved limited sales because, by now, percussion weapons were being rapidly superseded in the marketplace by the new generation of breech loading, metal cartridge weapons. His interest in breech loaders may have been stimulated by this lack of success, because in 1867, he went on to produce the center-fire breech loading revolver adopted by British armed forces in 1872 as the "Breech Loading revolver, Mk II." He was also awarded the contract for converting the War Department's stock of Beaumont-Adams revolvers to breech loading as the "Breech Loading revolver, Mk I."

FACTORY EQUIPMENT

Equipment within the Adam's Patent Small Arms Company's premises was impressive for such a small company and included several important innovations Adams himself had patented. The machinery consisted of four sets of milling wheels and centering jigs that produced the lock frame forging in four separate operations. There was a second machine—also with four stations—used to produce the cylinders, although the remaining components seem to have been produced by the more usual techniques of the gun trade.[8] With the parts finished, the weapon was put together by the "action-maker" and sent for proof (this is in contrast to his brother's process, where it is recorded that the barrels and cylinders were proofed before the action was fitted). On its return, it was disassembled and the components smoothed, then it went in turn to the stocker, then the polisher. With all these processes complete, it was reassembled and placed in stock, ready for sale.

By 1880, John Adams was no longer involved with the company and it had become "The Adam's Patent Small Arms Manufacturing Co" and was owned by William Locke.

WEBLEY'S BIRMINGHAM FACTORY

Initially, Webley revolvers were produced by "piece" workers, who made the separate components by hand before sending them to the factory for assembly. From about 1874, however, the factory was equipped with hydraulic presses with a working pressure of around ten tons and a variety of steam-driven planers, lathes, borers, and jigs. These were general-purpose tools and were set up as required for the specific revolver being manufactured. Few details of the processes involved are currently available, but it is known that Webley's drilled their cylinder chambers singly, rather than five or six simultaneously. Final assembly, polishing, and stocking were done presumably by hand, in a manner similar to the Adams's factory. The history of Webley's earlier production—between 1860 and 1890—is obscure, and it has been observed that many revolvers with a Webley stamp may well have not been produced in the company factory.[9]

COLT'S LONDON FACTORY

Colt began his London operations by leasing a factory adjacent to Bessborough Place, Pimlico, in 1851, although no revolvers were produced here until January 1853. His production methods differed significantly from his English competitors, in that he employed about 200 unskilled British workers to act as machine minders, with a subsidiary force of approximately 30 American assemblers and supervisors who undertook the more skilled work.

Revolver production in Colt's factory was totally mechanized, all machinery being run from a 30hp steam engine situated in the basement and delivering power via a system of shafts and belts. Revolvers consisted of three main components: the barrel, cylinder, and frame, which only differed in size between models. Frame forgings and the blanks for hammers, triggers, and loading levers were stamped out of red-hot metal by "drop" hammers fitted with suitable dies, while the barrels and possibly cylinders were produced in a forging machine designed by William Ryder, a Lancashire spindle maker. After forging, barrels, cylinders, and frames were bored, milled, and finished as required, then all components were case-hardened, stress-relieved, and annealed in Colt's patent furnace. Cylinders and barrels were proofed in the usual manner at the London House and, upon return, the revolvers were finally assembled by hand before being sent for sale.

A number of writers have argued about whether the parts for Colt's revolver were truly interchangeable within any particular model. It seems probable they were, and a convincing case has been made for this view.[10]

REVOLVER CHARACTERISTICS

Distinguishing characteristics of the weapons described subsequently are listed here. Where such data is available, it is included under the relevant weapon and is, for the most part, self explanatory.

- Hand-made: In the context of these weapons, refers to an individual revolver produced in a gun maker's workshop, with a high degree of skilled hand finishing and parts that were not interchangeable; e.g., Lang revolvers.
- Machine-made: Refers to a factory-made arm with a minimum of hand finishing; e.g., Colt and Adams revolvers.
- English or British Patent numbers: Numbers assigned by the Patent Office to the patentee of a particular gun.[11]
- Frame/ Frame numbers: Frames are either open or solid. Number series and any frame markings are given where these are known. Such numbers may be true serial numbers, patent numbers (these are numbers used to calculate payments to those entitled to patent royalties: e.g., Hankey and Beaumont in connection with Adams revolvers), or production numbers. Particularly during the early percussion period, revolver makers sometimes inscribed their weapons with higher frame numbers than production warranted. It has been suggested that this was done to convince prospective customers that the weapons enjoyed a greater popularity than they actually did. Many makes of revolver (for example: Adams, Colt, and Le Mat) will bear numbers on components other than the frame. When dispatched from the factory, these parts will have been stamped with the same number, so any variation—such as a revolver in which cylinder and frame numbers do not match—may affect the value of the weapon.
- Barrel: Shape and caliber, with corresponding lengths, barrel addresses, and other relevant details are given where known.
- Cylinder: Plain or fluted, chambering, decoration, and numbers are given where known.
- Loading lever/rammer
- Type and Patent number (where a separate English or British Patent applies)
- Model Designations: Designations here follow the most widely accepted system, which corresponds to that used by Robert Adams when advertising his original self-cocking revolvers.[12] Other makers may not have used these designations and where differences are known, they are included. The terms "Army" and "Navy" are more commonly applied to revolvers from American makers. These designations are used for convenience and to illustrate the scope of a company's products. They do not imply that the revolvers described were ever advertised or sold under these names.
- Holster, Dragoon or Army Model: This designation describes a revolver in any size from 24 bore (.577 caliber) to 54 or 56 bore (nominally, .45 or .44 caliber), regardless of barrel length.
- Belt or Navy Model: This designation describes a revolver in 80 or 90 bore (nominally, .38 or .36 caliber), regardless of barrel length.
- Pocket Model: This designation describes a revolver in 120 bore (nominally, .31 caliber) or smaller, regardless of barrel length. In general, caliber corresponds to barrel length, in that larger caliber weapons have longer barrels and vice-versa. Custom-made exceptions are frequent; however, large caliber weapons with factory-shortened barrels are the commonest variation.
- Value: Values quoted in this book are those found for the revolvers described at UK or U.S. auctions between 2007 and 2012. Two values are given corresponding to revolvers in NRA "Good" and NRA "Fine" condition (see Chapter 9: Collecting Antique Revolvers for definitions). Values for cased examples are included where they are known.

Frequency at UK auctions:
- Very rare – known to exist from the relevant literature, but not seen in a catalog search covering five years. Any revolver with this designation has not been given a value.
- Rare – Seen at least once in a catalog search covering five years.
- Common - Seen in most years at least once
- Very common – Seen more than once a year.

GLOSSARY

Included here are some of the specialist terms used in the text that apply most usually to revolving pistols and rifles.

Arbor: The axle upon which the cylinder rotates.

Breech (alternately breech lug or barrel lug): That part of a revolver frame between the cylinder and barrel. It bears the barrel, either screwed into the breech (Bentley revolvers) or forged with it (Adam's revolvers; the single piece frame protected by his 1851 patent). In open-framed revolvers, it is pierced by a rectangular slot that accepts the frame wedge. It may bear a "bullet cut" to facilitate loading the ball into the cylinder chamber.

Butt (aka Stock): The down-curving section of the frame gripped by the shooter when firing. Made in a wide variety of shapes: Conventional or "Target," with a flat base, and "Birdshead" or "Parrot-beak" being the most common.

Caliber: Caliber, bore, and gauge are all terms that indicate the size of ball that fits the bore and, in revolvers, the cylinder of any particular weapon. Caliber is expressed in inches (usually as a decimal), while bore and gauge are both measured in "balls per pound." Thus, a weapon of 120 bore shoots balls weighing 1/120 of a pound, or "120 to the pound," corresponding to .31 caliber.

In general, caliber is the designation used for American flintlock and percussion weapons, while bore is used for English weapons. Ammunition for metal case weapons is always described by caliber, whatever its country of origin. Table showing caliber as bore size.

Caliber (inches)	Bore (balls per pound)
0.58	24
0.5	38
0.44	54/ 56
0.38	80
0.36	90
0.31	120
0.28	240

Cartridge (aka metal cartridge or metal case): A brass cylinder, with a flat base, that holds the powder and ball used in a revolver. The base of the cartridge holds a highly volatile substance used to ignite the charge and fire the weapon, serving the same function as the percussion cap. There are three common types:

Rim-fire: These cartridges have the priming compound enclosed in the base of the cartridge, which is of thin brass. The hammer strikes the rim of the cartridge and thus fires the round. Due to the necessity for a thin base, rim-fire cartridges were not suitable for heavy powder loads.

Pin-fire: A rarer cartridge type than the other two, mostly confined to European arms. The cartridge case is fitted with a pin that goes through the wall of the case and ignites the primer. Cylinders fitted to these arms have a characteristic slot machined in the top edge of each cylinder to receive the pin of the cartridge. Such weapons are also, of necessity, always of open-frame design.

Center-fire: Revolvers using this type of cartridge are by far the most commonly encountered design; it is the cartridge of choice for most modern revolvers larger than .22 in caliber, although many early weapons were chambered for larger rim-fire rounds (.38, .32, .41). Center-fire cartridges consist of a hollow cylinder closed at one end by a substantial brass base plate termed the "head," which has a hole for the priming cap or primer to fit into the center of the base of the cartridge case. This primer consists of a metal cup, containing the priming material and, depending upon its design, an "anvil." Upon firing, the weapon's firing pin strikes the base of the primer, crushing the priming material between the cup and the anvil and firing the cartridge. This anvil may be either contained in the primer [Boxer primer] or manufactured as part of the case [Berdan primer].

Cylinder: As its name suggests, the cylindrical component that holds the powder charge or cartridge. It may have four, five, or six chambers and, in percussion revolvers, it is fitted at the end nearest the hammer with a percussion cone (aka: nipple), which holds the percussion cap. A plain cylinder is a cylinder left in the round, without fluting. A fluted cylinder is one in which the metal of the outside surface of the cylinder is machined out to form a groove with a semi-circular end, between the chambers, e.g., some Lang revolvers, later Colt Armys, 1861 Navys, and many metal cartridge weapons. A semi-fluted cylinder is a cylinder in which the fluting extends only a short distance across the surface of the cylinder, and is a feature of the Webley MkI-MkVI Government revolvers. A "church steeple" or steeple-fluted cylinder is a cylinder in which the ends of the fluting meet in a point instead of ending in a semi-circular configuration. Found in some early Webley "W. G." revolvers.

Cylinder bolt: The component of the lock mechanism that "bolts" the cylinder in line with the barrel and hammer prior to discharge. In any antique revolver bought for shooting, it is essential that this component, particularly, is in good condition. The cylinder should lock properly or "index" in the correct position when the hammer is cocked, without significant play between the cylinder and the barrel, which should also be clean and without too much wear to the rifling.

Flash Guard (aka recoil shield): The component molded or fitted to the frame behind the cylinder of both percussion and metal case revolvers to protect the user from the ignition flash of the percussion cap and cylinder charge. In metal cartridge revolvers, the right flash guard is frequently recessed to accept the loading gate.

Frame: The part of the revolver that holds the lock and trigger mechanism and to which the breech lug and barrel are attached. Open-frame refers to a revolver with only a single strap, either above or below the cylinder, joining the frame and the barrel. Solid-frame describes a revolver in which a strap is present above and below the cylinder. This may be a real solid-frame in one piece, as is found in Adam's revolvers. Alternatively, it may be a two-piece frame, superficially resembling a true solid-frame in which the top-strap and lower section of the breech lug locate in recesses in the lock frame. This type is found in Ball's revolver and some cheaper Adam's copies.

Frame Wedge (aka cross bolt in single shot pistols): The metal wedge that passes successively through slots in the breech lug and the middle of the cylinder arbor to secure the barrel to the lock frame.

Gate-loading: This describes a revolver fitted with a loading gate, usually on the right side, through which cartridges are pushed into the cylinder. This gate is then closed to retain the cartridges. Examples include the Colt Single-action Army (aka Model P, Peacemaker, Frontier), some early Tranters, and Webleys.

Hinge-Frame: A revolver in which the barrel lug and standing breech are joined by a substantial hinge. Found in the later Webley metal cartridge revolvers, such as the "W. G." and Webley Mk-Mk VI Government revolvers.

Loading Lever (aka rammer, lever ramrod): Usually mounted under the barrel or on the frame of a percussion revolver, although in early Colt and Tranter revolvers it was a separate component. Its function was to seat the load firmly in the chamber. Loading levers were often the subject of separate patents.

Lock Mechanisms: This book uses the following classification with reference to revolver lock mechanisms. It is the typical system for most British and some American publications.

1] Single-action: This refers to a revolver whose hammer has to be cocked manually before it is fired by pulling the trigger. Examples of this type of weapon are Colt, Remington, and Manhattan revolvers. It is by far the commonest type of action found in percussion and early metal cartridge revolvers.

2] Self-cocking: In this type of revolver, the weapon is fired by pulling the trigger, which causes the hammer to move backwards until automatically released, thus firing the charge in the chamber. The hammer cannot be cocked manually. Early Adams and Webley-Bentley revolvers are the most commonly encountered arm with this type of mechanism. Such weapons may be readily identified by the absence of a hammer spur. In some American publications, this system is referred to as "double-action."

3] Double-action: This mechanism, as its name suggests, is a combination of the two previous types. The hammer of a double-action weapon may be cocked and then fired or, alternatively, it may be fired by simply pulling the trigger. This mechanism combines the advantages of both types, in that rapid fire is possible by simply pulling the trigger, while if greater accuracy is required, the weapon may be used in single-action mode. Beaumont-Adams and 4th Model Tranter revolvers have this type of mechanism.

4] Hesitating: This type is a modification of the self-cocking mechanism, in that one pull of the trigger cocks the weapon, while the second pull fires it. It is much less common than the other types and examples include a few early Adams, Tranter, and Starr revolvers. Both Tranter and Starr revolvers, in fact, are equipped with two triggers—one to cock the weapon and the second to fire it.

Lock Plate: Plate covering the lock mechanism, removal of which allows easy access to the underlying hammer, trigger, and pawl assembly. Commonly found in revolvers from smaller manufacturers, especially Webley-Bentley (Bentley licensed) revolvers and Beaumont-Adams revolvers made under license by the Massachusetts Arms Co.

Marks (frame, barrel or cylinder): Gun Maker's or Manufacturer's mark: Mark stamped or inscribed on a weapon to indicate the maker: for example, "L.A.C" stamped on Beaumont-Adams revolvers to show they were manufactured by the London Armoury Company Ltd.
Patent mark: Mark stamped or inscribed on a revolver to show the English or British Patent it was made under, e.g., "Tranter Patent" or "Colts Patent." Patent marks do not usually include the patent number and are frequently followed by the frame or serial number.
Proof Mark: Mark stamped on a revolver (or any firearm) by the relevant Proof House, to show it had passed one or more stages of "Proof" (see Appendix One: Proof Marks, for further details).
Retail Mark: Marks inscribed on a revolver to show the retailer it was originally purchased from; for example, "P.Webley & Son" or "Deane & Son." Usually stamped or inscribed on the top-strap of solid-framed revolvers and on the barrel of other types.

Pawl: The part of the lock mechanism, usually in the form of a lever, that rotates the cylinder before it is "bolted" in place.

ENGLISH REVOLVERS

Prawl: Protrusion of the top section of a revolver butt designed to protect the user's hand from the recoil of the hammer in a self-cocking or double-action revolver.

Rebounding Hammer: In a gun using a rebounding hammer, when the trigger is pulled, the hammer springs forward and strikes the firing pin, as normal. It then springs backward, or "rebounds" slightly and comes to rest away from the firing pin. The hammer is then locked so the weapon cannot be fired unless the trigger is pulled; i.e., a sudden blow will not be against a hammer with its striker resting on the firing pin of a fresh cartridge. This does away with the need to remember to put the weapon at half-cock after firing.

Self-Extracting: In this design, spent cartridges are extracted automatically when the weapon is opened. Found in top-break revolvers, such as the later Webleys, Pryse, MkI-MkVI, and also Smith & Wesson and Tranter revolvers.

Sheath or Sheathed Trigger: In this design, the trigger guard is missing and the trigger returns to a hollow extrusion of the frame after firing. Cocking the mechanism of such a weapon, which is invariably single-action, causes the trigger to protrude from its "sheath," ready for firing.

Standing Breech: that part of a revolver that contains the hammer and lock mechanism.

Top-Break: A revolver in which there is a join between the top-strap of the frame and the lock mechanism that is opened to eject the spent cartridges. These revolvers are usually self-extracting and include the Webley MksI-VI and some early, large caliber Smith and Wesson revolvers.

Top-Strap: Metal bar joining the top of the lockwork to the barrel, bridging the cylinder space, in solid-frame revolvers. Frequently found inscribed or stamped with the name of a maker or retailer.

CHAPTER TWO

Smaller English Revolver Manufacturers

Revolver manufacture marked one of the first attempts at mechanized firearm production in Britain. Although previously barrels, lock plates, and stocks for military arms had been produced to a Sealed Pattern, the weapons still had to be assembled, or "set-up," and the variation between the components produced meant this could only be done by a gunsmith in his workshop.

Sam Colt changed all that. His plant in Hartford and the later London factory turned out revolvers whose parts were interchangeable, at least within a specific model, and this pointed the way for gunmakers like Robert Adams and William Tranter. These innovations did not affect the whole of the British trade, however, and in Birmingham, for example, revolvers sold by Joseph Bentley and the Webley brothers were hand-made by piece workers until well into the late 1850s.

Revolvers—unlike their forerunners, the single-shot flintlock and percussion pistols—could now be produced quickly and at reasonable cost by these industrial methods, although the initial outlay for the manufacturer was high. A Manton percussion pistol, for example, retailed at around £55 in 1830, while Colt was selling his Colt Dragoon revolver in London twenty years later for £6, which included a bullet mold and spanner for the percussion cones. This went up to £7.50 for a cased weapon, complete with accessories. Despite this cut-price policy, he still made sufficient profit to leave an estate worth $15 million when he died in 1862.

REVOLVER MANUFACTURERS & MAKERS

The weapons produced by the English revolver manufacturers listed here may be unfamiliar to all but the collector specifically interested in that model. Therefore, in order to avoid confusion, where a manufacturer has produced more than one weapon, each revolver is listed by patent date. Thus, for example, Joseph Bentley's earliest revolver is described as a "Bentley 1852 revolver." In this way, it is hoped that confusion over which weapon is being referred to will be minimized.

Pepperboxes, most of which are hand-made, will also be found included here, when they are the subject of a separate English or British Patent, as are several common, hand-made "transition" revolvers.

ADAMS, JOHN

Machine-made revolvers.
Brother of Robert Adams. His early percussion revolvers, which were produced by the London Armoury Co, are rare. Later, in 1864, he formed his own company, "The Adam's Patent Small Arms Co," at 391, The Stand, London, and it was this concern that made the Model 1866 percussion revolver and the breech loading, center-fire revolver, adopted by British armed forces in 1872 as the "Breech Loading revolver, MkII."

By 1880, the company had become "The Adam's Patent Small Arms Manufacturing Co" and was owned by William Locke.

ADAMS 1857 PERCUSSION REVOLVER

British. Pat. 2824/1857
Frame number series: Unknown, but probably in the low hundreds.

Frame made in two parts, the top consisting of the barrel, slotted top-strap, and recoil shield, which was then screwed to the lockwork and supporting barrel lug. John Adams used this design so as not to infringe his brother Robert's 1851 patent.

Solid-frame, double-action percussion revolver. The barrel is octagonal, 5¾ inches long, with either clockwise or counterclockwise three-groove rifling. Cylinder is plain, without decoration and chambered for five rounds. Weapons converted for rim-fire cartridges have been recorded. Usually fitted with "Harding Patent" under-barrel loading lever. This device consisted of a single thin rod, secured under the barrel by a narrow catch and at the breech end by a single screw, upon which both the lever and rammer head pivot. Being made by the London Armoury Co. Ltd, most of these revolvers will probably bear some form of their characteristic "L.A.C" mark on the frame or barrel.

Variations
Three variations known:

- Holster Model: Cylinder with five chambers, in 54 bore, 5¾ inch barrel.
- Belt Model: Cylinder with five chambers, in 80 or 90 bore, 5¾ inch barrel.
- Pocket Model: Cylinder with five chambers, in 120 bore, 5¾ inch barrel.

Values: Good: $3,700-$4,067
(£2,200-2,400)
Fine: $8,400-$9,300
(£5,000-5,500)
Rare at UK and U.S. auctions

ADAMS 1866 PERCUSSION REVOLVER

British. Pat. 1959/1866.
Produced at a time when percussion weapons were largely being replaced by cartridge arms, so few were produced. This is reflected in the small frame number range, which may not even reflect production.
Frame number series: 1-260

Trademarks found on John Adam's revolvers; these are taken from a 1867 center-fire revolver. *Courtesy of Collectible firearms.*

Solid-frame, double-action percussion revolver, in 54 bore. Barrel is octagonal, 5¾ inches long, with five-groove, right twist rifling. Cylinder chambered for six rounds, in contrast to Adam's 1857 revolver, and an under barrel loading lever fitted. Finish is blue overall, except the spurred hammer and loading lever, which are case-hardened (i.e., bright). London proof marks are present on barrel and cylinder.

Top-strap and barrel are inscribed:

ADAM'S PATENT SMALL ARMS COMPANY, 391, STRAND, LONDON

Lower right hand side of the frame bears the following inscription:

ADAM'S PATENT IMPROVED NO.

followed by the frame number.
John Adams's bilobed trade is also found stamped at the lower right side of the frame in later weapons.

Variations
Only the Model described is known.
Holster Model: cylinder with six chambers, in 54 bore, with 5¾ inch barrel.

Values: Good: $1,600-2,030
(£1,000-1,200)
Fine: $2,500-2,900
(£1,500-1,700)
Rare at UK and U.S. auctions.

ADAMS, ROBERT

Retail premises:
• 76, King William Street, London: 1858 – 1865 (declared bankrupt).
• 40, Pall Mall, London: 1866
Eng. Pat 13527 /1851 – Protects a percussion revolver, with barrel and frame in one piece
See "Adams" chapter.

BAILEY, THOMAS

Hand-made revolvers.

BAILEY MODEL 1858 PERCUSSION REVOLVER

British Pat. No. 1634/1858
Frame number series: Unknown
Very rare double-action, side hammer percussion revolver with solid, two-piece frame, only found in 120 bore.
Details of frame numbers not recorded. Barrel octagonal, 5 inches long. Plain cylinder, with five chambers and horizontal percussion cones.
This information based on a single example,[1] although no examples are now known.
Very rare at UK and U.S. auctions.

BALL, H.

Hand-made revolvers.
Best remembered for his "Anti-garroter" firearm, which was attached to a belt and could be fired at an attacker approaching from behind the wearer, he also registered a British patent for a percussion revolver.

BALL MODEL 1857 PERCUSSION REVOLVER

British Pat. No 1213/1857 (Provisional protection)
Frame number series: Unknown

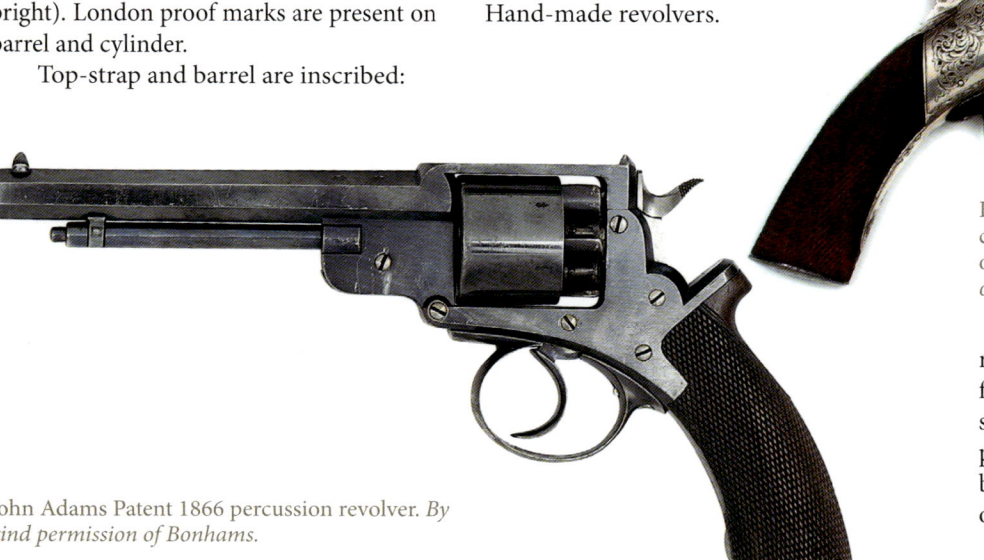

Ball revolver showing the square-ended cylinder arbor and "Ball's Patent" inscription on the bottom of the frame. *By kind permission of Bonhams.*

Solid-frame, double-action percussion revolver in 90 bore. Barrel is octagonal, fitted with fore and rear sight. Cylinder with six chambers. Birmingham proof marks are present. Frame is stamped on the right side breech lug with a small Patent mark in an oval format:

BALL'S
PATENT

John Adams Patent 1866 percussion revolver. *By kind permission of Bonhams.*

The frame was made in two parts: the first consisting of the butt and lockwork, which was joined to the second part, consisting of the top-strap, breech lug, and barrel, by a square-headed screw that passed through the cylinder to locate in a threaded hole in the lock-frame; this also served as the cylinder arbor. No recoil shield was fitted, but the frame bulged between the cylinder and the butt and gave some protection to the user's hand; there was a recess in the top of the frame to allow the cylinder's percussion cones to be capped. A loading lever was fitted, mounted on the left side of the frame, and is also subject to protection by British Pat. 1213/1857.

These revolvers were well made and engraved with scroll-work at the breech, on the top-strap, and on the rounded German silver frame.

Variations
Only the Model described is known.

- Belt Model: cylinder with six chambers, in 90 bore, 6-inch barrel.

Values: Good: $2,800-3,220
(£1,700-1,900)
Fine: $4,200-4,900
(£2,500-2,900)
Rare at UK and U.S. auctions

BEATTIE, JAMES

Maker of pepperbox revolvers as well as pistols. Brother Henry is also recorded, although he appears to have concerned himself more with retailing, rather than making, guns. Retail addresses:
James:
- 43, Upper Marylebone St, (1832 – 1835)
- Collinson Hall, 52, Upper Marylebone, St (1836-1846)
James Beattie & Son:
- Collinson Hall, 52, Upper Marylebone, St (1864-79)
James Beattie & Co:
- Collinson Hall, 52, Upper Marylebone, St (1881-1894)
Henry:
- Gun & Pistol Repository, 205 Regent St
James & Henry:
- Gunmakers, 205 & 223, Regent St, (1847)

Well made, ornately decorated, bar hammer, self-cocking percussion pepperbox pistols. Six-shot weapons have been recorded so far, although other types may have been produced. Action is inscribed:

J. BEATTIE
226, REGENT ST
LONDON

Lettering usually within an ornate box of scrolled foliage.

Values: Good: $1,180-1,360
(£700-800)
Fine: $1,860-2,120
(£1,100-1,250)
Common at UK auctions.
Rare at U.S. auctions.

BENTLEY, JOSEPH

British Pat. No 960/1852 – Self-cocking, 5-shot revolver
British Pat. No 2657/1857 – Double-action revolver.
(See "Webley Revolvers" for detail.)

CALLISHER & TERRY.

Birmingham gunmakers responsible for the manufacture of later Beaumont-Adams revolvers, as well as copies of Tranter and Webley cartridge revolvers.
Retail address:
- 22/ 24, Whittal Street, Birmingham.

The firm is recorded as War Dept. contractors at this address.

COCHRAN

Hand-made revolvers.

COCHRAN MODEL 1837 PERCUSSION REVOLVER

Eng. Pat 7286/ 1837 (Pat agent: M. Poole) These revolvers were never manufactured in the UK, although there was an English patent, which is the reason for their inclusion here. They were produced to Cochran's longarm design, with horizontal rotary cylinder, but made by C.B. Allen of Springfield, Massachusetts, who may have instructed Poole to take out the English patent. Cochran's rifle was also made and retailed by J. Wilkinson of Pall Mall.

Single-action, .36 caliber under-hammer, percussion revolvers. The cylinder is horizontal and hand-turned, with seven chambers. Further details of these interesting, American-made weapons are recorded in Flayderman.

James Beattie pepperbox. *Courtesy of Thomas del Mar Ltd.*

Cochran turret revolver, right side. Although not made in England, Cochran did have a British patent. Courtesy of James D. Julia Auctioneers, Fairfield, Maine (www.jamesdjulia.com).

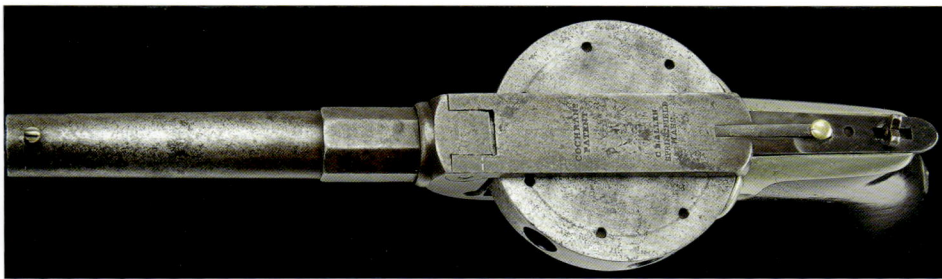

Cochran revolver showing the top-strap, securing device, and Patent and retail marks. Courtesy of James D. Julia Auctioneers, Fairfield, Maine (www.jamesdjulia.com).

Cochran revolver from the left side, showing the "under hammer" ignition system. Courtesy of James D. Julia Auctioneers, Fairfield, Maine (www.jamesdjulia.com).

Values: Good: $8,400-11,000
(£5000-6,500)
Fine: $25,400-30,500
(£15,000-18,000)
Very rare at UK auctions.
Rare at U.S. auctions.

COLLIER, E.H.

Retail addresses:
• Charterhouse Square (1818-1820)
• 6, Herbert's Passage, Beaufort Buildings, Strand (1820)
• Fountain Court, Strand (1822)
• Collier & Co, 54, Strand (1824)
• 3, North Side, Royal Exchange (1825-1827), retired.

Hand-made revolvers.

Collier's original revolver design was something of an innovation.

To operate the weapon, the cylinder's chambers were first loaded with powder and ball in the usual way and the priming magazine in the frizzen (or steel) filled with powder. The cylinder—the mouth of which was countersunk to allow it to be seated into a corresponding percussion cone on the barrel—was then drawn back against the pressure of the helical spring, which served to seat the cylinder and barrel firmly together when firing. With the cylinder drawn back, it was rotated counterclockwise against the pressure of a second spring. When this second spring had sufficient tension, the cylinder was allowed to re-engage the barrel cone.

In firing, the hammer was first cocked, which caused a small hook, linked to the hammer, to catch in a circular notched skirt attached to the rear of the cylinder. This hook then drew the cylinder back against the pressure of the helical spring, thus allowing the second spring to rotate the cylinder to the next chamber. As the chamber came opposite the barrel, the hook encountered one of the notches in the cylinder skirt, disengaged, and thus allowed the helical spring to push the chamber mouth on to the barrel cone. The frizzen or steel was then snapped down and a linkage rotated the plug in the bottom of the priming magazine, depositing a quantity of priming powder into the flash pan. Sufficient powder was carried in the magazine to charge the pan each time the frizzen was closed.

Unfortunately, Collier soon found this method of cylinder rotation too problematic to be reliable and most of his pistols and longarms have hand-rotated cylinders—the cylinder being simply pulled back, turned, then allowed to snap into place. Even without the mechanically-rotated cylinder, the guns were reliable and popular, although the design was never accepted by the military, despite Collier's efforts to elicit Royal favor. Sam Colt was also said to have got the idea for the original Paterson after he bought a Collier revolver in London.[2]

COLLIER MODEL 1818 FLINTLOCK REVOLVER

Eng.Pat 4315/ 1818

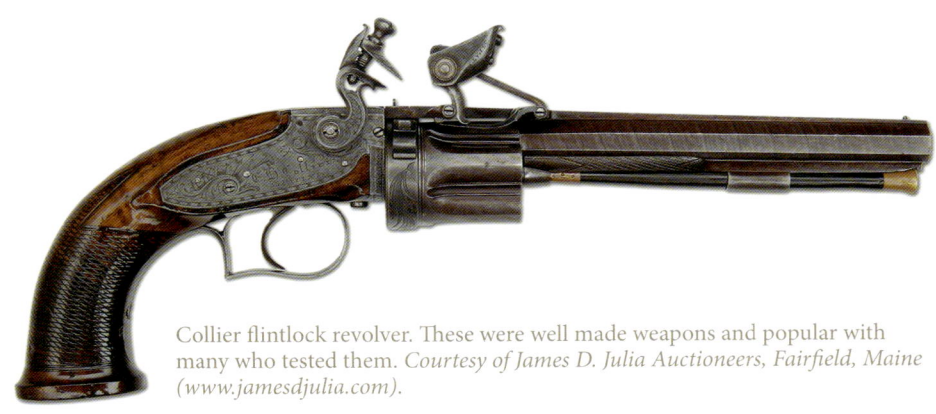

Collier flintlock revolver. These were well made weapons and popular with many who tested them. Courtesy of James D. Julia Auctioneers, Fairfield, Maine (www.jamesdjulia.com).

Frame number series: Unknown (all automatic cylinder weapons would have had low numbers, although there are no known existing examples of these early weapons).

Open-frame, single-action, flintlock revolver in 50 bore (.46 caliber), with frame open below cylinder. Early examples have a cylinder turned by a helical spring, but this system was quickly abandoned and most guns have hand-turned cylinders. A second spring is used to force the mouth of each chamber tightly against the end of the barrel.

Locks are inscribed:

E H Collier
Patent

An alternate lock mark is also found, which includes a serial or production number (XX); for example:

E H Collier
XX Patent

The barrel is octagonal, 6 inches long, fitted with post front sight and open rear sight. It is inscribed on the top flat:

E H Collier London

An alternative form of barrel address is also found, which includes the serial number:

E H Collier XX London

Both forms of address are usually surrounded by engraved scroll work.

The frizzen magazine may also be inscribed with the serial number:

XX Patent

The five-chambered, fluted cylinder has a single pan on an outer collar. It is rotated by hand, then moves forward, under the action of a strong spring, to seal against the barrel. Some examples have been found fitted with a cover over the front of the cylinder and attached to the barrel, which serves to keep the loads in place. Unfortunately, this circular plate was said by some users to have caused multiple firing of the chambers. A conventional wooden ramrod is fitted under the barrel, retained by a single, centrally mounted band and a tailpipe.

These are well made, very collectible guns, which is reflected in their auction values.

Collier flintlock revolver, showing the hammer, pan, and frizzen assembly. The linkage that operates the pan magazine is behind the frizzen. *Courtesy of Horst Held.*

Collier flintlock revolver, showing one design of the lock inscription. *Courtesy of Horst Held.*

Collier flintlock revolver, showing the hammer, frizzen, and cylinder assembly, as well as the second design of the lock inscription. *Courtesy of James D. Julia Auctioneers, Fairfield, Maine (www.jamesdjulia.com).*

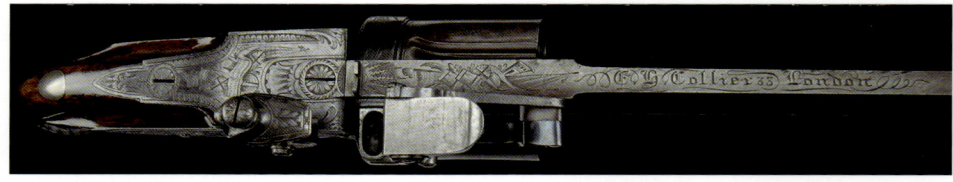

Collier revolver, showing the barrel address on the top flat of the barrel. *Courtesy of James D. Julia Auctioneers, Fairfield, Maine (www.jamesdjulia.com).*

Collier revolver, showing the opening of the frizzen magazine. *Courtesy of Horst Held.*

Variations

Two variations known:
- Automatically rotated cylinder model: cylinder with five chambers, in 50 bore, 6 inch barrel. The cylinder is rotated by a complex pre-wound spring, although all other features are similar. No existing examples are known.
- Hand-rotated cylinder model: cylinder with five chambers, in 50 bore, 6 inch barrel. Cylinder is rotated by hand, in

a way similar to the earliest pepperbox revolvers. Other features similar to the automatic cylinder model.

Values: Good: $6,400-8,500
(£3,800-£5,000)
Fine: $25,400-27,950
(£15,000-£16,500)
Cased $33,880 (£20,000)
Rare at UK and U.S. auctions.

COLT, SAMUEL

Factories:
• Bessborough Place, Millbank, London (1852-1857)
• 37, Chandos St, London (1857 -1860)
Offices:
• 1, Spring Gardens, London (1852-1855)
• 14, Pall Mall, London. (1855-1861)
Retail premises (trading as Colts Patent Firearms Manufacturing Co.):
• 14, Pall Mall, London (1861 – 1913).

Machine-made revolvers.
Colt Dragoon, Pocket, and Navy model percussion revolvers were produced in the UK. Colt maintained a retail outlet in Pall Mall until 1913, after his London factory ceased production in 1858.
Eng. Pat 6909/ 1835 – Paterson revolvers (never manf. in UK)
Eng Pat 12668/ 1849 – Pocket revolvers.

LONDON DRAGOON COLTS

Colt's London factory began manufacturing in January 1853, but it appears that what are referred to as "Hartford-London" Dragoon Colts were only ever assembled in London from parts made in America. They correspond to the design of the Hartford "Third" model.

LONDON MODEL DRAGOON REVOLVER

Serial numbers: in a range from 1-700, stamped on cylinder and frame.
Single-action, open-frame percussion revolver in .44 caliber. Barrels 7½ inches long, octagonal at breech, with a round barrel and seven groove, gain twist rifling.

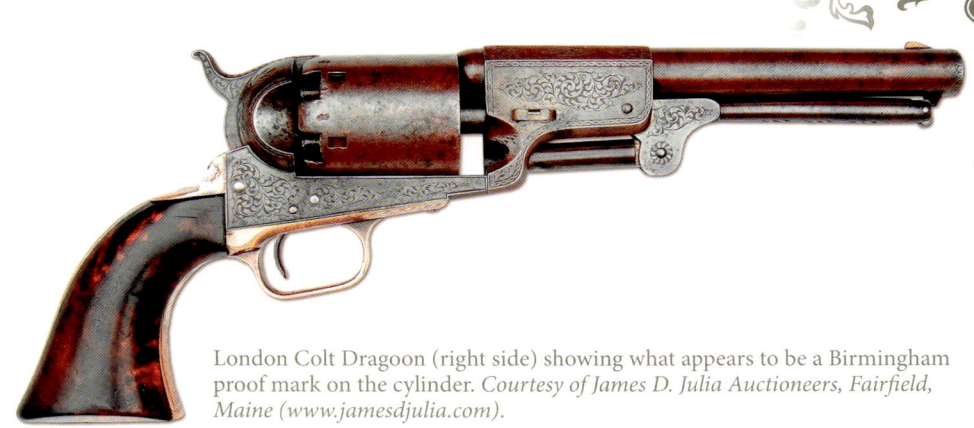

London Colt Dragoon (right side) showing what appears to be a Birmingham proof mark on the cylinder. *Courtesy of James D. Julia Auctioneers, Fairfield, Maine (www.jamesdjulia.com).*

Barrel addresses are found on the top barrel flat:

COL. COLT LONDON
(this address will always be inscribed rather than stamped) or

ADDRESS: SAM^L COLT, NEW-YORK CITY
(this address is stamped)

Cylinders have six chambers, with rectangular bolt stops, safety lugs between the percussion cones, and a rolled-on scene depicting Texas Rangers fighting Indians.
Frames are similar in shape to the later Navy, but slightly more massive.
Frames stamped on either the right or left side:

"COLT" or "COLTS'S PATENT"

Trigger guard and backstrap usually silver plated brass, with small decorative bows. Barrel, cylinder, and screws are blued, loading lever case hardened. Butt is one piece, in walnut.

Values: Good: $25,400-28,800
(£15,000-17,000)
Fine: $59,300-64,370
(£35,000-38,000)
Cased $76,200-101,640
(£45,000-60,000)
Common at UK and U.S. auctions

LONDON-MADE POCKET REVOLVERS

Although there is no certainty about the date in 1853 when Colt's London factory began to manufacture the Pocket revolver either, good evidence suggests that about 300 were initially assembled here from imported parts. Barrel addresses are also something of a mixture, in common with the Dragoons. Approximately 11,000 Pocket Model revolvers were produced in London.

London – Hartford Colt Dragoon cased with accessories. Rectangular cylinder bolt slots differentiate this from the earlier 1st Model. *Courtesy of James D. Julia Auctioneers, Fairfield, Maine (www.jamesdjulia.com).*

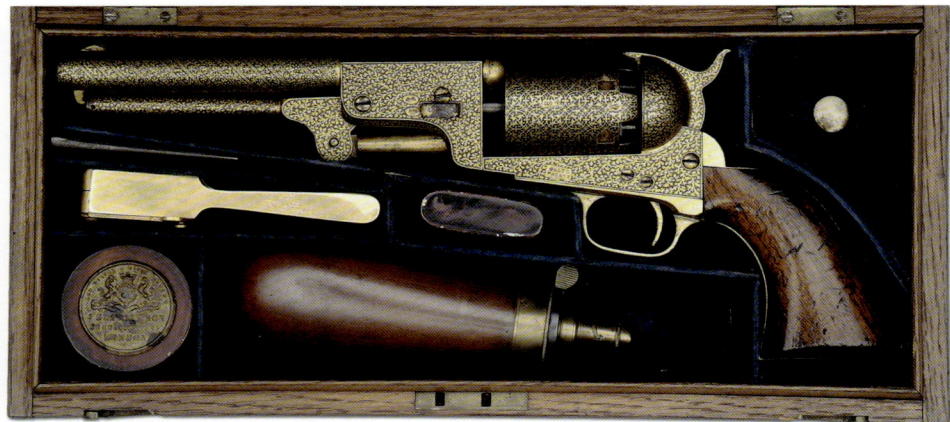

London Colt Dragoon showing the characteristic barrel address. *Courtesy of James D. Julia Auctioneers, Fairfield, Maine (www.jamesdjulia.com).*

Damasened London Colt Dragoon in its case with accessories. *Courtesy of James D. Julia Auctioneers, Fairfield, Maine (www.jamesdjulia.com).*

Higher magnification view of the gold inlaid Dragoon, showing that the gold finish has been applied after proof. *Courtesy of James D. Julia Auctioneers, Fairfield, Maine (www.jamesdjulia.com).*

COLT POCKET MODEL 1849 REVOLVER

Serial number series: 1-11000
Colt Pocket revolvers were all single-action, open-frame percussion revolvers in .31 caliber, with octagonal barrels of 4, 5, or 6 inches, and with a slight taper towards the muzzle and seven groove rifling which may be left or right hand twist. Barrel lugs were thin, with a plain bullet cut, although beveled cuts are found in very early and some later weapons. Brass, or occasionally copper, pin front sights were fitted, with the usual "V" notch in the hammer forming the rear sight. Cylinders were plain, with five chambers, and engraved with the "Stagecoach" scene and a stamped panel containing the words and serial number (XXXX):

COLT'S PATENT
N° XXXX

Colt Pocket Model revolver from the right side. *Courtesy of James D. Julia Auctioneers, Fairfield, Maine (www.jamesdjulia.com).*

SMALLER ENGLISH REVOLVER MANUFACTURERS

There were five safety lugs between the percussion cones and chamber mouths are beveled to facilitate seating of the ball and ensure a gas-tight seal. Percussion cone housings are a little deeper on the early London pistols. The cylinder circumference of London guns is also slightly larger than Hartford Colts, which means that cylinders are not interchangeable between the two types of weapon. Loading levers were of the thin latch pattern, with the screw entering from the left. There are slight differences in detail between the frame of London and Hartford-made Pocket Colts.[3]

Trigger-guards in early weapons are small, brass, and either round or oval. Later, they were slightly enlarged, before being superseded by iron trigger guards and backstraps that were found to be more popular with British customers. Brass mounts were often silver plated, although this is rare with the later iron furniture. Early weapons have Hartford "Slim Jim" butt plates, later replaced by what came to be known as the "London" butt plate, with its characteristic "bell-like" appearance. Usually made from American black walnut and stained and polished so as to appear "gold" when new, although this ages to brown or dark red in antique weapons.

Other slight differences include the pattern of the hammer knurl and the characteristic domed screws found on London guns.

Inspector's marks vary, depending on the component examined. Presence or absence does not reflect on the authenticity of the weapon in question (see Rosa for details). Proof marks are usually the crowned GP and V of the London Proof House, either in one line or one above the other, on both barrel and cylinder. Some Pocket pistols carry Birmingham proof marks and several have been encountered without proof marks.

FRAME STAMPS

Frame stamps differ, with several of the early weapons bearing "COLT" on the left side of the frame instead of the more familiar "COLT'S PATENT." Before purchasing any Pocket revolver claimed to be a London Colt, especially if the seller is asking a premium for such a weapon, it is wise to examine this frame stamp carefully. These stamps show certain specific defects that may help in determining the authenticity of any weapon inspected. Specifically, and most noticeable is the broken "S" in "COLT'S." In later weapons, both the first "T" and "E" in "PATENT" are damaged.[4] Later still, the stamps were changed, becoming smaller and showing no distinctive damage.

LONDON COLT POCKET MODEL REVOLVERS

London Colt Pocket revolvers form a serial number series separate from the Hartford-made weapons. Differences between the six models of London Pocket revolver are confined to the barrel address and minor modifications.

FIRST MODEL

These were manufactured from Hartford parts, then finished and marked in London.
Serial number range: 1-265 / 300
Barrel addresses:
  Group 1 - comprising serial number 1 to approximately 100: Each letter is individually hand-stamped on the top barrel flat:

  ADDRESS:
  SAM[L] COLT LONDON

  Group 2 – serial number 100 – approximately 300: each letter is hand inscribed, appearing as one of the following:

  COL. COLT LONDON
  or
  COLONEL COLT, LONDON
  or
  SAM[L] COLT LONDON

By about serial no. 200, London Pocket Colts had started to be marked with what was to become the standard London address, stamped with a die cut for the purpose:

  ADDRESS : COL. COLT
  LONDON

This form of address appears on the barrel of all other models.

SECOND MODEL

Serial number range: 265/300 to approximately 1,000
Trigger guards may be iron or brass, with Hartford and London-made weapons both present. Approximately 100 weapons in this serial range have an "X" suffix to the serial number, for reasons which are not clear.

THIRD MODEL

Serial number range: 1001 – 3000.
Large oval trigger guards were first fitted to this version. Bullet cuts are slightly enlarged, but not bevelled.

FOURTH MODEL

Serial number range: 3001-5000.
"London" pattern butt plates were first fitted to this model.

FIFTH MODEL

Serial number range: 5001-9000.
Weapons in this group may have slightly enlarged butt plates. Bullet cut modified, but not bevelled. Butt plate now that of the more common Hartford-made arms.

SIXTH MODEL

Serial number range: 9001-11000.
This group contains several weapons that are clearly Hartford-made, usually indicated by the use of the Hartford pattern serial number stamps.

Values: Good: $1,600-2,500
         (£1,000-1,500)
         Fine: $4,200-5,000
         (£2,500-3,000)
         Cased: $8,400-10,100
         (£5,000-6,000)
Very common at UK and
U.S. auctions.

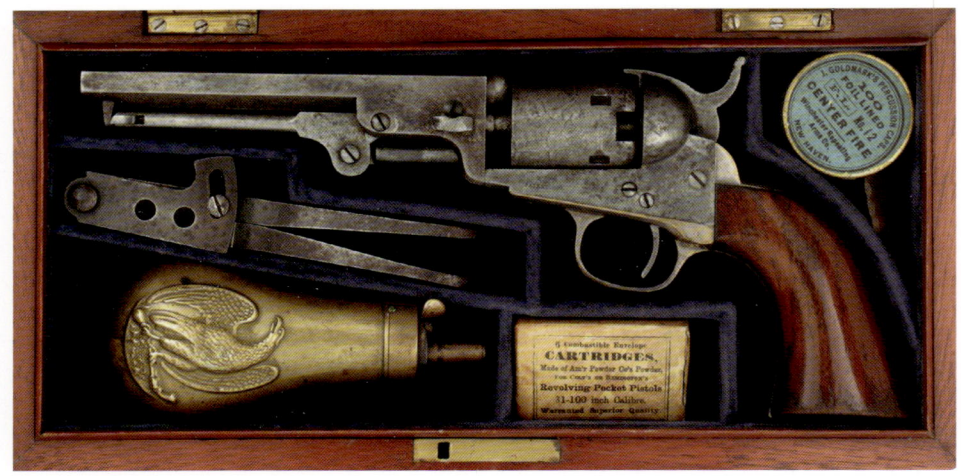

Colt Pocket Model revolver cased with accessories. This revolver is of later manufacture, because the case contains a box of foil cartridges used to facilitate reloading. *Courtesy of Thomas del Mar Ltd.*

Cylinders are plain, with six chambers and rectangular cylinder bolt stops. Engraving is die-rolled, depicting the usual naval battle, with a date given as:

16 May 1843

An engraved panel contains "COLT'S PATENT," with the serial number, and beneath this is inscribed:

Engraved by W.L. Ormsby New-York.

Safety lugs are found on the rear of the cylinder. A frame wedge goes through the center of the cylinder arbor, with the retaining screw above the wedge, and in this model, the loading lever screw

LONDON MADE COLT NAVY MODEL REVOLVERS

This group of revolvers is divided into four sub-models, all based on the Third Model of the Hartford Navy. Approximately 40,000 London Navys were produced with their own serial number range, with these numbers usually being found stamped on the frame and cylinder.

FIRST LONDON MODEL

Serial numbers: in a range from 1-1800 Single-action, open-frame percussion revolver in .36 caliber. The barrel is 7½ inches long, octagonal, with a brass pin forming the foresight and the usual hammer-notch rear sight.

The top barrel flat is inscribed:

ADDRESS : SAM^L COLT NEW-YORK CITY.
or
ADDRESS .COL: COLT. LONDON.

Colt Navy Model revolver cased with accessories, showing the Eley cap box and Dixon flask with graduated spout. *Courtesy of Thomas del Mar Ltd.*

Colt Navy revolver from the right side, showing more extensive engraving than usual, which was characteristic of a presentation gun. This particular weapon was presented to a Mr. Richard Green by Sam Colt and the butt strap is engraved to that effect. *Courtesy of James D. Julia Auctioneers, Fairfield, Maine (www.jamesdjulia.com).*

Colt Navy from the left side, showing the "COLTS PATENT" stamp, serial number, and a London Gunmakers Company "View" mark. *Courtesy of James D. Julia Auctioneers, Fairfield, Maine (www.jamesdjulia.com).*

SMALLER ENGLISH REVOLVER MANUFACTURERS

Butt strap inscription from the previously pictured Colt Navy. *Courtesy of James D. Julia Auctioneers, Fairfield, Maine (www.jamesdjulia.com).*

Disassembled Colt Navy. One of the advantages of Colt's early revolvers was their simple construction, with parts easily exchanged.

The engraving of a Colt Navy cylinder from a replica gun. The sails of the ship in the naval battle are just visible in the top left.

The loading lever latch of the Colt Navy revolver.

enters from the right. Trigger guards are small and round and made of plated brass. Squareback trigger guards are occasionally found fitted to weapons with serial numbers between 1-450, possibly because such parts were imported initially from Hartford. Backstraps are plated brass. Butts are one piece, "Slim Jim," and of varnished walnut, although some later pistols show the "bell" shape that has come to characterize London-made Colt revolvers. Pearl, ivory and other types of butt plate were never fitted to London Navy Colts as a factory option.

SECOND LONDON MODEL

Serial number range: 1800 – 3000
Identical to the first model, except that the barrel address only appears as:

>ADDRESS. COL: COLT. LONDON.<

Some weapons in this range have the loading lever screw entering from the left. Trigger guards may be of either iron or brass, with iron gradually predominating. Triggers themselves may be of either large or small type.

THIRD LONDON MODEL

Serial number range: 3000 – 37500
Commonest of the London-made Colt Navys and identical to the first and second models, except that the top barrel flat is stamped:

>ADDRESS. COL: COLT. LONDON.<

Bullet cuts are non-bevelled and trigger guards are large, round, and always of iron in this series, as are the backstraps. The loading lever screw always enters from left.

FOURTH LONDON MODEL (LATE HARTFORD – LONDON)

Serial number range 37500 – 42000. Similar to standard London Colt Navy Models except:

- The bullet cut is not bevelled
- Addresses did not have arrow heads
- Hammer knurl is cross hatched
- Ormsby's name is omitted
- Serial number numerals are of the Hartford type

The diameter of the cylinder differs, so that fourth Model Hartford-made cylinders will not fit London-made arbors and vice-versa.

Cased London Colts are much more rare than single weapons. Usual accessories were: a bullet mold, wood or iron ramrod, a Dixon or occasionally a Hawksley powder flask, combined percussion cone key and screwdriver, and a box of Eley Bros. percussion caps. Some cases will also include an oil bottle, again made by Dixon or Hawksley, and spare percussion cones, a mainspring, and occasionally a cylinder bolt or trigger. Boxes themselves are machine made in oak, mahogany, or rarely, birds eye maple. All were baize or velvet lined. A label giving instructions on loading and cleaning was pasted inside the lid and this can take a variety of forms. Later labels included details of Colt's foil cartridges.

Values: Good: $1,700-2,000 (£1,000-1,200)
Fine: $3,300-3,900 (£2,000-2,300)
Cased: $5,900-8,500 (£3,500-5,000)
Very common at UK and U.S. auctions

LATER LONDON-RETAILED COLTS

Colt's Bessborough Place factory closed in 1857, but he retained a London Agency in Pall Mall until 1913, and a number of percussion models were marketed from here, including the Model 1860 Army, Model 1861 Navy, Model 1862 Police, and the Model 1862 Pocket Navy (.36 caliber).

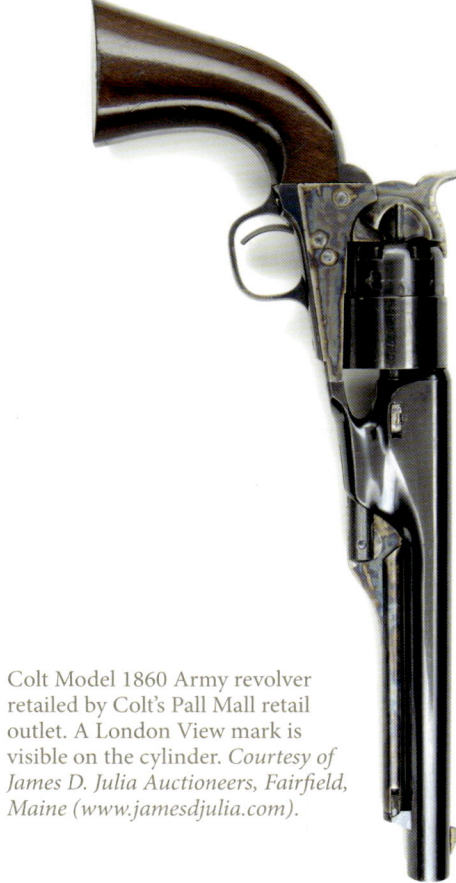

Colt Model 1860 Army revolver retailed by Colt's Pall Mall retail outlet. A London View mark is visible on the cylinder. *Courtesy of James D. Julia Auctioneers, Fairfield, Maine (www.jamesdjulia.com).*

Serial number ranges: These revolvers are found in a variety of ranges, but they are often characterized by the addition of a small "L," which indicates their origin.

They bear the usual marks, except the barrel address is stamped:

ADDRESS COL. COLT
LONDON

London proof marks are usually found stamped on the barrel and cylinder.

The company also sold the Model "P" from this retail outlet; these weapons only differ from the Hartford guns in having London proof marks and the barrel stamped:

PALL MALL LONDON

These weapons are described in Flayderman, but details of the serial number range for the London retailed "Model P" are not available.

Given the potential outlay, anyone seriously contemplating purchasing one of these guns would be well advised to consult Joseph Rosa's excellent and exhaustive book on the subject. Colt's London factory also made a number of presentation guns and these will have auction values significantly above the average.

As usual, guns with matching cylinder and frame numbers are usually considered to be worth more than guns in which these features do not correspond.

Values:
Percussion revolvers fetch prices similar to the earlier, British-made weapons. These are rare at UK and U.S. auctions. The Model "P" and later cartridge revolvers are very rare at UK and U.S. auctions.

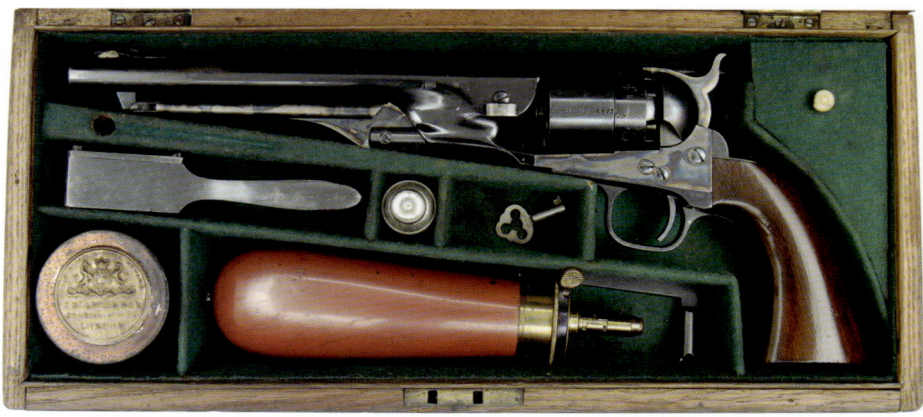

Colt 1860 Army Model revolver, cased with accessories and sold by Colt's Pall Mall retail outlet. *Courtesy of James D. Julia Auctioneers, Fairfield, Maine (www.jamesdjulia.com).*

COOPER J.R

Retail premises:
John, Richard Cooper & Co: "Gunmakers, 52, Eastcheap," (1850 -1853) is included in Blackmore's "Dictionary," though this may not be the same individual.

Maker of 6-shot pepperbox pistols.

COOPER 1840 PERCUSSION PEPPERBOX

Eng Pat 8347/1840: (Patent registered, although it is not clear what feature of the mechanism is covered; certainly not the lockwork.)
Hand-made pepperbox revolvers.

Well-made, six-shot percussion weapons with a ring trigger and under hammer that strikes forward. Often silver plated and inscribed on the side of breech enclosed in a decorative box:

J R COOPER'S
PATENT

Values: Good: $840-1,016
          (£500-600)
          Fine: $2,000-2,400
          (£1,200-1,400)
Common at UK auctions

DAW, GEORGE HENRY

Retail premises:

• Witton Daw & Co., 57, Threadneedle St, London: 1851- 1855: partner with Witton.

• Witton & Daw, 57, Threadneedle St, London: 1855-1860

• George Henry Daw, 57, Threadneedle St, London, from 1860.

PRYSE & CASHMORE MODEL 1855 REVOLVER (COMMONLY "DAW" REVOLVER)

An open frame Daw revolver (from the left) showing the wedge, with the upper securing screw and rear sight on the barrel.

Brit.Pat. 2018/1855 (registered to Pryse & Cashmore)

Largely hand-made revolvers, although some parts were machine-made.

Frame number series: 1 – 5500

No British patent was taken out for these revolvers under Daw's name; the mechanism is based on Pryse & Cashmore's British Patent 2018/1855. Pryse & Cashmore manufactured all of these weapons, either as complete weapons or partially finished for completion at Daw's London premises. The amount of hand finishing called for during construction priced this otherwise well-designed, sturdy revolver out of the government's lucrative contracts.

Cooper pepperbox, showing the distinctive name scroll.

Cooper pepperbox, showing detail of scrolled trademark.

Cooper pepperbox, showing detail of the under barrel trigger.

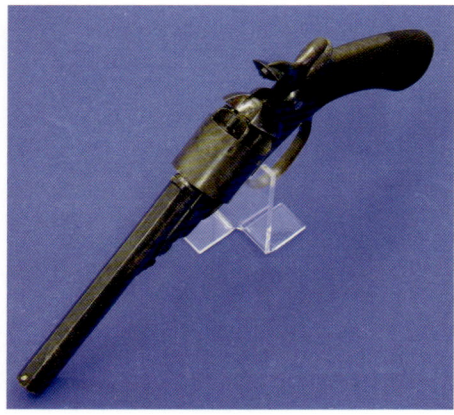

Daw revolver showing conformation of the hammer nose.

Double-action or self-cocking, open-frame percussion revolvers, with cylinders having five or six chambers in a variety of bores from 240 to 38. There are also some solid-frame examples, although these are rare. The frame is usually heavily engraved and the barrel may be octagonal or round, and is secured to the frame by a wedge through the center of the cylinder arbor, entering from the right. The weapon is capped via a "U"-shaped slot cut in the lockwork directly in front of the hammer, which also gives the hammer access to the percussion cap when firing.

Barrels are sometimes found inscribed on the top barrel flat with George Daw's address, although this is not found on all revolvers by this maker:

G.H DAW. 17, THREADNEEDLE ST. LONDON.

The cylinder is plain, inscribed with the serial number, and characteristically turns counterclockwise. Weapons chambered for 38, 54, 80, and 120 bore are known, and there is also a rare 240 bore (.28 caliber) variation. The cylinder bolt is in the form of a "plot," integral with the front face of the pawl. A hammer spur may be present or absent, depending upon the mechanism. The loading lever is similar to the under barrel type seen in revolvers made by Joseph Lang and may be based on Joseph Blisset's patent (Brit. Pat. No. 2069/1855), although another type, based on Pryse & Cashmore's patent, was also fitted. The butt is walnut, in one piece, and may be fitted with a lanyard ring.

Details of these weapons are complicated and a prospective buyer should consult Taylerson et al[3] for more detail before purchase.

A Daw revolver showing the London proof mark, frame, and cylinder number.

Variations
The following variations are recorded:[4]

- Holster Model: Open-frame, double-action revolver, cylinder with five chambers. Produced in 38 bore, with 6½ inch round or octagonal barrel.
- Army Models: Open-frame, double-action revolver, cylinder with five chambers. Produced in 54 bore, with 6½ inch round or octagonal barrel.
- Open-frame, self-cocking revolver, cylinder with six chambers. Produced in 54 bore, with 6½ inch round or octagonal barrel.
- Navy Models: Open-frame, double-action revolver, cylinder with five chambers. Produced in 80 bore with 5½ inch round or octagonal barrel, although this weapon may have been manufactured with other barrel lengths.
- Open or solid-frame, self-cocking revolver, cylinder with six chambers. Produced in 80 bore with 5½ inch round or octagonal barrel, although this weapon may have been manufactured with other barrel lengths.
- Pocket Models: Open-frame, double-action revolver, cylinder with six chambers. In 120 bore, with 5½ inch round or octagonal barrel.

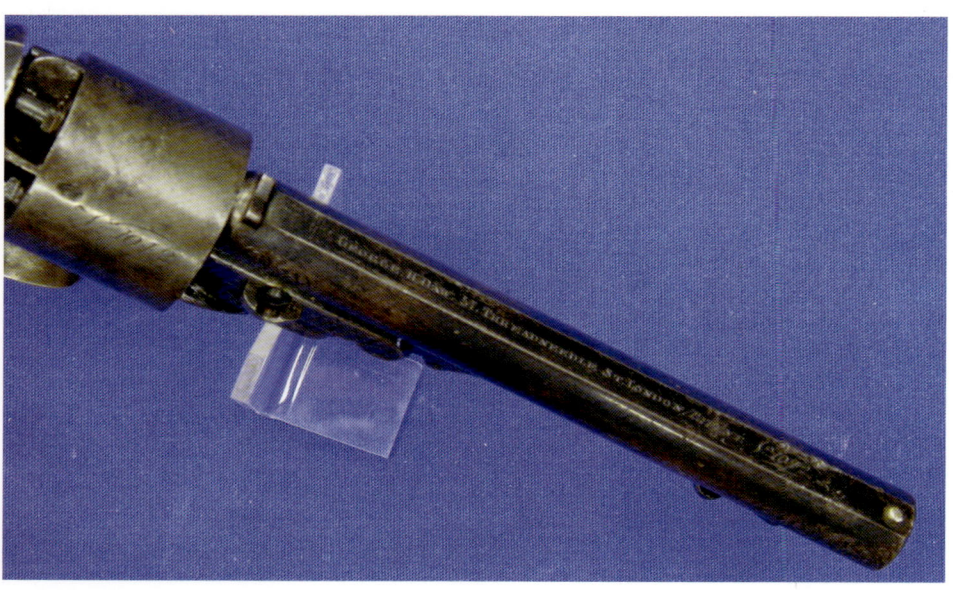

Daw revolver showing the retailer's name on the top flat of the barrel: "GEORGE H DAW, 57, THREADNEEDLE ST. LONDON."

SMALLER ENGLISH REVOLVER MANUFACTURERS

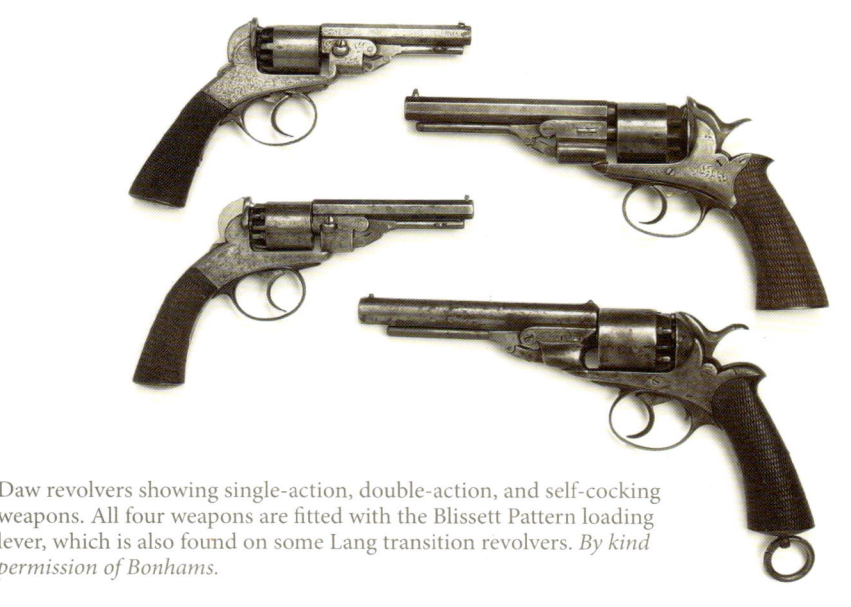

Daw revolvers showing single-action, double-action, and self-cocking weapons. All four weapons are fitted with the Blissett Pattern loading lever, which is also found on some Lang transition revolvers. *By kind permission of Bonhams.*

Collection of single-action, double-action, and self-cocking Daw revolvers. *By kind permission of Bonhams.*

Open or solid-frame, self-cocking revolver, cylinder with six chambers. In 120 bore, with 5½ inch round or octagonal barrel.

A small 240 bore (.28 caliber) weapon has been recorded, although these are rare.

George Daw also produced a solid-frame, rim-fire revolver,[5] as well as copies of both Tranter and Webley metal cartridge revolvers.

Values: Good: $1,700-2,400
(£1,000-1,400)
Fine: $3,300-3,900
(£2,000-2,300)
Cased: $5,000-6,800
(£3,000-4,000)
Common at UK auctions.
Rare at U.S. auctions

DEANE, JOHN / DEANE – HARDING / HARDING, WILLIAM

Successors to Deane, Adams & Deane: Retail address:

• 30, King William Street, London (1856-1873).

All these revolvers were manufactured under license from John Deane by Tipping & Lawden (1858), Pryse & Redman (1862), or Callisher & Terry (1863).

DEANE-HARDING MODEL 1858 REVOLVER

Machine-made revolvers
  Br. Pat. 669/1858 – Patent protected a loading lever fitted to Deane-Harding revolvers
  Br. Pat. 1159/1858 – Patent protected the two-part frame construction and lock mechanism of Deane-Harding's five-shot, double-action percussion revolver.

Deane-Harding percussion revolver in the 5000 L serial number range.

Frame number series:
  1-100 (Prototype serial range)
  5000L-7000L (Revolvers produced by Tipping & Lawden, may be stamped "T&L" internally)
  15000P-15600P (includes all the rim-fire weapons, probably produced by Pryse & Redman)
  25000–25200 (revolvers produced under license by Callisher & Terry)

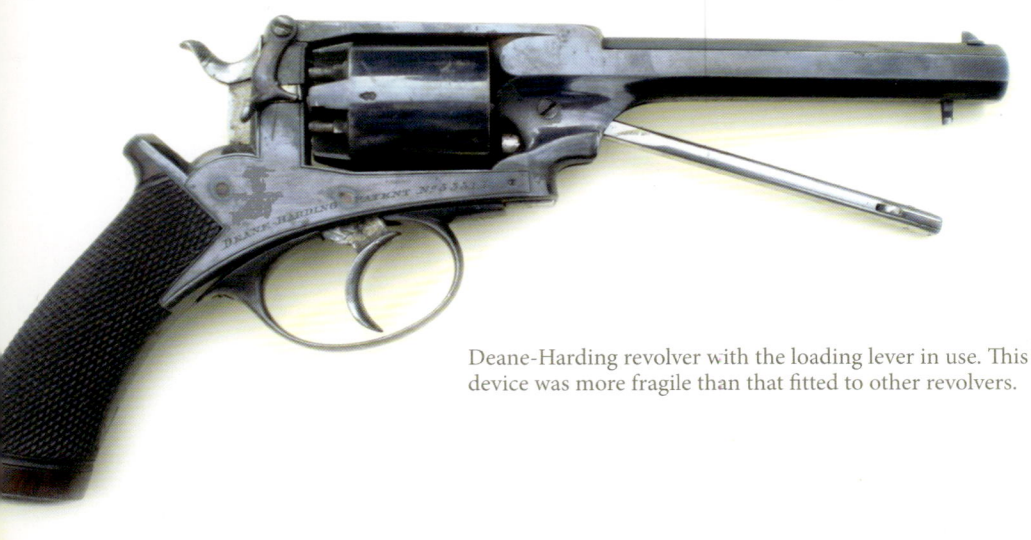

Deane-Harding revolver with the loading lever in use. This device was more fragile than that fitted to other revolvers.

Deane & Harding revolver showing the retail mark found on the top-strap of this revolver.

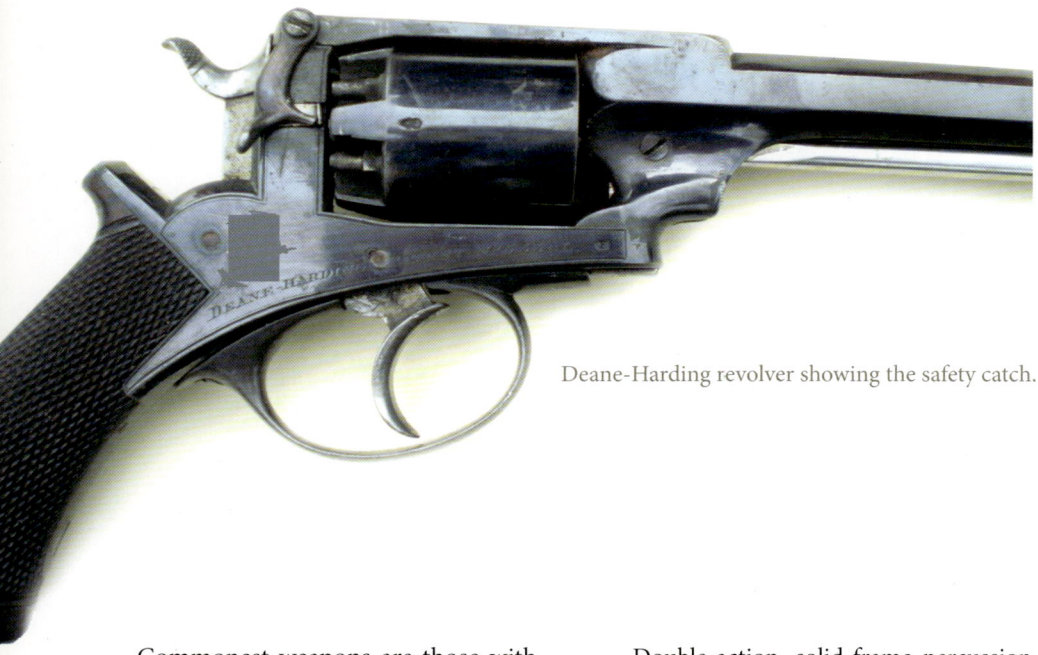

Deane-Harding revolver showing the safety catch.

Barrels are octagonal, usually rifled with three broad, clockwise grooves and fitted with a triangular blade front sight. Both barrels and cylinders usually bear London view and proof marks, although some rim-fire arms bear Birmingham proof marks.

Most weapons bear what is thought to be an acceptance stamp on the right side of the frame at the front and beneath the hook on the barrel lug, which appears to take the form of a conjoined "D" and "H." Cylinders in all percussion models have five chambers, with the rear end characteristically sloping inwards from the point of insertion of the percussion cones.

All Deane-Harding revolvers so far recorded are fitted with the "Harding Patent" under barrel loading lever. This device appears more fragile than the Colt or Kerr loading levers fitted to similar contemporary revolvers. It consists of a single thin rod secured under the barrel by a narrow catch and at the breech end by a single screw, upon which both the lever and rammer head pivot. There are two distinct patterns: an early, round "bulbous" type with a swelling at the muzzle-end of the lever; and a later type, in which the lever is either flattened or round, yet both having the same conformation throughout their entire lengths.

Revolvers in serial range 0-100:
All revolvers in this range are 54 bore, five-chambered percussion arms. A characteristic "L"-shaped safety catch pivots on the cylindrical pin that secures the frame. The securing pin itself has a vertical retaining screw that had to be removed before the frame pin could be withdrawn. To operate, the safety catch is pushed forward into the percussion cone well, locking the cylinder between chambers and ensuring a safe carry. The loading lever is of the early bulbous pattern.

The frame inscription on the right side reads:

THE DEANE-HARDING
PATENT No

This is followed by a frame or serial number. The top barrel flat is inscribed:

DEANE & SON . 30, KING WILLIAM ST, LONDON BRIDGE.

Butts are one piece, in chequered walnut.

Commonest weapons are those with frame numbers in an "L"-suffixed series from 5000L to approximately 7100L, although this may not reflect production. In addition, there was a very small early series from 1 to 100; a slightly larger "P"-suffixed series from 15000P to 15600P, which includes the six-shot percussion / rim-fire weapons; and another small series of wholly percussion arms in a range from 25000 to 25200.[6]

Double-action, solid-frame percussion or rim-fire revolver in 54 and 120 bore and rim-fire .442 and .32 calibers.

The frame is in two parts: a hook on the barrel lug engaging a recess in the front of the lock frame, while the rear of the top-strap in turn engages another robust lug on the top of the standing breech in front of the hammer. The assembly is locked together by a cylindrical retaining pin passing from right to left through the top-strap and the lug on the breech.

Revolvers in the 5000L – 7000L serial number range:
Produced by Tipping & Lawden, revolvers in this range include both 54 bore and 120 bore five-chambered percussion arms.

In weapons in this range, the frame securing pin has no retaining pin and in revolvers after 6070L, the pin is further refined, so that simply twisting the safety catch to the rear releases the barrel from the lockwork. This device proved susceptible to wear and a new frame securing pin was introduced from about serial no. 7110L, which consisted of a simple threaded screw passing through the top-strap and frame lug, but still carrying the arm of the hook-pattern safety catch. Loading levers were of the later type.

The frame inscription is on right side, in a single line, and includes the serial number:

DEANE-HARDING PATENT No

The top-strap is inscribed either:

DEANE & SON . 30, KING WILLIAM ST, LONDON BRIDGE.
or
DEANE & SON. LONDON BRIDGE.

The lower butt strap is usually stamped:

T&L

Butts are one piece, chequered walnut.

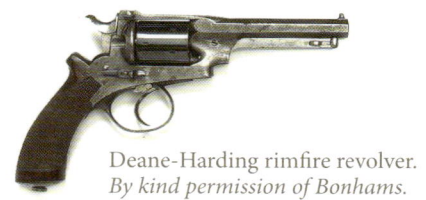
Deane-Harding rimfire revolver. By kind permission of Bonhams.

Revolvers in serial range 15000P- 15600P:
This range includes both percussion and rim-fire weapons, probably produced under license by Pryse & Redman. Percussion arms are in either 54 bore or 120 bore, with cylinders having five chambers, while the optional rim-fire arms were supplied with a recoil plate and second cylinder having six chambers in either .442 cal. rim-fire for the Army models and .320 cal. rim-fire for the Pocket model revolvers. The frame securing pin is the later threaded type. Loading levers were of the later type and rim-fire weapons have an additional rod-shaped case ejector screwed into the butt cap and a modified hammer.

The frame inscription is on right side, in a single line, which includes the serial number:

DEANE-HARDING PATENT No

The top-strap is inscribed either:

DEANE & SON . 30, KING WILLIAM ST, LONDON BRIDGE.
or
DEANE & SON. LONDON BRIDGE.

Rim-fire revolvers have a second frame and cylinder number with a "DHD" suffix.
Butts are one piece, chequered walnut.

Revolvers in serial range 25000 – 25200:
This range includes all weapons produced under license by Callisher & Terry.

Percussion revolvers in 54 or 120 bore and cylinders with five chambers. Two types of frame were fitted to revolvers in this series. The first was the type used by all previous Deane-Harding revolvers, with a pin securing the frame between the top-strap and standing breech. The second type replaced the top-strap pin with a permanent hinge and was secured by a vertical screw in the barrel lug that had to be completely removed before the frame could be opened. Loading levers were of the later type, and in weapons with the later frame, the previous hook pattern safety catch was replaced with a sliding catch inclined from the horizontal. The frame inscription is on the right side, in a single line that includes the serial number:

DEANE-HARDING PATENT No

The top-strap is inscribed:

DEANE & SON . 30, KING WILLIAM ST, LONDON BRIDGE.
or
DEANE & SON. LONDON BRIDGE.

Butts are one piece, of chequered walnut.

Variations
Four variations are known:

Army Model: Cylinder with five chambers, in 54 bore with a 6 inch barrel.
Rim-fire Army Model: Factory-made, 6 inch barrel, cylinders with six chambers in .442 rim-fire with a percussion cylinder and recoil plate supplied as an alternative.
Pocket Model: Cylinder with five chambers in 120 bore with a 4½ inch barrel. Pocket models are the rarest variation.
Rim-fire Pocket Model: Factory-made, 4½ inch barrel. Cylinders with six chambers in .320 rim-fire, with a percussion cylinder and recoil plate supplied as an alternative.

Original percussion weapons may also be found converted to use metal cartridges, using a system protected by William Tranter's Brit. Pat. No. 1889/1865.

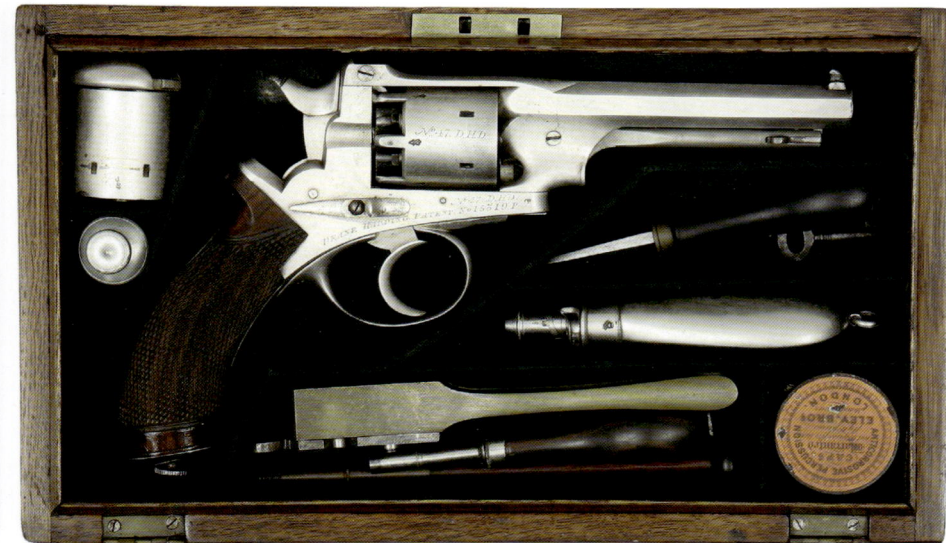
Deane-Harding revolver cased with accessories. This example is nickel-plated, with an additional rim-fire cylinder included in the case. It is in the 15000 P frame number range and is characteristic of these rim-fire/ percussion weapons. By kind permission of Bonhams.

Values:
Percussion: Good: $2,300-2,700
(£1,400-1,600)
Fine: $3,500-3,900
(£2100-2,300)
Rim-fire: Good: $2,900-3,400
(£1,750-2,000)
Fine: $3,970-4,300
(£2350-2,500)
Rare at UK auctions.

DIMANCEA, HARALAMB

Described in his 1885 British patent application as a "Captain of Roumainian (*sic*) Artillery" and resident at 299, Aston Street, Birmingham. Although some examples are stamped as being made at the Holford works of the Kynoch factory, it seems unlikely that serious production ever took place there. Revolvers with the "Kynoch" stamp were probably weapons left behind when the factory was purchased and marked with the company stamp before being sold to a retailer, simply to get rid of them.[7]

MODEL 1885 CENTER-FIRE REVOLVER

British Patent 9973/1885
Solid-frame, self-cocking (hammerless), metal cartridge revolver featuring a characteristic swing-out, self-ejecting cylinder with six chambers in .380 or .450 caliber. The barrel is round with a rib machined into the top surface.

The loading mechanism is unique to this revolver. A catch on the rear of the frame is moved backwards to allow the cylinder and barrel to pivot about a bolt located on the front of the frame, below the barrel/cylinder assembly. The barrel/cylinder assembly is then pushed to the left, clear of the frame, before being pulled forward to operate the self-ejecting mechanism. Once the chambers have been loaded, the barrel/cylinder assembly is pushed back into the frame.

Top rib of barrel stamped:

THE GATLING ARMS AND
AMMUNITION Co., LTD
or
KYNOCH GUN FACTORY ASTON
or
DIMANCEA PATENT

Butts in one piece, of walnut or gutta-percha.

Very rare at UK and U.S. auctions

DODDS, I

Hand-made revolvers.

DODDS MODEL 1835 PERCUSSION RADIAL REVOLVER

Eng. Pat 6826/1835
Single-action, 4-shot radial percussion revolver. This arm had chambers bored as radii in a circular metal plate, arranged vertically. No examples are currently known, but presumably may be identified by the presence of a "DODDS" patent inscription or stamp.

Very rare at UK auctions (the only examples so far recorded are museum pieces).

GREEN, EDWINSON, CHARLES

Hand-made revolvers, probably assembled from parts imported from Liege, Belgium.

A small gunmaker based in Cheltenham, Gloucester, Charles Green was responsible for one of the nineteenth century's most important revolver developments: the frame catch incorporating a side lever that was developed by Webley for their later hinge-frame revolvers. Webley and Carter patented this catch in 1885 (Br. Pat. 4070/1885), four years before Green registered his own patent protecting the design (Br.Pat. 20321/1889). Relations between Webley & Scott and Green became increasingly acrimonious and eventually resulted in litigation, although subsequently, Green was able to show that he had been making revolvers featuring the frame catch mechanism with its associated locking device since 1883. Webley probably settled out of court for an undisclosed sum, since revolvers made by them and fitted with this catch bear no number relating to royalties paid to Green; in contrast, for example, to the revolvers made under Michael Kaufmann's patents.

Retail addresses:
• E.C Green, 87 High Street, Cheltenham Gloucs.
• E.C Green & Son, 87 High Street, Cheltenham Gloucs.

The history and dates of manufacture of these revolvers is obscure, and for convenience they are described here as "Early" Model and Model 1883. Subsequent research may reveal this designation to be in error,[8] the later revolvers being made under the protection of Green's 1889 patent, despite having been produced from as early as 1883.

GREEN EARLY MODEL CENTER-FIRE REVOLVER

British Patent 20321/1889
Serial number range: Unknown

Hinge-frame, double-action metal cartridge revolver in .450 caliber, with a 5½ inch barrel and plain cylinder with six chambers. The frame locking catch is of a type described as a "half-pin" turn-over type, but in other features, the revolver resembles a Pryse revolver of the type made by the Belgian (Liege) trade. In particular, the lock mechanism does not have a broad, rectangular lug projecting out of the frame into the rear of the trigger guard and the cylinder release mechanism is a broad button engraved with an arrow.

The barrel top-flat is stamped with what is assumed to be the earlier address:

E.C. GREEN, HIGH STREET, CHELTENHAM.

Finish is usually blue and butts are one-piece, walnut, with a slight prawl behind the hammer. Birmingham proof marks are usually found on the barrel and cylinder.

SMALLER ENGLISH REVOLVER MANUFACTURERS

GREEN MODEL 1883 CENTER-FIRE REVOLVER

British Patent 20321/1889
It was probably his development and sale of this revolver that resulted in Green's letters to "Field" when Webley introduced their Mk I Government revolver.

Serial number range: Unknown

Hinge-frame, double-action metal cartridge revolver in .450 and Webley .455 caliber, with a 5½ inch barrel and semi-fluted cylinder with six chambers, although this weapon is of heavier construction than the Early Model. The frame locking catch is stirrup-shaped with a thumb-operated lever, and is similar to that found on the Webley Mk I Government revolver

The barrel top-flat is stamped with what is assumed to be the later address:[9]

E.C. GREEN & SON, CHELTENHAM AND GLOUCESTER.

Finish is usually blue and butts are two-piece, "Birds-head" configuration in walnut. Birmingham proof marks are usually found on the barrel and cylinder.

Variations
Green Model center-fire revolvers:
Green Early Model center-fire revolver: Chambered in .450, plain cylinder with six chambers, 5½ inch barrel.
Green Model 1883 center-fire revolver: Chambered in .450/ .455, semi-fluted cylinder with six chambers, 5½ inch barrel.
Very rare at UK and U.S. auctions.

HARVEY, WILLIAM JOSEPH

Hand-made revolvers.
Birmingham gunmaker responsible for a small number of these unexceptional revolvers.
• Br. Pat 1298/1853 – Hammerless, self-cocking revolver
• Br. Pat 2602/1854 – Transition-type revolver

HARVEY MODEL 1853 PERCUSSION REVOLVER

Frame number series: Unknown.
Rare, hammerless, self-cocking percussion revolver. Barrel is octagonal, 76 bore with 4 inch barrel or 54 bore with 5½ inch barrel. The cylinder of both types has five chambers. No loading lever is usually fitted. Both models usually have 8-groove, left twist rifling, although examples are known with 3-groove rifling.

Variations
Two variations known:
• Holster Model: cylinder with five chambers, in 54 bore, 5½ inch barrel.
• Belt Model: cylinder with five chambers, in 76 bore, 4 inch barrel.

Very rare at UK auctions,

HARVEY MODEL 1854 REVOLVER

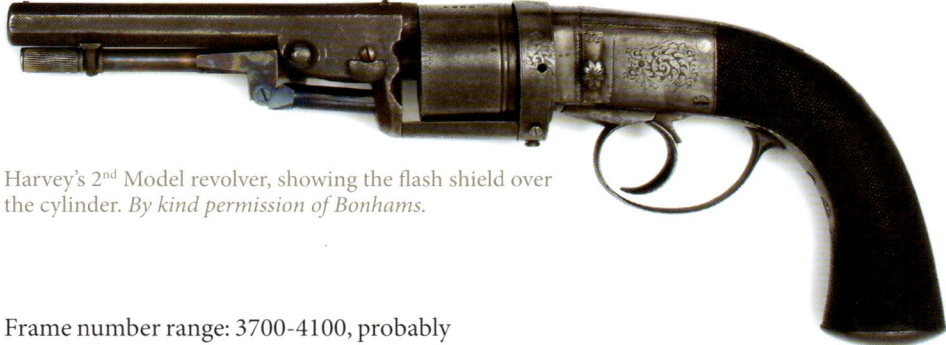

Harvey's 2nd Model revolver, showing the flash shield over the cylinder. *By kind permission of Bonhams.*

Frame number range: 3700-4100, probably not reflecting production.
Self-cocking, hammerless, transition-type percussion revolvers in 80 bore.
The serial number is found between the second and third words of the barrel address and on the cylinder. Barrels are octagonal, with a rear and fore sight fitted and secured by the frame wedge entering from the left, as in Colt's revolvers, with the screw above the wedge.
Patent information is usually inscribed on the top barrel flat, although occasionally this may be missing:

Harvey's Patent (serial no) Breech Loading Revolving Pistol:

Cylinders are plain, undecorated, with six chambers, sometimes numbered "1" to "6," and fitted with a circular shield protecting the hammer and the percussion caps. A "Harvey's Patent" loading lever is fitted under the barrel, which is similar in conformation and operation to Colt's device. These revolvers usually bear Birmingham proof marks on the barrel and cylinder. Butts are one-piece and of a narrow, saw-handle pattern with a hinged butt-trap cover.

Variations
One variation is recorded, although Harvey may have made other models:

Pocket Model: Cylinder with 6 chambers, in 80 bore, 6 inch barrel.

Values: Good: $1,300-1,700
(£800-1,000)
Fine: $2,000-2,300
(£1,200-1,350)
Rare at UK auctions.

KERR, J

Factory and retail addresses:
Factory:

London Armoury Company Ltd, Henry Street, Bermondsey. (Premises leased from Robert Adams, upon dissolution of Deane, Adams & Deane).

Later retail address:

James Kerr & Co, 114 Queen Victoria Street, London E.C. (also as "The London Armoury Company" until 1894). This company was never associated with the manufacture of the Kerr revolver.

Machine-made revolvers with some hand finishing, so parts are not readily interchangeable.

The London Armoury Company Ltd [L.A.C] appointed James Kerr as foreman of the works during Robert Adams's tenure as manager. His designs seem to have been well received because, in addition to his revolver, the company also adopted (and paid patent royalties for) a loading lever that bears his name and is used on most of the later Beaumont-Adams revolvers. Adams and the L.A.C parted company in 1858, following a dispute over the production of Adams's revolver, and Kerr's weapon may have been manufactured to replace the Beaumont-Adams, although it is undoubtedly a good weapon in its own right. Whatever its origins, this revolver was produced in significant quantities by the L.A.C and sold principally to the government of the Confederate States of America. Records show that the South bought over 10,000 Kerr revolvers, so the Confederate soldiers must have been enthusiastic about them. A few privately owned, cased examples are also known.

Kerr's design was a useful weapon for the Confederate Army, because one of his initial intentions was to produce a revolver that was simple enough to be easily repaired by a rural gunsmith or military armorer. Lockwork was a robust, self contained, "back-action" lock—as found on many Enfield muskets—with a side hammer, and the frame and barrel were in two pieces, secured together by screws. They were well finished, reliable weapons, produced in both single and double-action mode.

Care should be exercised when examining any Kerr revolver, as American buyers will pay a large premium for weapons with a Civil War history and revolvers with altered frame marks are known. It should be noted in this context that there is apparently no possibility of linking any serial number series in these weapons to any weapon used by the Confederacy.[10]

James Kerr later formed his own company (James Kerr & Co.), trading as ammunition manufacturers and agents for American firms such as Colt, Merwin Hulbert, and Winchester.

KERR MODEL 1858/1859 REVOLVER

The left side of a Kerr revolver, possibly Confederate issue, showing the side-hammer lockwork. Courtesy of James D. Julia Auctioneers, Fairfield, Maine (www.jamesajulia.com).

The right side of the Kerr revolver. The protruding cylinder arbor can clearly be seen in this well preserved example. Courtesy of James D. Julia Auctioneers, Fairfield, Maine (www.jamesdjulia.com).

Br.Pat No. 2396/1858 - Single-action revolver
Br.Pat No 242/1859. - Double-action revolver
Frame numbers: 100 - 11000, in a complex series of ranges.

There is no clear differentiation between single- and double-action weapons, apart from their operation, and they appear randomly in all frame number ranges. One authority suggests that double-action weapons are more common, although others claim the opposite.[11]

Both were solid-frame, side hammer percussion revolvers, with a "back action" lock plate screwed to the butt. They were produced in 54 and 80 bore (approximately .44 and .36 calibers, respectively), with 5¼ inch barrels and 5-grooved, left twist rifling. Cylinders were plain, with five chambers, and both cylinder and barrels will usually be found with London proof marks. In addition, barrels frequently bear a small "LAC" stamp. Cylinder arbors locate through a hole in the rear of the lock frame and protrude past the hammer, giving a characteristic appearance. Loading levers were fitted and are an original design by Kerr, although it is claimed they are not so robust as the patent design he sold for use on the Beaumont-Adams revolvers.

Frames are inscribed on the lower left side, in small script:

'LONDON ARMOURY'

It is inscribed on the right side, below the cylinder:

'KERR'S PATENT'

SMALLER ENGLISH REVOLVER MANUFACTURERS

This is followed by a frame or possibly a serial number.

Lock plates may be inscribed:

LONDON ARMOURY Co.

After 1867, James Kerr went into business on his own and revolvers made after this date are sometimes inscribed:

LONDON ARMOURY CO. , JAMES KERR & CO. , SUCCESSORS

One of the commonest marks seen on revolvers with a claimed Confederate history is the "JS over anchor," found scratched on the woodwork of a number of Kerr's revolvers. Several origins have been suggested for these marks, including the possibility that they may be a stocker's mark (of one J. Smiles, who had a workshop in London at the time,[12] or alternatively, the stamp of a Confederate arms inspector). An inspection mark seems most likely, and it is perhaps significant in this context that similar marks are also found on a number of Enfield rifles, with both London and Birmingham proof marks.[13] This makes the possibility of the "JS over anchor" being a stocker's mark unlikely, as Enfield rifles proofed in the Birmingham house would probably not have been set up by a London "stocker."

Whatever their origin, the marks found on Kerr revolver butts are quite shallow and do not seem particularly difficult to duplicate, although how they were originally applied is difficult to say. Once again, as

The patent mark on the Kerr revolver frame. *Courtesy of James D. Julia Auctioneers, Fairfield, Maine (www.jamesdjulia.com).*

The "JS over anchor" mark from a Kerr revolver. The careless way in which this mark has been inscribed is characteristic of the many Confederate weapons on which it is found. *Courtesy of James D. Julia Auctioneers, Fairfield, Maine (www.jamesdjulia.com).*

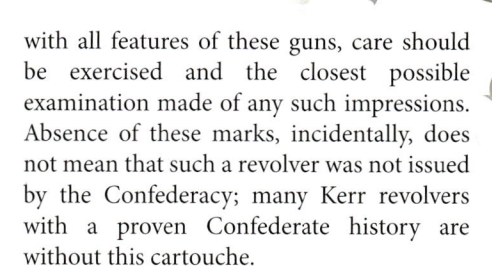

A Kerr revolver cased with accessories and showing London Armoury Co. frame marks. *By kind permission of Bonhams.*

with all features of these guns, care should be exercised and the closest possible examination made of any such impressions. Absence of these marks, incidentally, does not mean that such a revolver was not issued by the Confederacy; many Kerr revolvers with a proven Confederate history are without this cartouche.

There are few cased examples, and these were economy revolvers made for a military market.

Variations

Two variations are known:

- Double-action Model: Cylinder with five chambers, in 54 and 80 bore, 5 ¼ inch barrel.
- Single -action Model: Cylinder with five chambers, in 54 and 80 bore, 5 ¼ inch barrel.

Specification is similar in these two models, except for the variation in mechanism. They appear randomly throughout the various serial ranges, probably reflecting the L.A.C's somewhat haphazard production methods.

Values: Good: $2,000-2,300
(£1,200-1350)
Fine: $3,500-4,300
(£2,100-2,500)
Cased: $5,000-6,420
(£3,000-3,800)
Rare at UK auctions.
Common at U.S. sales.

LANG, JOSEPH

London premises:

- Gun & Pistol Repository, 7, Haymarket (1825 – 1852)
- Joseph Lang & Sons, 22, Cockspur Street, SW 1 (1853 – 1874)

Joseph Lang was a London gunmaker with a workshop listed in *Kelly's Directory* at 7, Haymarket from 1825–1852. He exhibited some four and six-barrel revolvers (presumably pepperboxes) at the Great Exhibition of 1851, and it may have been the increased business as a result of this which caused his subsequent move to 22, Cockspur Street, SW 1. The company remained there from 1852 until 1874, and at some point during this period, the name was changed to Joseph Lang & Son. Lang himself died in 1869 and probably gave up work at some earlier date, leaving his son to carry on the business.

No British patent appears to have been recorded by this maker, so the revolver was probably made using features from other makers and could not be the subject of a new patent.

LANG MODEL 1852 REVOLVER

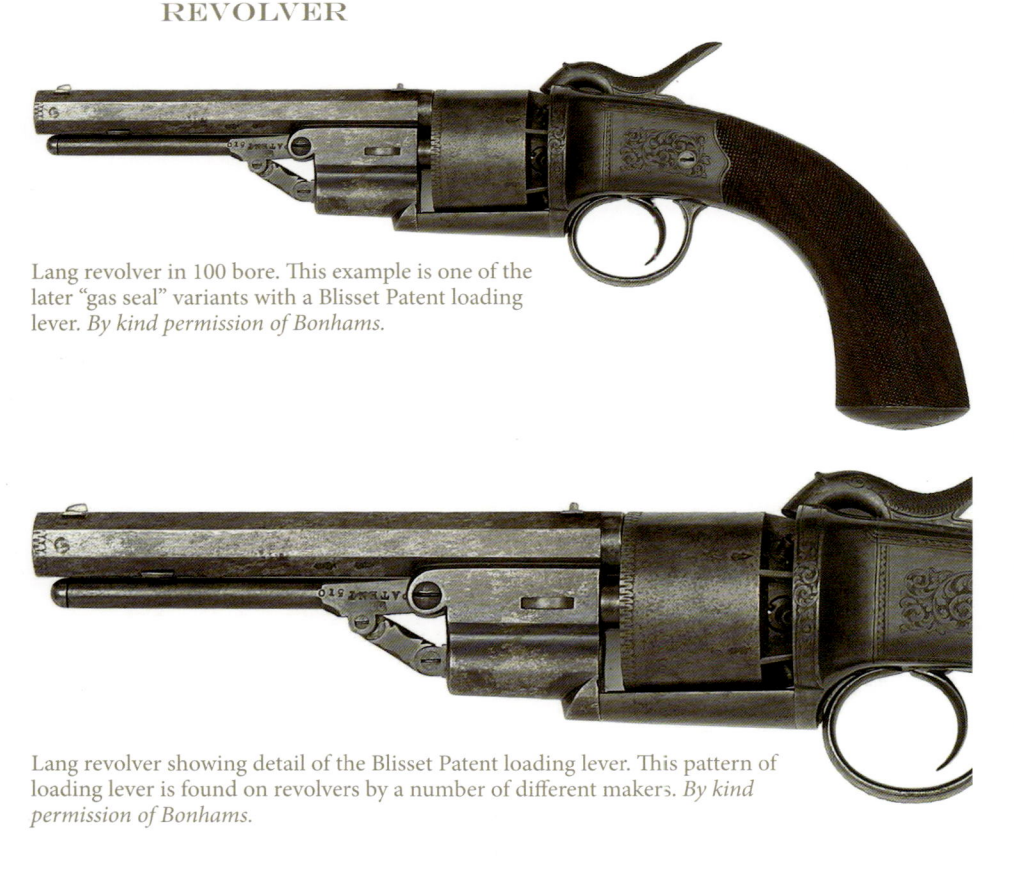

Lang revolver in 100 bore. This example is one of the later "gas seal" variants with a Blisset Patent loading lever. By kind permission of Bonhams.

Lang revolver showing detail of the Blisset Patent loading lever. This pattern of loading lever is found on revolvers by a number of different makers. By kind permission of Bonhams.

Hand-made transition revolvers (much copied).
Frame numbers: In range 1-9575. Frame numbers are stamped on all major components when present. It is not clear whether these are the manufacturer's serial numbers or retailer's stock numbers, although they are unlikely to be serial numbers and so do not reflect production.

This is an open-frame, single-action, transition-type percussion revolver in several calibers. The hammer is within the frame, but offset, with both breech and hammer usually ornately engraved. An octagonal, rifled barrel with front and rear sights on all calibers is fitted (rifling may be five, twelve, fourteen or twenty groove, depending on the maker). The barrel is retained in position by a wedge locating through the center of the cylinder arbor, entering from the right.

Maker's address, when present, is inscribed on the top barrel flat, for example:

J. LANG 22, COCKSPUR ST.

A retailer's name may also be found inscribed on the barrel flat, in place of the maker.

Cylinders may be plain or fluted, with six chambers fitted with the usual arrangement of vertical percussion cones typical of a "transition" pattern revolver.

Early examples may be without a loading lever, while later weapons have an under-barrel loading lever thought to be the subject of a separate patent owned by James Blissett. Revolvers of this type may also be found fitted with a loading lever by Pryse & Cashmore, although these are rare. Butts are usually walnut, in one piece, with fine chequering and case hardened butt "trap" (for percussion caps) with an engraved, hinged cover. Some later examples were made with a "gas seal" refinement to the lock mechanism similar in operation to that found in Collier's flintlock revolver, in that it operates to push the mouth of a chamber on to the end of the barrel, thus effecting a "gas seal."

Retailers/Makers

Seven retailers have been recorded so far, all London firms, although there may very well be others:[14]

T.K, Baker 88 Fleet St,
J Beattie, 205, Regent St,
J. Blanch & Sons, Gracechurch St,
J. Blissett, 16 & 321 High Holborn,
J. Lang 22, Cockspur St,
Parker Field & Sons,
233 High Holborn
Witton, Daw & Co, 57 Threadneedle St.

Names were inscribed on the top barrel flat; for example:

WITTON DAW & CO.

These businesses were able to make and sell copies of this weapon, presumably because the relevant mechanical features of Lang's revolver were copied from other weapons and so could not be covered by an English patent. Significantly, there is no British patent bearing Lang's name for such a revolver, although that does not necessarily mean the weapon could not have been subject to an original patent, if the inventor had wanted to go to the expense of making an application.

This revolver is typical of the type known to collectors as a "Lang" revolver, although similar weapons were produced by a number of other makers. This is a better quality transition revolver, having the frame secured by a wedge through the arbor in a manner reminiscent of a Colt revolver and fitted with a robust loading lever. Courtesy of Thomas del Mar Ltd.

Variations
Several variations known, although these are not part of a rational system:

A cylinder with 6 chambers in 44, 52, 58, 60, 70 , 80, and 120 bore, with barrels varying in length from 7 to 4½ inches; smaller caliber revolvers usually have shorter barrels, although variations from this pattern are known. Some later examples in all bores were fitted with the "gas seal" refinement, and this mechanism is described in Taylerson *et al*,[14] which also includes details of the development of these interesting revolvers.

Lang's revolver is another weapon that reflects the nature of the English revolver trade during this early period. Gunmakers probably produced these revolvers in calibers and barrel lengths to suit the customer, which was easy enough to do in a small workshop, rather than to any sort of coherent pattern. So it follows that trying to produce a system for collectors to categorize these revolvers would be problematic at best.

Values: Good: $2,000-2,400
(£1,200-1,400)
Fine: $3,000-3,400
(£1,800-2,000)
Cased: $4,200-4,600
(£2,500-2,700)
Rare at UK auctions

LEMAT'S "GRAPESHOT" REVOLVER

Invented by Dr J.A. LeMat and first patented in America in 1856, with later British Patents in 1859 and 1862, the prototypes of these unusual revolvers were made in Philadelphia by John Krider. Krider never manufactured any of these weapons commercially and large-scale production was eventually begun in Europe, where they were made by the Paris firm C.F Giraud & Cie, amongst others. Some revolvers were also made under license in Britain, probably by smaller gunsmiths working in the Birmingham gun quarter.

LeMat revolvers were of a characteristically massive, open-frame design with a nine-chambered cylinder and two barrels, and incorporating a single-action mechanism. In this initial design, the lower, shorter smoothbore barrel, upon which the cylinder revolved, was approximately .60 caliber and designed to fire a charge of shotgun pellets. Cylinders were plain, in an unusual .40 or .42 caliber, firing through the upper barrel, which had conventional rifling. The hammer was fitted with a pivoting head that could be positioned to strike either a cylinder chamber percussion cone or the single percussion cone in the top of the "grapeshot" barrel. All models had a blue finish, with a case hardened hammer and loading lever. The butt consists of two plates in chequered walnut, although in some early first models the chequering was absent.

Two models are commonly encountered, although there is also a prototype with a "Krider" barrel address, of which only a few are recorded in collections.

KRIDER PROTOTYPE

Krider prototype.
Frame number range: Unknown.

Production is claimed to be approximately 25, with five still accounted for. This first prototype was made by John Krider of Philadelphia.

Two of these weapons are well documented.[15] The first, sold from the estate of M. Auguste Francotte in 1891, bears a barrel address:

MADE BY JOHN KRIDER,
PHILADA. LE MAT'S GRAPESHOT
REVOLVER PATENT.

In addition, this weapon also bears the inscription "No 1" on the frame.

The second weapon, which came to light in northern France in 2004, bears a barrel inscription:

JOHN KRIDER &CO.,
PHILADELPHIA MAKERS COL. A.
LE MAT'S GRAPESHOT REVOLVER
PATENT NO. 2 (inscription in a
single line)

"Krider" Pattern LeMat made in Liege by Auguste Francotte, showing the early pattern rammer and the characteristic bolt stops on the surface of the cylinder.
Courtesy of James D. Julia Auctioneers, Fairfield, Maine (www.jamesdjulia.com).

Krider Pattern LeMat from the left side. A small wedge, which appears to secure the loading lever, is visible at the top left, together with its securing screw.
Courtesy of James D. Julia Auctioneers, Fairfield, Maine (www.jamesdjulia.com).

These weapons are of similar construction and differ significantly from the later models made for the Confederacy.

Barrels are octagonal over the whole length and have a 1st Model pattern loading lever mounted on the right side, with a securing screw in the barrel. They are nine shot, with a .41 caliber revolver cylinder and barrel and an 18 bore "grapeshot" barrel. Trigger guards are spur-less, the lanyard ring is fixed, and although similar in operation, the linkage between the rammer head and the operating lever differs in shape from that fitted to the 1st Model. Cylinders also have nine cylinder bolt slots visible on the external surface; these are absent from the later arms and indicate that a different method of locking the cylinder in position was used in these Krider revolvers, similar to that used in a Colt revolver. In addition, the hammer spur has a more acute angle and the join between the butt plates and the lock frame has an angular configuration, instead of the semi-circular shape of both later models. Finally, the junction between the barrel lug and the lock frame takes the form of an interlocking "key-way," which, on these Krider prototypes, also serves to hold the barrel and lock the frame together. In both later models, the barrel lug and frame simply butt together, secured by a slot and lever fitting in the 1st Model and a pin through the barrel lug and into the frame in later arms.

Copies with a very similar conformation were also made in Belgium by M. Auguste Francotte of Liege, their main difference being the form of the junction between the frame and the barrel lug. Five are recorded and significantly, none bear the inscription "A.LeMat," which was stipulated in the original contract between Le Mat and Beauregard to safeguard Le Mat's patent payments. Several of these weapons also have Liege proof marks. Francotte was certainly responsible for copying a number of British and European arms, including Adams and Beaumont-Adams revolvers. However, he manufactured Robert Adams's revolvers under license and these weapons are always inscribed with the relevant patent information. Some Belgian copies of the Krider prototype of Le Mat's revolver are unmarked, although the superior quality of manufacture is reminiscent of M. Francotte's work.

1ST MODEL (MANUFACTURED: 1860-1861)

Very early 1st Model LeMat (serial no. 7) with the characteristic barrel catch, trigger guard, and lanyard ring. *Courtesy of James D. Julia Auctioneers, Fairfield, Maine (www.jamesdjulia.com).*

Early 1st Model LeMat revolver with its characteristic right mounted loading lever. *Courtesy of James D. Julia Auctioneers, Fairfield, Maine (www.jamesdjulia.com).*

Krider Pattern Le Mat, showing the characteristic junction between the lower lock frame and the barrel lug. In later revolvers, this was a butt joint, secured with a lever or pin. The "crowned AF" is the trademark of M. Auguste Francotte. *Courtesy of James D. Julia Auctioneers, Fairfield, Maine (www.jamesdjulia.com).*

SMALLER ENGLISH REVOLVER MANUFACTURERS

Frame numbers: range: 1 - 562
Total production: Approximately 450– 490.

Made under LeMat's European Patents, including British Patent 1081/1862, in a serial or frame number range of 1 to approximately 562.[16] Frame numbers may also be found on the barrel and cylinder, with the last two digits stamped on other components. Frames typically also bear LeMat's first trademark—a conjoined "L" and "M" in script letters enclosed in a circle, and apparently applied as a single stamp. Details of this stamp are often not clear.

Characteristically round with an octagonal section at the breech lug, the upper, rifled barrel has the early pattern loading lever mounted on the right and a substantial, internally-threaded ring brazed on to its lower flat. This ring fits on to the threaded end of the lower barrel, which also serves as the cylinder arbor. The barrel is screwed on to the lower barrel or arbor, and when correctly positioned and flush with the lock frame, it is secured by a lever on the frame that locates into a slot on the barrel lug. Shot barrels are .60 (or .62) caliber and approximately five inches long, with the .40 (or .42) caliber revolver barrels longer at 6¾ inches and marked on the top flat:

COL. LeMAT'S PATENT

Two 1st Models are also known, marked "1" and "4," with a barrel address in the following form:

LEMAT'S PATENT

Some examples of this model also bear a Liege proof mark in the form of an "E" over an "LG" with a star beneath, all contained in an oval ring. These proof marks are often stamped on the front of the cylinder and may be difficult to interpret correctly. No 1st Model is recorded with either London or Birmingham proof marks.

Cylinders are round, plain, and undecorated, with nine chambers. They have no cylinder bolt slots on the outer surface, although there are circular depressions on the rear of the cylinder that engage the small, fragile cylinder bolt. Loading levers fitted to 1st Model Le Mat revolvers consist of a hollow lever that moves the loading lever head into the cylinder via a substantial linkage. A second, conventionally designed rammer for the shot barrel is contained in the hollow lever of the first device.

Early form of barrel address. Courtesy of James D. Julia Auctioneers, Fairfield, Maine (www.jamesdjulia.com).

Early form of trademark. Courtesy of James D. Julia Auctioneers, Fairfield, Maine (www.jamesdjulia.com).

A spurred trigger guard is always found on this model, together with a swivelling lanyard ring. A front sight is fitted, along with a hammer notch rear sight.

Rare at UK and U.S. auctions.

2ND MODEL (MANUFACTURED: 1861-1862)

Similar in conformation to the 1st Model, with nine rounds in the cylinder and a shot barrel under the longer, rifled upper barrel.

2nd Model LeMat, this one made in England and bearing Birmingham proof marks. Courtesy of James D. Julia Auctioneers, Fairfield, Maine (www.jamesdjulia.com).

Three frame number ranges are recorded:[17]

1195 – 1845
2003 – 2412
8016 – 8974

2nd Model LeMat revolvers showing the characteristic loading lever and fixed lanyard ring. By kind permission of Bonhams.

London barrel address found on guns made in England. *Courtesy of James D. Julia Auctioneers, Fairfield, Maine (www.jamesdjulia.com).*

These ranges are reported to be characterized by differing barrel addresses, although there is some overlap:

- Col. Le Mat Bte s.g.d.g. Paris (nos. 1195 -1950)
- SYSTME LE MAT BTE S.G.D.G. PARIS (nos. 2003 – 2412)
- LeMat & Girard's Patent London (nos. 8016 – 8974)

Frame numbers may be found additionally on the barrel and cylinder, with the last two digits stamped on components like the loading lever. The trademark, when present, is also stamped:

L*M

Its position is variable; it may be found either on the barrel or the cylinder. Often poorly struck, the star and both letters appear to have been applied with three separate stamps. In addition to the trademark, London proof marks have been recorded,[18] as well as the names of British and French retailers stamped on the shot barrel.[19]

The revolver barrel is octagonal over its whole length, with the loading lever mounted on the left side by a single screw into the lower section of the barrel lug. The lever itself is hollow and contains a conventional rammer for the shot barrel. The barrel screws on to the cylinder arbor in a similar manner to the 1st Model, but the barrel and lock frame are secured in position by a large-headed, thick-bodied retaining pin machined flat on one side. This passes through the barrel lug and into the frame, where it is retained by a substantial, spring loaded lug that locates in the flat of the retaining pin, thus preventing its accidental removal. The shape of the retaining pin's head may have a number of forms and occasionally bears the last two digits of the frame number. Cylinders are similar in conformation to the 1st Model, with cylinder bolt slots on the rear of the cylinder. Trigger guards are round and spurless on the 2nd Model, and a more robust, fixed lanyard ring is incorporated into the lock casting at the butt. Front and rear sights are identical to the 1st Model.

TRANSITIONAL OR INTERMEDIATE VARIATIONS

Intermediate Model Le Mat revolver with a 1st Model spurred trigger guard and frame lock, but a 2nd Model loading lever mounted on the left side. *Courtesy of James D. Julia Auctioneers, Fairfield, Maine (www.jamesdjulia.com).*

Barrel address from an Intermediate Model. *Courtesy of James D. Julia Auctioneers, Fairfield, Maine (www.jamesdjulia.com).*

As well as the two models already described, there are a number of variants, usually described as "Transition," "Army," "Navy," or "Artillery" models. Given the nature of nineteenth century revolver manufacture in general and M. Giraud's rather inept and unlucky operations in particular, these were probably not specifically designed transitional models. They are much more likely to have been made up from parts left over from the 1st Model's production run, so as not to waste those remaining components already available.

The major components of a Le Mat revolver that show structural differences between the 1st and 2nd Models are the loading lever, butt and lock frame assembly, the barrel, and the trigger guard. The 1st Models seem to have been of adequate quality, most of the criticism being levelled at the 2nd Models delivered to the Navy. These 2nd Models were often poorly made throughout, and it may be that the changes to the loading lever, modifications to the trigger guard, and other features were incorporated to cut costs, rather than improve performance. If this is the correct explanation, the following variations could be expected:

1] 1st Model spurred trigger guard, frame (i.e., with the swivelling lanyard ring), round barrel and early barrel/frame securing device, but 2nd Model loading lever. (This variation is recorded.)

2] 1st Model spurred trigger guard and barrel/frame securing device, but 2nd Model barrel and loading lever (this variation is recorded with frame number 767).

3] 1st Model spurred trigger guard but 2nd Model frame, barrel, and loading lever (this variation is also known; Le Mat frame no. 941[20]).

Frame numbers on these early variations are in ranges between the first and second models, as might be expected if such variations can be explained by their production history, rather than as specific designs.

Incidentally, this mixing of components is a feature of a number of nineteenth century revolver manufacturers' production. Robert Adams produced his Beaumont–Adams revolver with frames left over from the production run of the earlier, self-cocking

42   SMALLER ENGLISH REVOLVER MANUFACTURERS

arm and William Tranter followed a similar system with his later revolvers. Many of the variants produced by Colt are also known to be the result of expediency rather than design. This was a particular feature of some of the later London Colts, in which Hartford-made parts were used to supplement parts made in the London factory for the final batch of 4th Model London Colt Navys.

Rare at UK and U.S. auctions.

"BABY" LE MAT

Frame numbers: In a unique range from 1 to approximately 100

Similar in conformation to the larger revolver, nine shot .32 caliber cylinder with an upper 4¼ inch, octagonal revolver barrel and a lower, 2¾ inch, .41 caliber grapeshot barrel. All features identical to the 2nd Model, with loading levers and furniture reduced in size to suit the smaller weapon. Barrels are inscribed on the top flat:

SYSTEME. LE MAT BTE S.G.D.G. PARIS

This indicates that the smaller revolver may have been part of the production run of larger revolvers in the second serial range (2003–2412), although their design and production history remain obscure. Correspondence has been cited showing that 2,000 of these revolvers were ordered, although records show that only about 100 were actually delivered.[21]

Le Mat revolvers were also produced as both pin-fire and center-fire weapons, although neither type was ever made in Britain. There was also a percussion carbine and a good reproduction percussion revolver.

THE "ENGLISH-MADE" GUNS

If any Le Mats were made in Britain, they were almost certainly copies produced by small gunsmiths, probably in the Birmingham Quarter, either clandestinely or under license to Giraud & Cie. There is also recent evidence suggesting those revolvers in the 8000-9000 serial range were made by Tipping & Lawden.[22] They were originally a London firm that had offices and a factory in the Birmingham Gun Quarter,[23] which would explain why all their Le Mats had Birmingham proof marks. They were taken over in 1877 by P Webley & Sons.[24] Incidentally, these

Reproduction Le Mat revolver from the left side to show the loading lever and hammer positioned to fire the center barrel.

Reproduction Le Mat revolver, right side. The hammer nose is set to fire the lower barrel.

Reproduction Le Mat revolver disassembled into its main components.

English-made revolvers have two different mechanisms for cycling and bolting the cylinder, depending on their origin.[25]

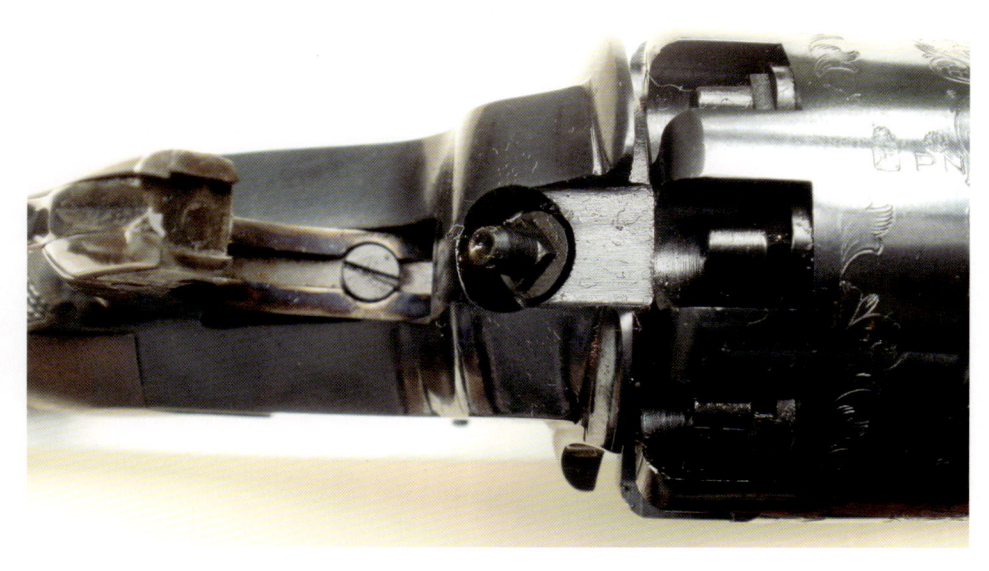

Reproduction Le Mat revolver showing the lock mechanism for the upper and lower barrels.

Reproduction Le Mat revolver showing the barrel address. This address is characteristic of the earliest 1st Models, while the reproduction is clearly based on the 2nd Model.

Reproduction Le Mat revolver showing the cylinder bolt stop slots. This cylinder is similar to Le Mat's later design.

It is extremely unlikely that either the London Armoury Co. (L.A.C) or the Birmingham Small Arms Co (BSA) were making Le Mat revolvers during this period, although Huse claimed that one of Girard & Cie's early revolvers was inspected by the L.A.C. The London firm was wholly occupied in producing Enfield rifles and Kerr revolvers for the Confederacy and had even parted from its manager, Robert Adams, because the Board wanted to concentrate on the more lucrative rifle manufacture, rather than Beaumont-Adams revolvers. BSA is an even more unlikely candidate, since the company was formed in 1861 by a collection of Birmingham gunmakers expressly to obtain and fill British government arms contracts. And even if either company wanted to do business with Giraud or the Confederacy, the cost of the plant to produce Le Mat revolvers by machine would have been prohibitive, to say the very least.

Le Mat and Giraud almost certainly produced their guns in the old-fashioned, time-honored way—with a number of small contractors producing parts and setting up the guns—while Giraud & Cie were middle men, assembling some of the weapons in their Paris factory and managing the shipping and contracts.

Values:
 1st Model:
  Good: $50,800-54,150 (£30,000-32,000)
  Fine: $76,150-84,600 (£45,000-50,000)
 Intermediate Models:
  Good: $34,000-37,200 (£20,000-22,000)
  Fine: $45,700-50,800 (£27,000-30,000)
 2nd Models:
  Good: $42,300-45,700 (£25,000-27,000)
  Fine: $54,100-59,200 (£32,000-35,000)
 Rare at UK auctions.
 "Baby" Le Mat:
  Good: $42,300-45,700 (£25,000-27,000)
  Fine: $54,100-59,200 (£32,000-35,000)
 Common at U.S. auctions.

SMALLER ENGLISH REVOLVER MANUFACTURERS

MOORE, W & HARRIS, W

One of the smaller Birmingham gun making firms.
Hand-made percussion revolvers.
Most usually found as the makers of fine flintlock and percussion sporting guns, Moore & Harris also made a small number of revolvers.

MOORE & HARRIS MODEL 1852 REVOLVER

British Patent No 69/1852
Frame number series range: 1-104

Self-cocking percussion revolver featuring a barrel that tipped up on a frame hinge for the removal of the cylinder, in 90 bore. The barrel is octagonal, with fore sight fitted and retailer's details inscribed on the top flat, as in the following example:

Retailed by H. Hand (Late with Manton & Son), London, No. 104, Circa 1852

The frame incorporated a spring-loaded barrel catch on the lower right side, allowing the barrel to tip up for loading. Right of frame is inscribed:

'Moore & Harris Patent A.D. 1853, no. 104'

The cylinder has six chambers and this example bears London proof marks.
The revolver is fitted with an angular butt (commonly referred to as a "saw handle"), similar in configuration to that seen on some Mortimer dueling pistols.
These guns appear to have been made in small numbers. They are extremely rare and no further information has currently become available regarding their specific features.

Variations
Only one known (the example described).
Pocket Model: chambered in 90 bore, with a 7½ inch barrel.

Moore & Harris revolver showing the saw-handle butt and hinged frame. By kind permission of Bonhams.

Values: Good: $3,400-3,700
          (£2,000-2,200)
          Fine: $5,900-6,800
          (£3,500-4,000)

Rare at UK sales, but typically only found as very rare museum pieces.

PENNELL, THOMAS

One of the smaller Birmingham gunmakers of hand-made transition revolvers
Revolvers with a completely encased lock mechanism. These weapons were well made and often highly engraved, although they are rare. Although Pennell never finalized his patent application, he did produce a number of self-cocking revolving pistols and rifles to this design.

PENNELL MODEL 1853 REVOLVER

British Patent No. 1038/1853
Frame number range: Unknown

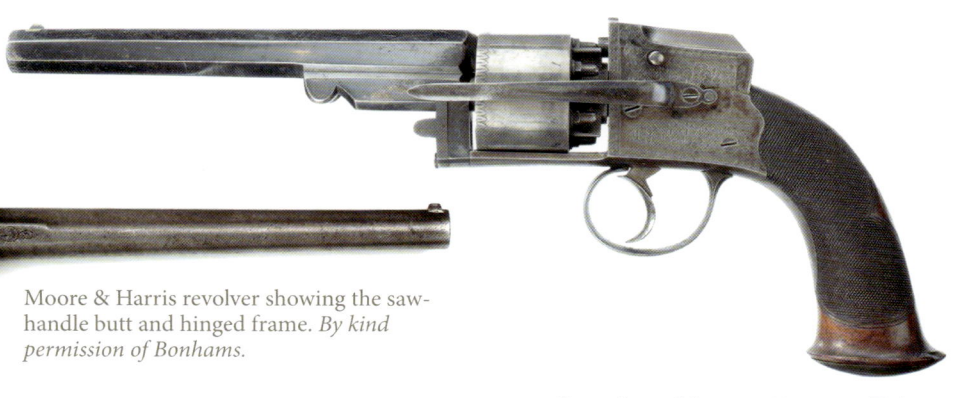

Pennell revolver of the transition type. This example is fitted with a belt hook. Courtesy of Peter Finer.

Pennell revolver from the right side. Courtesy of Peter Finer.

Open-frame, self-cocking percussion revolver with enclosed hammer. It may have a safety catch on the left side of the frame. The barrel is blued, octagonal, and fitted with fore and rear sight; 54, 56, and 60 bore examples are known, with barrel lengths of 6½ and 7½ inches, respectively. Shorter barrels probably correspond to the smaller bore weapons, as is the case with other revolvers, but details are so far unavailable.

A retailer's name is often inscribed on the top barrel flat, for example:

W. CHANCE, SON & CO

Cylinders were chambered for six rounds, with chambers numbered "1" to "6," and percussion cones horizontal. Detachable loading levers were fitted, located beneath the barrel and secured

Pennell revolver showing the retailer's name: "W. CHANCE.SON & Co." *Courtesy of Peter Finer.*

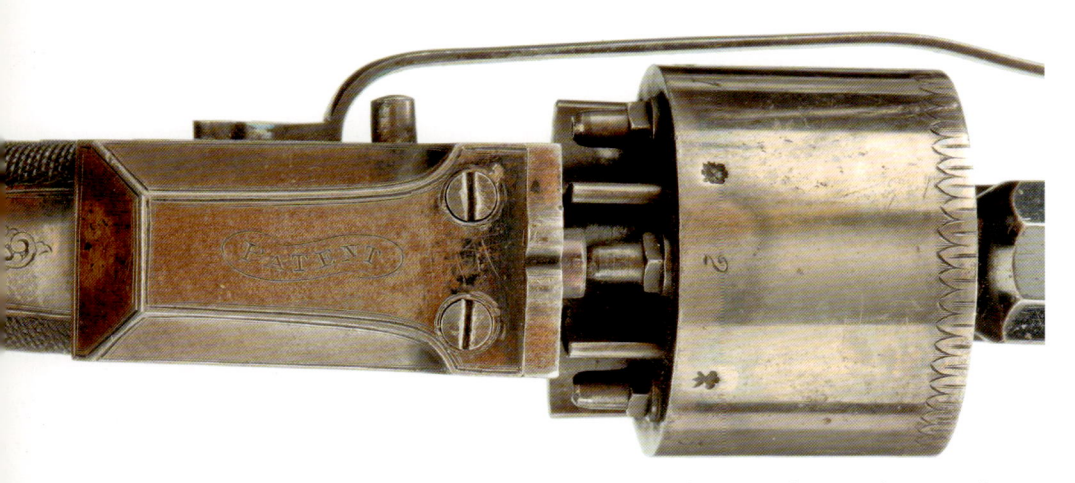

Pennell revolver showing the "Patent" lettering, cylinder numbering, and Birmingham Proof marks. The Proof marks are not very clear, which is typical of such marks for this period. *Courtesy of Peter Finer.*

Reeves revolver. This weapon is fitted with the Reeves Patent loading lever and hammer spring safety. *By kind permission of Bonhams.*

Reeves revolver showing the characteristic safety catch, Birmingham proof marks on the cylinder, and the frame number. *By kind permission of Bonhams.*

by a pivoting catch. The butt is chequered walnut or other hardwood. Belt hooks, silver frames, and butt-boxes for percussion caps were also sometimes fitted.

Variations
Two variations of the Holster Model are known:

• Cylinder with 6 chambers, in 54 or 56 bore, 7½ inch barrel.
• Cylinder with 6 chambers, in 60 bore, 6½ inch barrel.

Values: Good: $4,200-4,600
(£2,500-2,750)
Fine: $6,700-8,000
(£4,000-4,750)
Rare at UK auctions.

PRYSE, CHARLES

Birmingham gunsmith responsible for a number of important nineteenth century revolver patents. However, all the patents for his Webley-Pryse revolver were the property of Belgian gunsmiths and manufacturers.[26]

Trade associations:
• Pryse & Cashmore: Charles Pryse and Paul Cashmore registered a British patent in 1855.

British Patent 2018/1855 protects what has come to be known by collectors as the "Daw" revolver, as well as a number of loading lever designs.
• Pryce & Redman: Recorded at 84, Aston Street, Birmingham. A partnership between Charles Pryse and Richard Redmond. They produced the percussion/rim-fire versions of the Deane-Harding revolver under license from John Deane.

REEVES, CHARLES

Charles Reeves was one of the smaller Birmingham gunmakers. He also produced "Trade" revolvers, or copies of the products of larger manufacturers.

REEVES MODEL 1857/1858 REVOLVER

British Patent No 3156/1857
British. Patent No 1623/1858
Hand-made revolvers.
Both Patents refer to a 5 shot, 54 bore revolver.
There is a second, very rare Reeves revolver recorded fitted with a refinement of the previous double-action mechanism, although details of this weapon are scanty (British Patent No. 2690/1857).

Frame numbers: In range 500–2000 (may not reflect production).
Solid-frame, double-action percussion revolver with an inspection plate on the left side. Number on the right of frame, without patent information, while the left of frame is inscribed:

46   SMALLER ENGLISH REVOLVER MANUFACTURERS

Reeves Patent

Only examples of the 54 bore Model, with 6½ inch octagonal barrels, are known. Barrels rifled with five grooves, clockwise, although an example with unique rifling is also recorded.[27] The cylinder is plain, unfluted, and has five chambers. Often fitted with a Reeves Patent hinged loading lever and a sprung safety catch that operates by engaging the hammer, rather than locking the cylinder, as is more usual. These revolvers have been recorded with Birmingham proof marks, although a number are known that do not bear any proof marks.

Reeves is also recorded as having produced a rim-fire revolver, although examples are extremely rare, and the firm was also responsible for Trade copies of rim-fire and center-fire weapons by a number of makers.

TIPPING & LAWDEN

Recorded at 40, Constitution Hill, Birmingham; gunmaker responsible for manufacture of the Deane-Harding revolver, under license to John Deane. One of the 20 members of the Birmingham Small Arms Trading Company Ltd (BSA). Amalgamated with Webley and Sons in 1877, possibly to take advantage of certain British patents then held by Tipping. Also thought to have produced the Le Mat revolver under license.

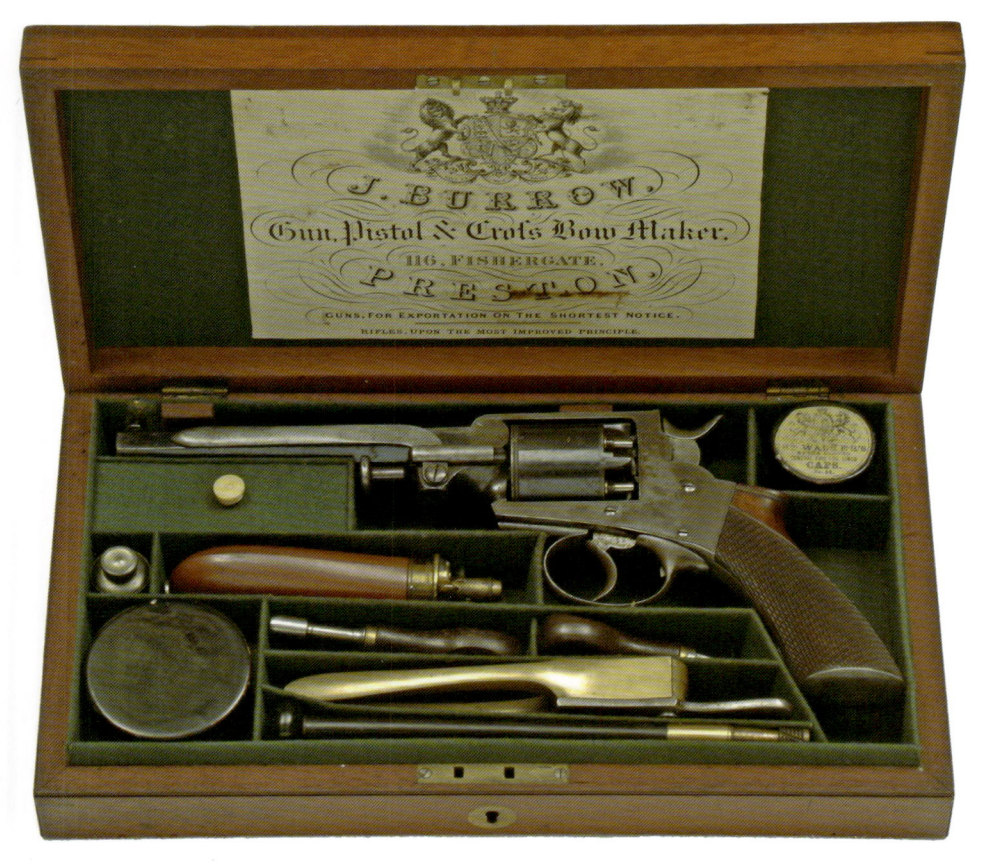

Reeves revolver cased with accessories. This example is fitted with a Kerr Patent loading lever. Retailed by "J. Burrow" of Preston. This case also includes an unusual cap box by R. P Walker. By kind permission of Bonhams.

Variations
Holster Model:

Cylinder with five chambers, in 54 bore; 6½ inch barrel with 5-groove, clockwise rifling.

Values: Good: $2,180-2,500
(£1,300-1,500)
Fine: $5,000-5,500
(£3,000-3,250)
Rare at UK auctions.

TRANTER, WILLIAM

(see "Tranter revolvers")

WALLIS, C.E

Patent address:
Millman Street, Bedford Row,
Holborn, London.
Hand-made revolvers.

WALLIS MODEL 1863 PERCUSSION REVOLVER (TRANSITION TYPE)

British Patent 2248/1863: A revolver with a cylinder fitted with two rows of six percussion cones.
British Patent 624/1864: Refinements to Patent 2248/1863.

Two models are known. Both are clearly recognizable as "transition" type revolvers, but the arrangements of the percussion cones vary between the two models. Very rare and detailed information about their features is unavailable.

Serial number range: Unknown.

Open-framed with a bar hammer, although they look distinctly unlike a conventional transition-type revolver. Both models have octagonal barrels and are without either front or rear sights.

Wallis's patents described a revolver with two rows of percussion cones, one behind the other, fitted to the cylinder to fire the "double-charged" chambers. The weapon's long bar hammer was also arranged to slide so as to be able to fire the rear loads after the front charges had been cleared. Cylinders in the early model are plain. In the later model, the cylinder features narrow ribs on the external surface, with the rear row of percussion cones covered by a protective band. These percussion cones are also sited much further forward on the earlier model. The loading lever on both models is similar to Kerr's device, with the lower arm of the lever being screwed to the frame, while the rammer head is screwed to the middle of the lever itself.

Examples of these weapons are in the E.M Perry and J.B Bell collections, with existing specimens now probably confined to museums.[28]

Very rare at UK and U.S. auctions.

WEBLEY

(see "Webley revolvers")

WESTLEY-RICHARDS, WILLIAM

Birmingham gunmaker who produced hand-made pepperbox and conventional revolvers. They later produced Martini-Henry rifles, Webley revolvers, and Lee-Enfield rifles under Government contract. They are still in business (2013) as makers of fine hand-made shotguns.

PEPPERBOX REVOLVERS

Hand-made pepperbox revolvers.
Six-barrelled, bar-hammered, pepperbox percussion revolver, in 54 bore. The barrel block is sometimes inscribed "1" to "5," with the maker's name in decorative "ribbon" on the left side of the breech, and may also feature an engraved percussion cone cover. Well made arms with heavy engraving.

Values: Good: $1,600-2,300
(£1,000-1,375)
Fine: $4,800-5,300
(£2,900-3,150)
Rare at UK auctions.

CONVENTIONAL REVOLVERS

Hand-made revolvers.

WESTLEY-RICHARDS MODEL 1852 REVOLVER

English Patent No 14027/1852
Frame number range: Approximately 1-350
Self-cocking percussion revolvers with cylinders chambered for five shots and an unusual frame configuration, being open below the cylinder. Hammers may be centrally mounted or, more rarely, as a side hammer. Examples with frame numbers between 30 and 323 have been recorded, although there may be others.

The barrel is octagonal and has a narrow, blade front sight, while a groove in the top-strap serves as the rear sight. The plain cylinder is chambered for five rounds with characteristically angled percussion cones. They are often engraved, and chambers may also be numbered. They are fitted with Richards's rack and pinion loading lever protected under British Patent 993/1854, when such a device is present. Butt is in one piece, of walnut, and may be fitted with a cap-box.

Variations
Holster Model:
• Cylinder with five chambers, in 36 bore, 7 inch barrel.
Belt Model:
• Cylinder with five chambers, in 80 bore, 5½ inch barrel.
• Also a rare Belt Model in 90 bore with a 4 inch barrel.

Values: Good: $2,000-2,500
(£1,200-1,500)
Fine: $3,300-4,700
(£2,000-2,800)
Rare at UK auctions.

WESTLEY-RICHARDS MODEL 1855 REVOLVER

British Patent No 911/1855 – Single-action, side hammer revolver.
Frame numbers: Below 100
Open-frame, single-action percussion revolver with a unique lock assembly, the hammer being mounted on a plate formed in the frame. Only weapons with numbers below 100 have been recorded. Found in 52 and 60 bore, both with 6 inch barrels rifled with 21 grooves. The cylinder is plain and unfluted, with six chambers.
Richards's own patent loading lever is usually fitted (British Patent No. 993/1854).

Variations
Holster Models:
• Cylinder with five chambers, in 52 bore, 6 inch barrel.
• Cylinder with five chambers, in 60 bore, 6 inch barrel.

Very rare at UK auctions.

Westley-Richards open framed, self-cocking revolver, Model 1852. It is unusual in having a side-mounted, spur-less hammer. *By kind permission of Bonhams.*

Westley-Richards Model 1853 self-cocking revolver showing the lockwork. *By kind permission of Bonhams.*

SMALLER ENGLISH REVOLVER MANUFACTURERS

CHAPTER THREE
Adams and Beaumont-Adams Revolvers

Adams's self-cocking revolvers made their first public appearance at the Great Exhibition in 1851. Although manufacture of Adams's revolver had begun some time previously under his British patent 13527/1851, only a single, silver plated, ebony-stocked revolver was displayed on the stand of his former employers, George & John Deane. Adams and John Deane were already in partnership with Deane's son as Deane, Adams & Deane, but strangely, this company, which would be the future manufacturers of Adams's revolvers until 1856, exhibited no revolvers of any kind, offering only a collection of patent gun locks and peculiar "raised rib" rifles.

By contrast, in the American Pavilion, Adams's main competitor, Colonel Samuel Colt, exhibited hundreds of his machine-made, single-action, percussion revolvers and his stand seems to have aroused much interest, especially amongst the military.

As a result of their success at the Exhibition, a public test of Adams's revolver and Colt's Dragoon model took place at Woolwich on 10 September 1851, before the British Government's Committee on Small Arms and a number of other interested parties, including the inventors. Adams's revolver appears to have proved superior to the Colt in every test, although whether the statements in a pamphlet circulated later by Adams, in which he claims superior accuracy for his weapon, are true, remain to be seen.

Despite this, the Board of Ordnance found neither revolver suitable for service use. In the case of the Adams, this may have been because these early weapons had no loading lever, the ball being seated in the cylinder by thumb pressure alone. Such an arrangement works if the lead ball is new and uncorroded, although when using poor quality ammunition seating the ball well enough to prevent it being jolted out of the cylinder is extremely difficult.

Having failed to gain the military contract, in June 1852, Adams was forced to arrange a loan from Hankey's, the London merchant bank, so he could expand his business. In order to do this, he granted T.A. Hankey of that firm a 1/8 share in English Patent 13527/1851, which covered his revolver. With this loan, Adams and his partners began their new, steam-powered manufacturing operation at a factory sited at No 2, Weston St, although they also retained their old retail premises at No. 30, King William St, London Bridge.

Early in this Deane, Adams & Deane partnership, lack of manufacturing capacity obliged Adams to grant a number of manufacturing licenses to UK and Belgian gunsmiths in order to meet demand for his revolver. These licenses usually allowed the manufacture of complete weapons, although in some cases, the arrangement also involved the manufacture of parts to be assembled at the London factory of Deane, Adams & Deane. William Tranter, Hollis and Sheath, and Joseph Brazier were the main British licensees and suppliers during this period.[1]

Deane, Adams & Deane continued manufacturing the self-cocking revolver and some early double-action weapons in their Weston Street factory until 1856, when, coinciding closely with Adams's purchase of Lt. Beaumont's patent for a modification to the internal mechanism, the partnership was dissolved and Adams transferred his assets, including his patents, to the London Armoury Company (Limited). Here he began manufacturing the double-action Beaumont-Adams—the type most usually thought of as characteristic of Adams's revolver design.

Approved by the British Army, it was a robust, reliable weapon. However, many users thought it was not as accurate as Colt's revolver, although there seems to have been little real difference between them. Colt revolver sights consist of a simple "V" notch cut in the top of the hammer and a brass pin for the foresight, so it is difficult to see how any subsequent manufacturer could fail to improve upon such an arrangement. The double-action mechanism of the Adams must also have endeared it to many, especially at close quarters, while the single-action option makes it as accurate as Colt's Navy Model, at least over sensible revolver ranges.

These later Beaumont-Adams had several other improvements over the earlier design, apart from the action. Most importantly, they now left the factory with some type of loading lever fitted, which greatly improved their loading characteristics.

Service orders for this improved revolver are recorded as beginning on 3 January 1856, and details of these transactions between the War Department and the London Armoury Company are included in Chamberlain and Taylerson's excellent and exhaustive book.[2] It will, however, be sufficient to say here that quantities of Beaumont-Adams revolvers were ordered by the War Department for experimentation and service use between 1856 and 1861, and that these weapons will usually have frame or production numbers in the B3600/19000R – B20000/36000R range, although revolvers from the earlier "14000R" range were also purchased. A letter from a Captain Caffin RA (Naval Director General of Artillery) in January 1856, confirms that the price for an Adams revolver, delivered as part of a contract lot of 2,000, was the princely sum of $14 (£2 17s 6d) each. Prices, sad to say, have risen a little since that time!

Adams's revolvers were clearly considered an excellent weapon by many in the military. One officer in the 88th

Regiment was so impressed that he was moved to write to the inventor, showing, as the L.A.C advertisement put it, "...the efficiency of the Revolver in the heat and excitement of battle..."

> Army and Navy Club,
> 6th January, 1855
> Sir,
> In these days of warfare, any invention of improvements in firearms should be patronized and assisted, and with that view I write you this letter.
> I had one of your largest-sized Revolver Pistols at the bloody battle of Inkermann, and by some chance got surrounded by Russians. I then found the advantages of your pistol over Colonel Colt's, for had I to cock before each shot, I should have lost my life; but with yours, having only to pull the trigger, I was able to shoot four Russians, and thereby save my life.
> I should not have had time to cock, as they were too close to me, being only a few yards; so close that I was bayoneted through the thigh immediately after shooting the fourth man.
> I hope this may be of service to you, as I certainly owe my life to your invention of the Revolver Pistol.
>
> I have the honour to be,
> Your obedient servant,
> J. G Crosse,
> 88th Regiment[3]

Robert Adams's association with the London Armoury Co. ended in 1858, when he resigned as manager and returned to his own business, selling revolvers from his address at 76, King William Street. This dislocation appears to have come about because of arguments over the relative importance of revolver production in the firm's future, and probably explains why Adams revolver production after 1861 is somewhat disjointed, the "B" prefix and "R" suffix having been abandoned at the 21000/36000 range. The Beaumont number itself was also discarded at around 23000/38000, presumably coinciding with the lapsing of the Lieutenant's patent in 1862. After this period, revolvers with frame numbers in the ranges 30000, 39000, 40000, 41000, 50000, 51000, 60000P, and 100000 are all encountered, although this is not an indicator of the level of production.

AMERICAN REVOLVERS

A number of Beaumont-Adams revolvers were also exported to America in 1857, four years before the start of the Civil War.

Adams's agent, Roswell Ripley, sold the U.S. Ordnance Department 100 imported Adams in March 1857. These weapons were of .36 caliber and they do not appear to have been of very good quality. Despite these problems, the U.S. Ordinance Dept. ordered another 500 Adams revolvers, this time to be manufactured by the Massachusetts Arms Co (Mass.Arms.Co), with all of these weapons to be of either .36 or .31 caliber. American Adams revolvers, either imported or of Mass.Arms.Co manufacture, were all of either .36 and .31 calibers,[4] despite published claims to the contrary. Adams also had some involvement with the "Adams Revolving Arms Company" of New York between 1857 and 1859, although it is doubtful whether this concern ever produced any revolvers.[5]

Sales of Beaumont-Adams revolvers began to slow around 1863, with the appearance of excellent weapons made by Webley and Tranter, amongst others. Robert Adams was ordered to surrender in bankruptcy as of January 1865, and he closed his London premises in 1866.

He died on Tuesday, 13 September 1870, at the home of a friend in Westwood Park, Forest Hill, London.

REVOLVER PRODUCTION

Adams revolver manufacture during the period of their production tended to be somewhat erratic. They were often supplied in both the caliber and type required by a particular customer, so a coherent account of every revolver a buyer is likely to encounter would be difficult, if not impossible. Nor would it be particularly useful.

However, all Adams revolvers have production/frame numbers and these series are probably the best aid to identifying the date of manufacture and manufacturing history of any particular weapon. Such numbers are not serial numbers in the normal sense, and they appear to have been simply stamped on the guns to give an exact count of weapons produced under any given patent agreement to ensure that correct payment was made to the relevant parties.

These numbers do, however, fit into a clearly defined chronology, with low numbers being on the earliest weapons, allowing their use as the basis for identification and a description of the history of the early Adams self-cocking revolver and later Beaumont-Adams. They are stamped on both cylinder and frame, and weapons in which they match usually have a higher value than those whose numbers do not correspond. Characteristics described for any particular class of production numbers are for guidance only. Exceptions are frequent, and where known, are included here.

ADAMS SELF-COCKING PERCUSSION REVOLVER MODEL 1851 (MANUFACTURED 1851-1856)

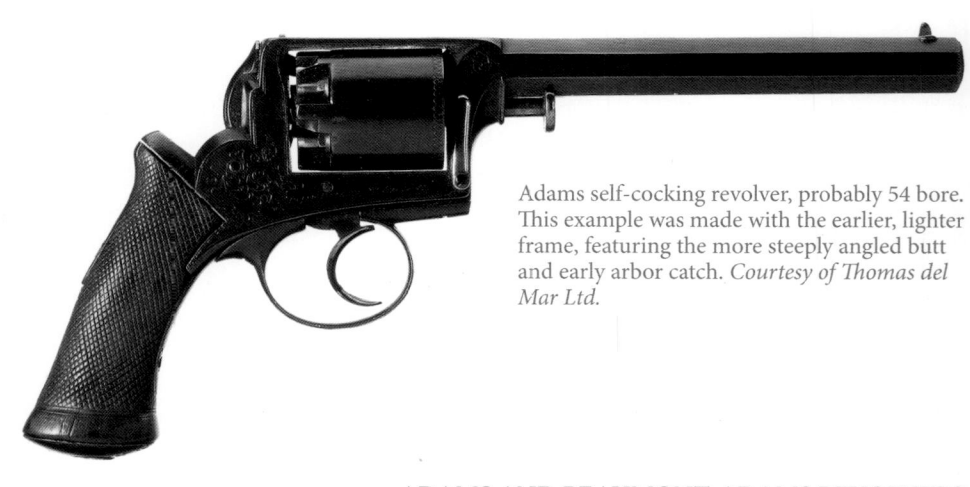

Adams self-cocking revolver, probably 54 bore. This example was made with the earlier, lighter frame, featuring the more steeply angled butt and early arbor catch. *Courtesy of Thomas del Mar Ltd.*

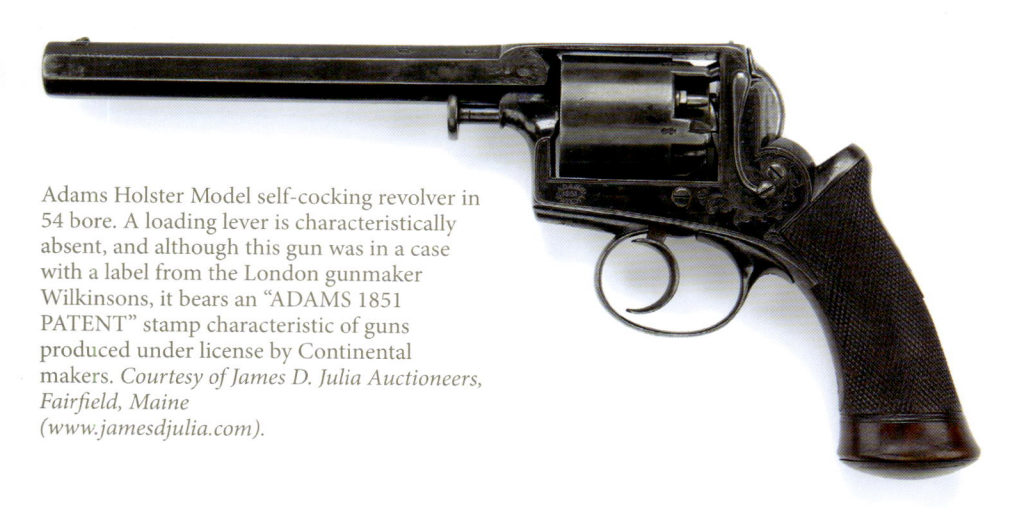

Adams Holster Model self-cocking revolver in 54 bore. A loading lever is characteristically absent, and although this gun was in a case with a label from the London gunmaker Wilkinsons, it bears an "ADAMS 1851 PATENT" stamp characteristic of guns produced under license by Continental makers. *Courtesy of James D. Julia Auctioneers, Fairfield, Maine (www.jamesdjulia.com).*

English Patent 13527/1851: Protecting Adams's one piece frame design.

British Patent 2645/1854: Protecting Adams's loading lever, later safety bolt, and arbor catch.

Solid-frame, self-cocking percussion revolver, with a plain cylinder having five chambers and produced in a variety of bores and barrel lengths.

All Adams revolvers were made under the protection of the first patent. It covered various improvements in firearms, including longarms, but is most significant for protecting the production of a self-cocking percussion revolver with a solid-frame forged from a single piece of malleable cast iron (aka "Marshall's Iron"). Unusual for revolvers in this era of erratic black powder, flash or recoil guards were not fitted. The first design of spring safety and cylinder bolt are also part of this patent application, which expired in 1865.

Adams and Beaumont-Adams revolvers were machine-made, although the parts are sometimes not fully interchangeable.

FRAME TYPES

There are two frame types: the early type found in revolvers up to the 14000R series and the later, more massive "Improved" type. The "Improved" frame differs from the earlier type in having a less steeply raked butt and slightly deeper lock section below the hammer. It is usually considered to be more characteristic of Beaumont-Adams revolvers and is associated with the introduction of three-groove rifling.[6]

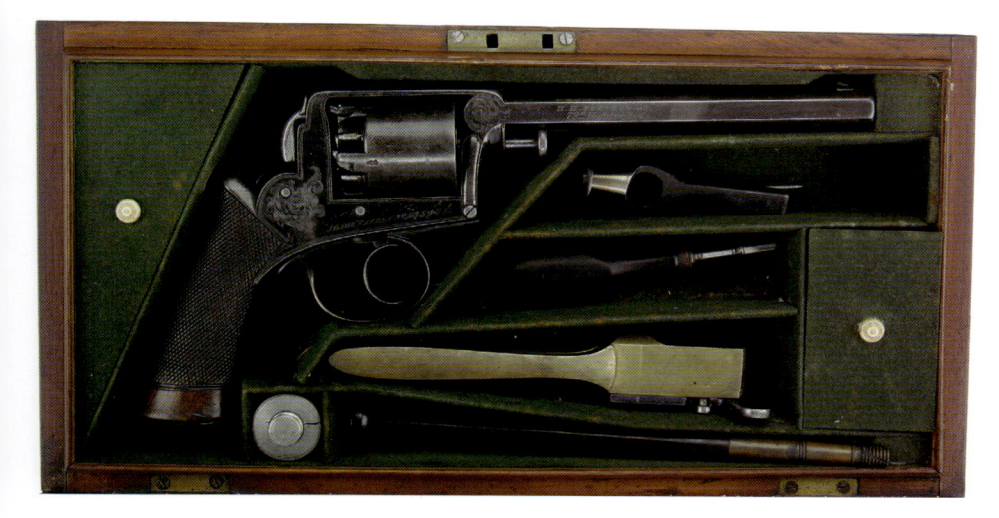

Adams revolver cased with accessories. *Courtesy of James D. Julia Auctioneers, Fairfield, Maine (www.jamesdjulia.com).*

ARBORS

Early weapons have a simple "pull-out" arbor, which, as its name implies, is disengaged by pulling the arbor forward against the pressure of its securing spring. Later weapons have an arbor secured by a screw on the right side of the breech; the head of this screw has a number of different configurations.

SAFETY BOLTS

Safety bolts were of two types. The earliest was a simple piece of spring steel with a cylindrical knob fixed to the end nearest the hammer that went through a hole in the left side of the frame. When the hammer was pulled back slightly, it allowed this spring to be pushed forward, moving the knob through the hole in the frame and preventing the hammer striking the cap and causing a fatal misfire. Pulling the trigger allowed the revolver to be fired normally. This safety bolt was also used while loading the revolver—in place of a more conventional half-cock mechanism—but it turned out to be quite unsatisfactory, since with time and wear it could not be relied on to retain the hammer in a safe position when subjected to a sudden jolt. Adams's later device was a much better design, comprising a short steel lever dovetailed into the frame, which when pushed forward, engaged the cylinder in such a way as to prevent the hammer coming into contact with the percussion cap. It also prevented the revolver being fired if the trigger was pulled accidentally. Weapons may be encountered fitted with both types.

RIFLING

Revolvers made by Adams and his licensees seem always to have had rifled barrels, although there may be unrecorded exceptions. In the pre-13000R series, weapons may be found with either five- or three-groove clockwise rifling, except in the 120 gauge weapons that were always manufactured with a three-groove clockwise rifling, at least amongst those recorded so far. Weapons in the 13000R and later frame number series were usually manufactured with three-groove clockwise rifling, although a very few five-groove examples have also been recorded.

FURNITURE AND FINISH

Little significant variation is seen in the finish found on Adams revolvers. Barrels, frames, and trigger guards are invariably heat blued, this finish often being retained quite well on many antique weapons. Similarly good retention of the finish are found on the cylinders, which may be heat blued or color case hardened, and on many lock components, which are most frequently bright case-hardened. Butts are walnut, cross hatched, and usually constructed in one piece, with a prawl to protect the shooter's hand. In addition, a number of both types appear to have been made to special order and are decorated with gold or silver inlay, jewel encrusting, or Damascening.

ADAMS REVOLVERS WITH FRAME/PRODUCTION NUMBERS: 0–3000

Some weapons in this range may be "R" suffixed. The early revolvers in this range usually have production numbers without letters as either prefix or suffix, and are considered to mark the period before Adams's involvement with Hankey's. They are rare and the frame number range also includes some self-cocking longarms (rifles or muskets) and shotguns.

These are solid-frame self-cocking percussion revolvers, with barrels approximately 7½ inches long, octagonal, and rifled with five broad grooves, twisted clockwise, in 34, 38, 52, and 54 bore. Revolvers with frame numbers above 500 are also encountered with six inch barrels (most often 52 bore with five-groove, clockwise rifling). Butts were usually manufactured in one piece, not as two butt plates. Early models included a cap box in the butt, although this may not always be present. Weapons are London proofed unless proof marks are wholly absent, although this is uncommon. Examples may be encountered that have proof marks only on the cylinder, not the barrel. Adams revolvers in the 0-500 range have percussion cone recesses as truncated cones, not parallel cylinders as in all later models.

The right side of the frame below the cylinder is inscribed:

Adams patent revolver No.

followed by the frame number. On revolvers with numbers above 500, this inscription reads:

Adams Patent No.

followed by the frame number. Either the production number or the last two digits of that number appear on most components.

Revolvers after no. 500 also occasionally have an internal "WT" or "H & S" stamp, showing that William Tranter or Hollis & Sheath supplied some of the parts for their construction.

Variations
- Holster Model: Cylinder with five chambers, in 34, 38, 52, or 54 bore, with a 7½ inch barrel and 5-groove rifling.
- Belt Model: Cylinder with five chambers, in 52 bore, with a 6 inch barrel and 5-groove rifling.

Very rare at UK and U.S. auctions.

ADAMS REVOLVERS WITH FRAME /PRODUCTION NUMBERS: 4000R – 17000R

This range overlaps that of the early Beaumont-Adams revolvers. This is by far the most likely serial range that a collector will encounter and its manufacture is closely related to the beginning of Adams's involvement with Hankey's bank.

Apart from a few early arms suffixed "R" or "Y" in the 0-3000 range, the Robert Adams "R" suffixed frame or production number range began at 4000R, marking the introduction of the 120 bore "Pocket" revolvers. It had reached 17000R when the Deane, Adams & Deane partnership was dissolved in 1856. Some Beaumont-Adams revolvers will also be found with later numbers in this series.

Frame or production number format is variable.

Prior to the 6000R series, the right frame wall below the cylinder is usually inscribed:

Adams's Patent No (serial No) R

During and after the 6000R series, the frame legend, still on the right, was changed to:

Adams' Patent No (serial No) R

Early in the series, weapons may have either a large "R" inscribed on the lower butt strap, with an unsuffixed number on the frame or, alternatively, a bracketed suffix to the frame number. All or part of the frame number may be found inscribed on the cylinder of Adams and Beaumont-Adams revolvers.

The most usual format is simply the addition of an "R" suffix to the frame or production number found on the right frame wall. Revolvers will also be found with a "WT" or "H&S" mark, or Joseph Brazier's name somewhere on the frame, denoting the origin of some or all of the parts used in the weapon so marked.

Caliber or gauge is more diverse than in the preceding series; 54 gauge weapons certainly predominate, although 38, 56, 80, 90, and 120 gauge weapons are not uncommon. Rarities, such as 24 gauge (0 .577" Enfield Minie caliber) and the occasional 240 bore weapon, may also be encountered.

Barrel lengths and rifling tend to be uniform in bore size, although factory-shortened examples of the larger gauge weapons are not uncommon.

Until 1855, Adams's self-cocking revolvers invariably left the factory without loading levers. The ball and wad were seated on top of the powder by pressure from the user's thumb. It was not uncommon, however, for an early model to be returned to the factory in order to have a loading lever fitted. These were similar to those found on the later Beaumont-Adams revolvers.

RETAILERS

In this frame/production number range, Messers. Deane, Adams & Deane are the most commonly encountered retailer, although weapons supplied by other gunmakers are not uncommon.

Deane, Adams & Deane used a number of retail marks, with two common examples being:

DEANE, ADAMS & DEANE, 30, KING WILLIAM ST, LONDON BRIDGE
and
DEANE, ADAMS & DEANE (MAKER'S TO H.R.H. PRINCE ALBERT), 30, KING WILLIAM ST LONDON BRIDGE

Retail marks of this sort are invariably found inscribed on the top-strap of the frame and the size varied to allow the requisite number of letters and numerals to be included. They were sometimes italicized.

Variations
Five basic variations are known, apart from special order or custom-made weapons.

- Holster Model: Cylinder with five chambers, in 38 bore, usually with a 7-7½ inch barrel, 3 or 5-groove rifling.
- There is a second, holster-caliber Model: Cylinder with five chambers, in 54 or 56 bore, usually with 6½ -7 inch barrel, 3 or 5-groove rifling.
- Belt Model: Cylinder with five chambers, in 80 or 90 bore, usually with 6 inch barrel, 3 or 5-groove rifling.
- Pocket Model: Cylinder with five chambers, in 120 bore, usually with 4½ inch barrel and 3-groove rifling.

Values: Good: $1,600-2,000
 (£1,000-1,200)
 Fine: $4,200-5,000
 (£2,500-3,000)
Rare at UK and U.S. auctions.

A number of other variations to the standard construction of Adams revolvers are infrequently encountered.[7] These include:

- A 54 gauge revolver with a needle-fire mechanism, recorded as No 10349 R.
- Several with counterclockwise cylinder rotation (all constructed under William Tranter's license).
- Revolvers (and longarms) with a "hesitating" lock mechanism.
- A small number of later, self-cocking revolvers fitted with a hammer spur to facilitate operation of the early model safety catch.

Unfortunately, it is unlikely that such rare weapons will be available for purchase by the amature collector. Values would probably also be prohibitively high.

OTHER LICENSED MANUFACTURERS

FRAME/PRODUCTION NUMBERS: 1000-17000 CONTINENTAL MANUFACTURERS

Adams revolver cased with accessories. Made by Pirlot Brothers of Liege, the case is especially well made. Unlike contemporary English cases, the interior has been molded to fit the gun and accessories, rather than being simply divided into compartments. *Courtesy of James D. Julia Auctioneers, Fairfield, Maine (www.jamesdjulia.com).*

Pirlot-made Adams from the right side, showing the characteristic frame inscription "Adams Patent No 9072." This frame number format is characteristic of Adams revolvers produced by Continental makers, who had their own frame number series (0-17000), without either prefix or suffix. *Courtesy of James D. Julia Auctioneers, Fairfield, Maine (www.jamesdjulia.com).*

Pirlot-made Adams from the left side, showing the characteristic frame stamp, oval "ADAMS 1851 PATENT," and the early form of the safety bolt. Courtesy of James D. Julia Auctioneers, Fairfield, Maine (www.jamesdjulia.com).

This serial range of numbers was set aside for those revolvers manufactured outside the UK, usually by Belgian gunsmiths, although a few weapons of Austrian or German origin may occasionally be found at auction.

DISTINGUISHING FEATURES

The most obvious characteristic of these weapons is the frame legend, which takes the form of an oval "ADAMS" with a lower "PATENT," enclosing the date "1851."

Pirlot-made Adams showing detail of the Continental frame stamp characteristic of guns produced under license by Continental gunmakers. Courtesy of James D. Julia Auctioneers, Fairfield, Maine (www.jamesdjulia.com).

This is always stamped on the left side of the frame. Such weapons are characterized by Liege proof marks and a distinctive top-strap legend denoting the manufacturer of the weapon:

Manuf by Ancion & Cie. Licensed by Deane, Adams & Deane.

Ancion seems, on balance, to be the most prolific of these Continental licensees and his retail mark is found in a number of forms.

Most common weapons in this serial range appear to be a 54 gauge with a 6 inch barrel and a 120 gauge revolver with a 4½ inch barrel.

Variations
Only two are commonly seen, although there may be others:

- Holster Model: Cylinder with five chambers, in 54 bore, usually with a 6 inch barrel.
- Pocket Model: Cylinder with five chambers, in 120 bore, usually with a 4½ inch barrel.

Values: Good: $2,500-3,400
(£1,500-2,000)
Fine: $4,200-4,500
(£2,500-2,700)
Rare at UK and U.S. auctions.

TRANTER-MADE ADAMS REVOLVERS

William Tranter began revolver manufacture in 1853, producing Adams self-cocking revolvers under a patent license from Robert Adams. These early self-cocking Tranter revolvers are of two types.

The first are single trigger Adams-framed revolvers made under license and in

Pirlot-made Adams revolver showing the maker's name on the top-strap. Courtesy of James D. Julia Auctioneers, Fairfield, Maine (www.jamesdjulia.com).

ADAMS AND BEAUMONT-ADAMS REVOLVERS

Adams's "R"-suffixed range, although some "Y"-suffixed weapons are also known. As well as the Adams frame or production number, weapons in this group also bear a "WT" internally on one side of the hammer slot and a second Tranter frame number on the other side. There is also a second, smaller group using the Adams single-trigger mechanism that bear "T"-suffixed frame numbers.

Tranter's second group—assigned frame/production numbers beginning at 20000 and with a "Y" suffix—are based on the Adams frame, but incorporate Tranter's double trigger mechanism (British Patent No 212/1853) and are described in the "Tranter Revolvers" chapter.

ADAMS SELF-COCKING REVOLVERS PRODUCED UNDER LICENSE BY TRANTER

Frame/production numbers: "R"-suffixed, within Adams's 4000R – 17000R range

Adams revolvers in this series have been recorded in 50, 54, and 56 bore, with 7½ inch barrels, although there may be exceptions. They bear frame numbers in the "R"-suffixed range and may be distinguished from Robert Adams's own revolvers by the "WT" and production number in the hammer slot. All are self-cocking revolvers with Adams's single-trigger mechanism.

Variations
Only one is known:
- Holster Model: Cylinder with five chambers, in 50, 54, or 56 bore, usually with a 7-7½ inch barrel. Frame number: "R"-suffixed.

Values: Good: $2,200-2,500
(£1,300-1,500)
Fine: $4,800-5,200
(£2,900-3,100)
Rare at UK and U.S. auctions.

FRAME/ PRODUCTION NUMBERS 2200 T

This is the second, much rarer Tranter series, with the Adams single-trigger mechanism.

The frames of revolvers in this series are claimed to be much more massively constructed than a normal Adams, although they were still manufactured under Adams's license, English Patent no 13527/1851. They all use the Adams, single-trigger, self-cocking mechanism and have so far only been found in 54 bore with a 7½ inch barrel.

Variations
Only one is known:
- Holster Model: Cylinder with five chambers, in 54 bore, usually with a 7-7½ inch barrel. Frame number: "T"-suffixed.

Very rare at UK and U.S. auctions.

ADAMS AND TRANTER FRAME NUMBERS

These frame number ranges are not absolutely discrete. Some of Tranter's double trigger revolvers also appear in the 4000 – 17000 "R"-suffixed range and, adding to the confusion about their production, Tranter-made Adams single-trigger revolvers may also be found with a "Y"-suffixed production number, usually characteristic of Tranter's Adams-framed, double trigger revolvers (see Tranter chapter). In addition, a number of Beaumont-Adams revolvers also appear in this "Y" range, some with the additional "B"-prefixed Beaumont Patent number.

FRAME/PRODUCTION NUMBERS 30000 B / L : BRAZIER-MADE ADAMS REVOLVERS

This series was allocated to Joseph Brazier, a well respected Wolverhampton lock and gunmaker, and is found in revolvers manufactured by him prior to 1854.

Brazier had a "B"-suffixed series for his own use, but his revolvers are also occasionally found with an "L" suffix or even within Adams's 4000-17000 "R"-suffixed range. These revolvers are usually 54, 80, or 120 gauge, with barrel lengths corresponding to Adams's "R" series, and three or five groove rifling.

Brazier's revolvers—not surprisingly, given his manufacturing base—carry Birmingham proof marks on cylinder and barrel and are often fitted with Brazier's patent loading lever.

Deane, Adams & Deane is the most commonly found retailer of this series, although several of the London retailers, such as Wilkinson & Son, also sold Brazier-made guns.

Rarely, Brazier's own retail mark is found inscribed:

Joseph Brazier & Son, Wolverhampton

Variations
Four basic variations are known, apart from special order or custom-made weapons:

- Holster Model: Cylinder with five chambers, in 38 bore, usually with a 7-7½ inch barrel, 3 or 5-groove rifling.
- There is a second Holster-caliber Model: Cylinder with five chambers, in 54 or 56 bore, usually with 6½-7 inch barrel, 3 or 5-groove rifling.
- Belt Model: Cylinder with five chambers, in 80 or 90, usually with 6 inch barrel, 3 or 5-groove rifling.
- Pocket Model: Cylinder with five chambers, in 120 bore, usually with 4½ inch barrel and 3-groove rifling.

Values: Good: $2,500-2,800
(£1,500-1,700)
Fine: $4,700-5,200
(£2,800-3,100)
Rare at UK and U.S. auctions.

FRAME/PRODUCTION NUMBERS 4000 – 6000X: HOLLIS AND SHEATH-MADE ADAMS REVOLVERS

Weapons with the "X" suffix, although manufactured by Hollis and Sheath, do not belong to a separate production range; rather, the firm had taken revolvers for their own use from the weapons they were making for Adams under his "R" suffix range. Thus, they lie in Adams's 4000R –17000R range of production numbers, except the suffix "X" is used instead. Weapons with frame numbers 4873X, 5485X, 5639X, and 6320X have been recorded, all in 38 gauge. Hollis & Sheath also retailed weapons in Adams's "R"-suffixed range and occasionally used "Brazier" stamped frames.

Variations
- Holster Model: Cylinder with five chambers, in 38 bore, 7½ inch barrel. Very rare at UK and U.S. auctions.

BEAUMONT-ADAMS MODEL 1856 REVOLVER (MANUFACTURED 1855-1865, POSSIBLY LATER)

BRITISH-MADE REVOLVERS:

Beaumont- Adams revolver in 90-bore, showing the loading lever in shooting position and the early safety catch. *Courtesy of Mr. Ronald Birnie.*

British Patent No. 374/1855 – This patent protects Lt. F.B.E Beaumont's modification of Adams's lock mechanism, turning it from self-cocking to double-action operation.

British Patent No. 1722/1855 – This patent protects Kerr's loading lever.

FRAME/PRODUCTION NUMBER RANGE 14000R – B3600/19000R

Detailed view of the Beaumont-Adams later safety bolt. Proof marks are visible on two of the cylinder's chambers and the frame number can just be seen on the top of the cylinder. *Courtesy of Mr. Ronald Birnie*

Beaumont-Adams revolver showing the later safety catch and early frame number format, without the "B"-prefixed frame number.

ADAMS AND BEAUMONT-ADAMS REVOLVERS

The later serial number format for Beaumont-Adams revolvers. *Courtesy of Mr. Ronald Birnie.*

Adams rammer in loading position. *Courtesy of Mr. Ronald Birnie.*

This range overlaps that of the earlier Adams revolvers and Beaumont-Adams revolvers are known with frame numbers as early as 14000R, either with or without a "B"-prefixed number inscribed above it. In addition, later Adams and Beaumont-Adams revolvers may also be found with frame numbers above 19000R, but with no "B"-prefixed number.

Most of the revolvers in this range were manufactured by Deane, Adams & Deane, before Adams's transfer to L.A.C., although some later weapons may be of early London Armoury Co manufacture and will bear the appropriate stamp.

These are solid-frame, double-action revolvers with spurred hammers; this is the most obvious difference between Adams and Beaumont-Adams revolvers.

Frames are usually of the later "Improved" type and cylinders are plain, with five chambers. Gauges and corresponding barrel lengths are similar to the earlier self-cocking Adams revolvers, usually with three-groove, clockwise rifling, although exceptions to this may be encountered. Adams or Rigby loading levers are usually fitted, although occasionally later weapons with a Kerr or Brazier loading lever are encountered in this range. Butts are in one piece, crosshatched walnut, and correspond in most features to the earlier model. Safety bolts are fitted, with the "New" type being most common, although both types may be found on the same revolver.

Top-straps of revolvers in this serial number range are most commonly inscribed with the following:

Deane, Adams & Deane, London.
or
Messrs Deane, Adams & Deane
or
Messrs Adams & Company
or
Messrs Deane, Adams & Deane, 30, King William St. London Bridge

In addition, a minute "DA&D," followed by the bore size, will be found stamped on the frame of those revolvers produced with the "Improved" frame.

Variations
Six basic variations are known, apart from special order or custom-made weapons:

- Holster Model: Cylinder with five chambers, in 38 bore, usually with a 7½ inch barrel and 3-groove rifling.
- There is a second Holster-size Model: Cylinder with five chambers, in 54 or 56 bore, usually with 6½-7 inch barrel and 3-groove rifling.
- Belt Model: Cylinder with five chambers, in 80 or 90 bore, most frequently with a 6 inch barrel and 3-groove rifling.
- Pocket Model: Cylinder with five chambers, in 120 bore, usually with 4½ inch barrel and 3-groove rifling.

Values: Good: $2,500-2,800
(£1,500-1,700)
Fine: $4,200-4,600
(£2,500-2,750)
Cased: $6,700
(£4,000-5,000)
Very common at UK and U.S. auctions.

Beaumont-Adams revolver showing detail of the "Improved" frame, Adams loading lever, and early safety catch. *Courtesy of Mr. Ronald Birnie.*

Early retail mark on the Adams revolver.

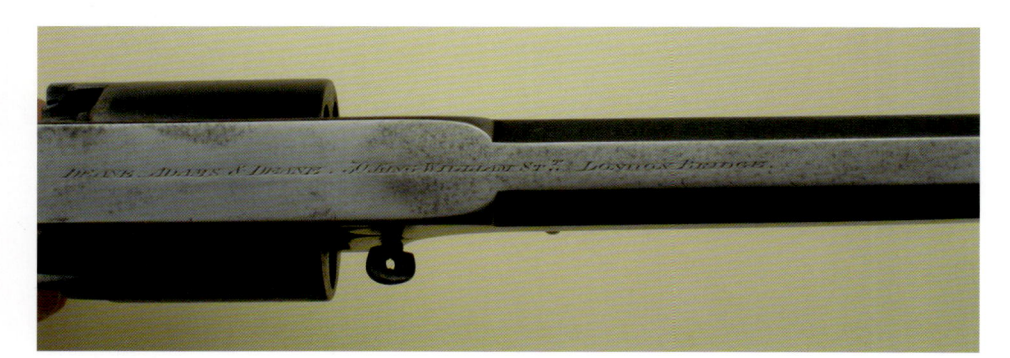

Alternative retail mark. This revolver has the later arbor catch, forward of the cylinder.

BEAUMONT-ADAMS REVOLVERS IN FRAME/ PRODUCTION NUMBER RANGE B3600/19000R – B20000/36000R

A Beaumont-Adams Belt Model revolver (90 bore, six inch barrel) from the right side. It is highly decorated, with the later arbor catch and spring safety bolt. *Courtesy of James D. Julia Auctioneers, Fairfield, Maine (www.jamesdjulia.com).*

ADAMS AND BEAUMONT-ADAMS REVOLVERS

Beaumont-Adams Belt Model revolver (90 bore, six inch barrel) from the left side, showing the Kerr loading lever. Courtesy of James D. Julia Auctioneers, Fairfield, Maine (www.jamesdjulia.com).

Beaumont-Adams Belt Model revolver (90 bore, six inch barrel) cased with accessories. Eley Bros caps and Tranter "Lubricating bullets" tins are both frequently found included in English revolver cases. Courtesy of James D. Julia Auctioneers, Fairfield, Maine (www.jamesdjulia.com).

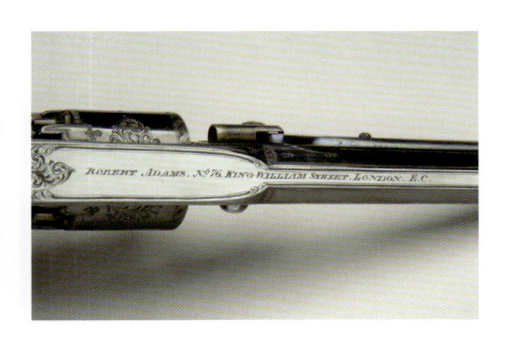

Unusual, highly decorated Beaumont-Adams. The short barrel suggests this is probably in 120 bore. By kind permission of Bonhams.

Beaumont-Adams Belt Model revolver (90 bore, six inch barrel) showing the maker's address on the top-strap. Courtesy of James D. Julia Auctioneers, Fairfield, Maine (www.jamesdjulia.com).

Revolvers in this serial range were all manufactured in the years between 1857 and the end of 1860 by the London Armoury Co. Approximately 17,000 revolvers were produced in this range, although many were converted to breech loading, for both the Army and private individuals. They do not differ significantly from weapons in the production number range 14000R – B3600/19000R, except frames are always of the "Improved" type, with calibers and barrel lengths corresponding to the earlier models.

Almost invariably, Kerr loading levers are fitted to revolvers in this series range, while all other features are predominantly the same as the earlier series.

RETAILERS' MARKS AND NAMES

Most commonly encountered is the London Armoury Company inscribed on the top-strap of the revolver:

London Armoury Company (Limited)
or
London Armoury Comp^y
or
London Armoury

Another mark which may be encountered—usually on weapons with frame numbers after B5400/21000R—is the "LAC" stamp. The early form of this is a small crowned shield, surrounding the letters "LA" over "C" and stamped above the arbor latch. Later weapons bear a simple, linear "LAC" stamped on the barrel, just forward of the proof marks.

As with revolvers in the previous 14000R – B3600/19000R frame number range, the London Armoury Company also supplied unmarked revolvers to retailers so that they could inscribe their own marks, usually on the top-strap of the revolver. One of the most commonly encountered is that of Robert Adams's ex-partners, the Deanes, trading from their old retail premises at 30, King William St. These revolvers are inscribed on the top-strap:

DEANE & SON

Robert Adams also retailed these revolvers from his 76, King William Street address and these weapons are inscribed on the top-strap:

ROBERT ADAMS. No 76. KING WILLIAM. STREET LONDON. E.C.

There were also a number of other English retailers during this period, including the Birmingham gunsmiths Calisher and Terry.

Adams also sold his revolvers in America through a New York agent; these weapons are marked on the top-strap in the following form:

R. Adams, London—Francis Tomes & Sons – Agent , New York

It has been suggested that Schuyler, Hartley and Graham, New York, the well known military equipment suppliers, may also have stocked Adams revolvers. Their 1864 catalog does not include any entry for Adams revolvers, however, and the only corroborated reference to their involvement with Adams is a customs dispute over a box of pistols imported from Britain without an invoice.[8]

Finally, many Beaumont-Adams revolvers of this period will be found with the broad arrow "WD" mark, usually stamped on the right side of the frame, indicating that they were War Department weapons. Not all Beaumont-Adams of War Department origin will be so marked, however. It has been suggested that this is because the "W/|\D" mark was not stamped on newly issued weapons, but only on those returned for repair, refinishing, or conversion to breech loading.

Variations
Six basic variations are known apart from special order or custom-made weapons.

- Holster Model: Cylinder with five chambers, in 38 bore, usually with a 7½ inch barrel, 3-groove rifling, and a Kerr Pattern loading lever.
- There is a second, holster-size Model: Cylinder with five chambers, in 54 or 56 bore. Most frequently with 6½ - 7 inch barrel, 3-groove rifling, and a Kerr Pattern loading lever.
- Belt Model: Cylinder with five chambers, in 80 or 90 bore, usually with a 6 inch barrel, 3-groove rifling, and a Kerr Pattern loading lever.
- Pocket Model: Cylinder with five chambers, in 120 bore, usually with 4½ inch barrel, 3-groove rifling, and a Kerr Pattern loading lever.

Values: Good: $2,100-2,500
(£1,250-1,500)
Fine: $4,200-4,500
(£2,500-2700)
Cased: $5,900-6,700
(£3,500-4,000)
Very common at UK and U.S. auctions.

FRAME/PRODUCTION NUMBERS 3000B AND A9000

Brazier-manufactured Beaumont-Adams are occasionally encountered with serial numbers in his 30000B range, a separate A9000 range, and several un-prefixed frame number ranges. Loading levers on these weapons were invariably of Brazier's own design and also had their own serial number in the 200-300 range.

Variations
Probably similar to those already described, but clear data confirming this is not available.
Very rare at UK and U.S. auctions.

BEAUMONT-ADAMS REVOLVERS IN LATER FRAME NUMBER RANGES

Frame number ranges: 30000/39000, 40000, 41000, 50000, 51000, 60000P, 61000, and 100000 (numbers almost certainly do not reflect production)

The London Armoury Company ceased production of Beaumont-Adams revolvers some time in 1862—probably because of their commitments to the Confederacy—and Beaumont-Adams revolvers made after this date were manufactured either in Birmingham or Liege. These revolvers do not differ in any important features from weapons in the B3600/19000R – B20000/36000R serial range, except for their frame stamps. All have 5-groove rifling, except those weapons made in Liege, which have 3-groove rifling.

It is difficult to assign specific manufacturers to each range, but the list below follows a generally accepted scheme:[9]

- 30000 and 39000 frame number range: Various Birmingham gunmakers, but may have either London or Birmingham proof marks.
- 40000 and 41000 frame number ranges: Various Liege gunmakers, in particular M. Auguste Francotte, although weapons in this group are often inscribed with English retail marks. They often bear the "Adams"

Beaumont-Adams Holster Model revolver fitted with a Brazier loading lever. By kind permission of Bonhams.

frame stamp characteristic of weapons made in Liege and have 3-groove rifling, while all other revolvers in these later frame number groups have 5-groove rifling. They may bear London, Birmingham or Liege proof marks.

- 51000 and 51000 frame number ranges: Few revolvers were made in these ranges and their manufacturing origin is not known.
- 60000P frame number range: All revolvers in this range are thought to be manufactured by Pryse & Redman, Birmingham, and bear the appropriate retail marks and Birmingham proof marks.

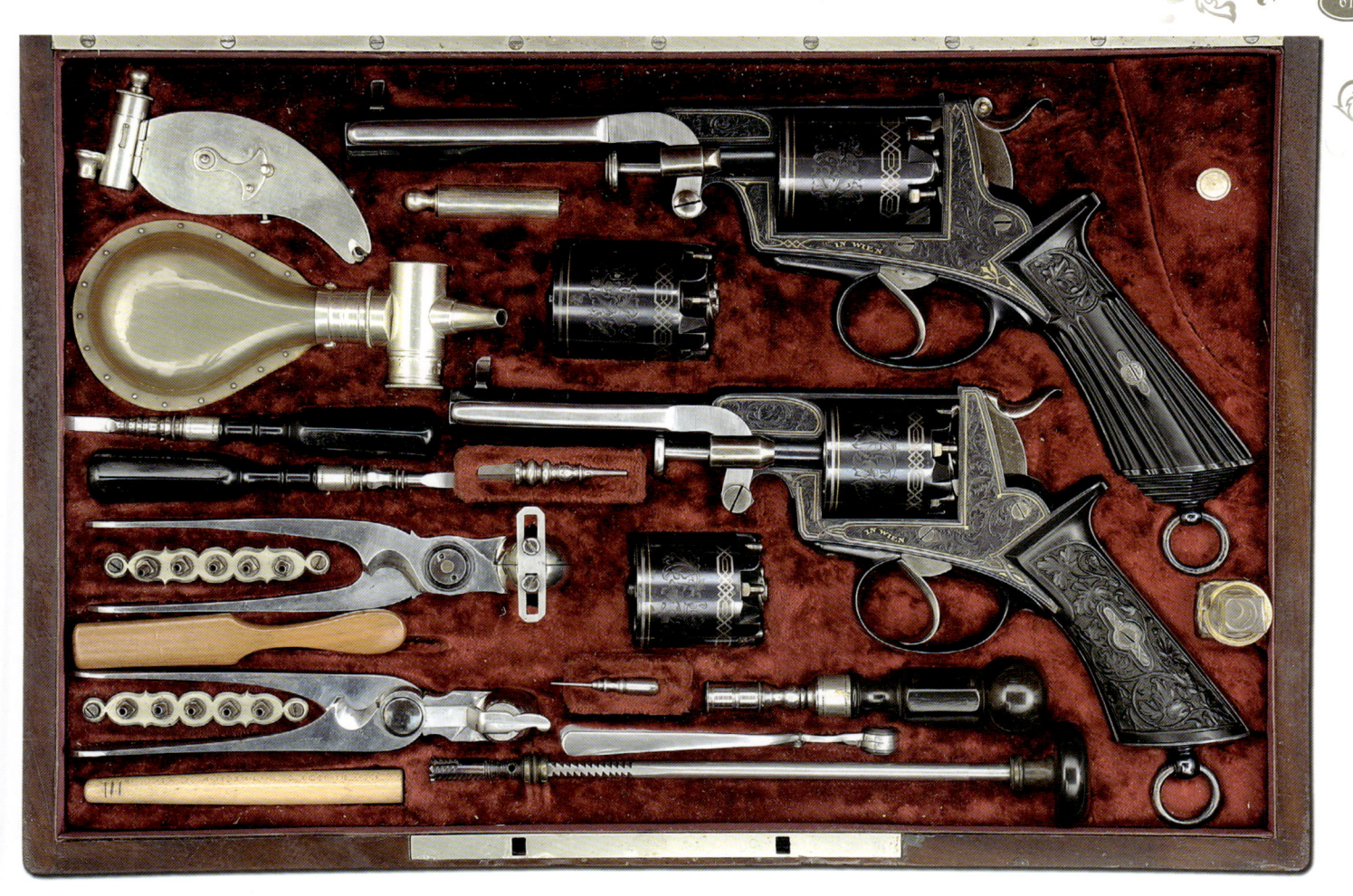

Cased pair of Beaumont-Adams revolvers of Continental manufacture (L. Gasser of Vienna), including a characteristic powder horn and spare cylinders. These two revolvers have different barrel lengths, but the same .548 caliber bore. *Courtesy of James D. Julia Auctioneers, Fairfield, Maine (www.jamesdjulia.com).*

Gasser-made Beaumont-Adams revolvers, both in .548 caliber: the upper has a six inch barrel, while the lower is shorter at five inches. The spare cylinders also match the guns—that for the five inch barreled gun being shorter—and the frame conformation, with its angular butt, is characteristic of Continental revolvers. *Courtesy of James D. Julia Auctioneers, Fairfield, Maine (www.jamesdjulia.com).*

Gasser-made Beaumont-Adams revolver showing the right side, with the maker's name replacing the more usual frame number. The "ADAM 1851 PATENT" stamp characteristic of revolvers made under license to Continental makers is also missing from the left side. *Courtesy of James D. Julia Auctioneers, Fairfield, Maine (www.jamesdjulia.com).*

- 61000 frame number range: Few weapons are recorded from this range, so a manufacturer is not known, although some may have been made by Pryse & Redmore.
- 100000 frame number range: All revolvers in this range are probably manufactured by Callisher & Terry, Birmingham, and will bear appropriate retail marks, as well as Birmingham proof marks.

Variations

As previously described, although examples in 54 bore with either 7 or 7½ inch barrels appear to predominate.

Values: Good: $1,700-2,100
(£1,000-1,250)
Fine: $3,800-4,200
(£2,300-2,500)
Rare at UK and U.S. auctions.

BEAUMONT-ADAMS REVOLVERS MANUFACTURED IN AMERICA

Mass. Arms Co. Beaumont-Adams in .31 caliber, showing the angled safety catch, which is characteristic of these Mass. Arms copies. Courtesy of James D. Julia Auctioneers, Fairfield, Maine (www.jamesdjulia.com).

American retailed, London-made Beaumont-Adams revolver; this example has a 40000 frame number. Courtesy of James D. Julia Auctioneers, Fairfield, Maine (www.jamesdjulia.com).

Pair of Mass. Arms Co. Beaumont-Adams revolvers in a case with accessories. These are .36 caliber revolvers, and the loading lever securing catch, which differs from the London guns, is shown top left. Although this pair has a characteristic "American Eagle" powder flask, it has two "Eley" cap boxes, more usually found with the London-made revolvers. Courtesy of James D. Julia Auctioneers, Fairfield, Maine (www.jamesdjulia.com).

Frame number range: Separate for Pocket and Navy Models. (A Pocket Model is recorded with a frame number of 4563, although it is not clear this reflects actual production.)

Manufactured under license by the Massachusetts Arms Company between 1857 and 1859, such weapons are found in .36 caliber with a 6" octagonal barrel or .31 caliber with a 3¼ inch octagonal or, rarely, a 4¼ inch, round barrel. Both calibers are usually found with a Kerr loading lever, although conformation of the lever latch at the end of the barrel in

Detail of the frame number from the American retailed revolver. This is in the "40000" range, usually found on guns made under license on the Continent. Courtesy of James D. Julia Auctioneers, Fairfield, Maine (www.jamesdjulia.com).

ADAMS AND BEAUMONT-ADAMS REVOLVERS

Detail of the retail mark (on the frame) on the American-retailed Beaumont-Adams, which reads "B.KITTERIDGE & CO CIN.O". Courtesy of James D. Julia Auctioneers, Fairfield, Maine (www.jamesdjulia.com).

the .36 caliber weapon differs from the standard British pattern. In contrast to the London Beaumont-Adams, there is a lock plate on the left side of the frame and these guns may also bear a government inspector's mark on the butt, with "LCA," "WAT," and "JT" being the most usual. The later, recessed safety catch is fitted and serves as another point of difference, since it is more steeply angled away from the horizontal than is common in the London-made guns.

These features, together with the absence of an "Adams's Patent" number below the cylinder on the right side, differentiate the American weapons from the imported product, although in all other respects they do not differ significantly from revolvers described in the B3600/19000R – B20000/36000R range.

Variations
The manufacturer's name is stamped on the top-strap of these revolvers, in the place usually reserved for the retailer in English-made arms.

Navy Model: Serial range 1-1000, possibly not reflecting production. Cylinder with five chambers, in .36 caliber, usually with a 6 inch barrel and 3- or 5-groove rifling. Top-strap stamped:

MANUFACTURED BY
MASS. ARMS CO.
CHICOPEE FALLS

Left frame stamped:

ADAMS PATENT
MAY 3 1858

Right frame stamped:

PATENT
JUNE 3 1856

The loading lever lever may also bear the inscription:

KERR'S PATENT
APRIL14 1857

Pocket Model: Serial range 1–4500, possibly not reflecting production. Cylinder with five chambers, in .31 caliber, usually with 3¼ inch, octagonal barrel and 3-groove rifling. Top-strap stamped:

MADE FOR ADAMS REVOLVING ARMS CO.
BY MASS.ARMS CO. CHICOPEE FALLS
PATENT MAY 3 1853. JUNE 1856. APL 7 1857

There is a second, much rarer Pocket Model that has a 4¼ inch round barrel. It corresponds in all other features to the model with the octagonal barrel.

Values:
Pocket Good: $2,200-2,500
        (£1,350-1500)
        Fine: $3,700-4,850
        (£2,200-2,875)
Navy   Good: $1,600-2,500
        (£1,000-1,200)
        Fine: $3,000-3,500
        (£1,800-2,100)
Rare at UK and U.S auctions.

ADAMS COPIES

Wedge-framed Adams copy, probably by one of the smaller Birmingham gunsmiths. This example is fitted with a Kerr loading lever.

The top-strap legend of the Adams wedge-framed copy.

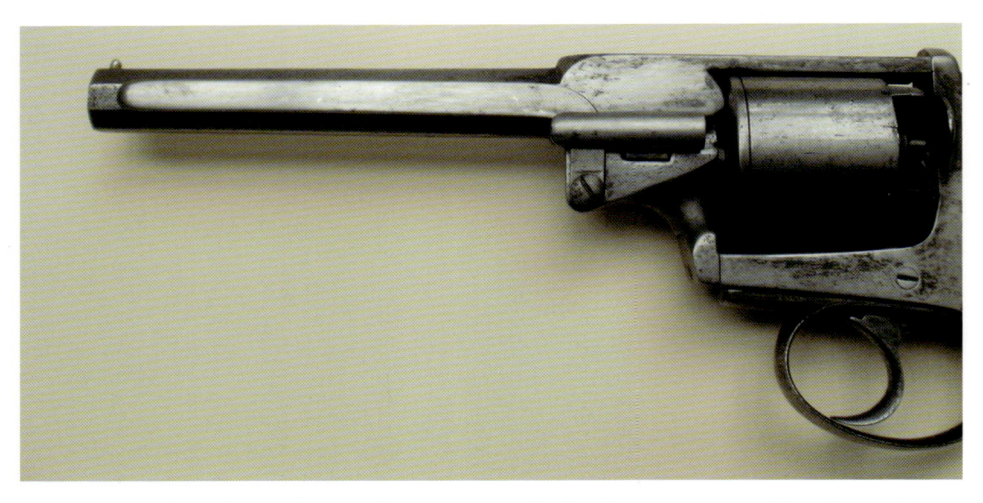

Adams wedge-framed copy showing the Kerr pattern loading lever in carrying/shooting position.

Adams revolvers were extensively copied by both the London and Birmingham trade, usually as wedge-framed revolvers. They bear a variety of frame and barrel marks that serve to distinguish them from Adams's product, as does their quality of manufacture.

REVOLVER VARIATIONS AND FRAME NUMBERS

Although the models of Adams and Beaumont-Adams revolvers are recorded under their various frame number groups with corresponding caliber and barrel lengths, many authentic variations to the configurations described will be encountered, usually as large caliber weapons with shorter barrels.

With regard to these frame number series, it should not be thought that there is any very clear division between serial number series that include Adams self-cocking revolvers and the later Beaumont-Adams. Indeed, a number of early Beaumont-Adams will be found in the 4000R – 17000R series, some with the extra "B" serial number. Adams self-cocking revolvers may also be found with serial numbers as high as 20000R, without an accompanying "B" prefixed number, and fitted with a factory loading lever from new.

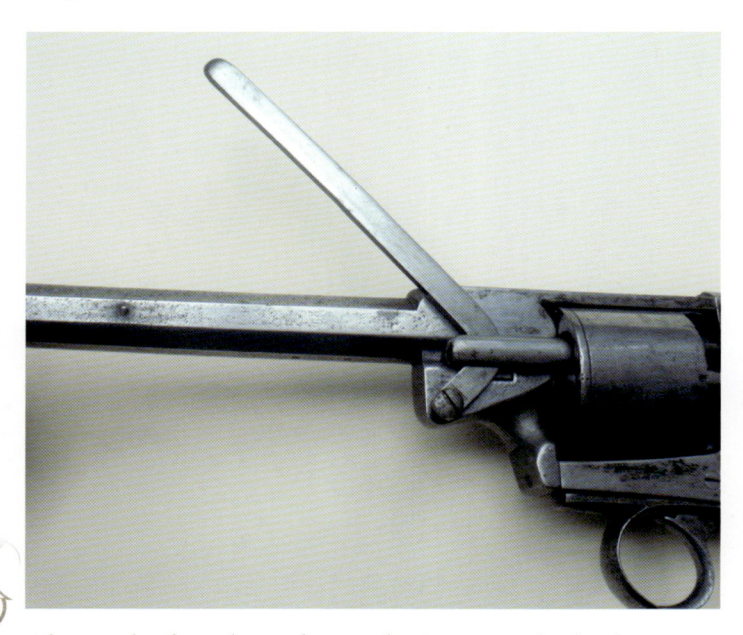

Adams wedge-framed copy showing the Kerr pattern loading lever prior to ramming the charge.

Adams wedge-framed copy showing the Kerr pattern loading lever with the charge fully home.

ADAMS AND BEAUMONT-ADAMS REVOLVERS

CHAPTER FOUR

Tranter Revolvers

William Tranter began his association with the Birmingham gun trade as an apprentice to the firm of Hollis Bros. in 1830, when he was fourteen. Leaving Hollis in 1839, he bought the business of Robert Dugard, at Whittall St, Birmingham, in the Gun Quarter. By 1844, he was back with the Hollis Bros., now as a partner in Hollis Brothers & Co at 10-11 Weaman Row, Birmingham. This association ended cordially enough in 1848, when Tranter seems to have begun the manufacture of military weapons, and by 1851, he had a factory of his own at 13, St Mary's Row, still in the heart of the Birmingham Gun Quarter. He moved again in 1854 to Loveday Street, where he had premises with steam-driven machinery installed, making him one of the first of the Birmingham trade to use such equipment for firearm production. In 1867, he moved into his own purpose-built premises, "The Tranter Gun and Pistol Factory," at 31, Lichfield Road, Birmingham; this became his main manufacturing outlet, although some business was carried on at the St Mary's Row premises until 1875.

In addition to being a gunmaker and inventor, Tranter was also a shrewd businessman, being one of the founders of the Birmingham Small Arms Company, which was initially set up in 1861 to produce rifles to fill government contracts.

His first Registered Design—for a pepperbox lock mechanism—appeared soon after the end of his partnership with the Hollis Brothers in 1849, and he continued producing innovative ideas for firearms until his retirement in 1885. These included patents for bolt-action rifles and machine guns, as well as his revolvers. He was also involved in the design of the Enfield MkI service revolver, although this contribution was never fully acknowledged. He died five years after retiring, on 7 January 1890.

Tranter's involvement with revolver manufacture really began in 1853, when he started producing Adams self-cocking revolvers under license. He became Robert Adams's most prolific supplier during the latter's Weston Street years, producing Adams frames, lock components, and complete revolvers under license and selling them to the London Bridge retail outlet. He also used the robust Adams frame to develop his own double trigger revolver, which he then sold under license from Adams. Tranter revolvers, like the Adams, appear to have been predominantly chambered for five shots, although there were later six-chambered models.[1]

OPERATION

To fire a Tranter double trigger revolver, the lower trigger, below the guard, is first squeezed, which raises the hammer to full-cock. Pressure on the upper trigger, which is within the guard, then releases the hammer and fires the weapon. Holding the upper trigger back and operating the lower causes the weapon to fire as soon as it reaches the full-cock position. Intermediate between a single-action and a true double-action revolver, this mechanism is termed a "hesitating" action in UK publications.

Early Tranter percussion revolvers are of two types, both with Adams frames. Later 2nd, 3rd, and 4th Models are nearly all based on a frame of Tranter's own design, and bear frame/serial numbers in a "T"-suffixed range.

Unlike a number of other percussion revolver manufacturers, Tranter made a successful transition to metal cartridge revolvers, producing weapons designed for both rim-fire and center-fire cartridges, one of which was bought in small numbers by the British Army.

TRANTER PERCUSSION REVOLVERS

Tranter revolvers were predominantly machine-made, with solid-frames, cylinders with five chambers and, like the Adams, without a flash or recoil shield. Despite this, parts are not always easily interchangeable, even between weapons of the same model. In common with revolvers fitted with the more usual self-cocking mechanism, 1st, 2nd and 3rd Models did not have a hammer spur.

Although the classification described here follows that first presented by J.N. George,[2] it is clear that the production of the so-called 1st, 2nd, and 3rd Models does not follow a chronological series with specific design improvements associated with later weapons. The three models are distributed randomly throughout all the earlier frame number series and moreover, it is clear that 1st and 2nd Model revolvers were sold simultaneously in one period, according to the customer's preference of pattern for the loading lever.[3]

TRANTER 1ST MODEL (PRODUCTION BEGUN: 1853-1854)

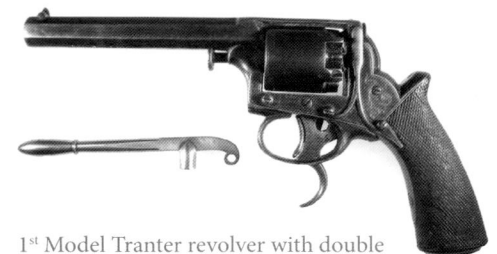

1st Model Tranter revolver with double trigger and made using the Adams frame. The rammer is shown detached from the frame peg.

1st Model Tranter showing the frame and "Y"-shaped safety catch.

Adams framed revolvers with the Tranter double trigger mechanism (1st and a few 2nd Models, although there are also some Tranter-made, single-trigger Adams revolvers in this range).

Frame number ranges: 1000Y, 2000Y, 06000Y, 07000Y, 10000Y, and 20000Y

Frame/production numbers are inscribed on the right side of the frame, below the cylinder in the same place as a conventional Adams as:

TRANTER'S PATENT

This is followed by the frame number.

They also bear a "WT" and production number in the hammer slot. A second identifying mark appears on the trigger assembly, stamped in an oval format:

TRANTER'S
PATENT

This refers to Tranter's patent for the hesitating mechanism (Brit. Pat. 212/1853) and is found stamped on the trigger of all four models.

The Tranter frame stamp found on most of the revolvers made by this company.

The Tranter Patent stamp found on the upper trigger of revolvers fitted with the "hesitating" mechanism.

Adams-framed revolvers with the Tranter "hesitating" mechanism were produced in 38, 50, 54, 80, 90, and 120 bore, with barrels varying in length from 7½ inches to 4½ inches; larger caliber weapons were commonly those with longer barrels.

Loading levers were produced under another of Tranter's patents (Tranter's British Patent 2921/1853). This model consisted of a separate, one-piece device that was carried in the pocket and attached to a straight round peg screwed into the frame below the cylinder when in use. Rotating the assembly on this peg forced the load into the chamber. Loading levers are also stamped:

TRANTER'S
PATENT

The 2nd, 3rd, and 4th Models all bear this inscription on their loading levers, whatever the design fitted.

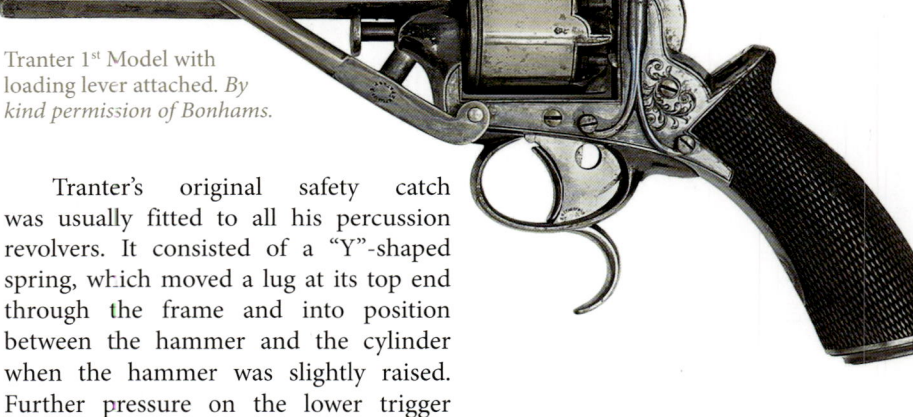

Tranter 1st Model with loading lever attached. By kind permission of Bonhams.

Tranter's original safety catch was usually fitted to all his percussion revolvers. It consisted of a "Y"-shaped spring, which moved a lug at its top end through the frame and into position between the hammer and the cylinder when the hammer was slightly raised. Further pressure on the lower trigger raised the pawl and cammed the safety out of alignment, allowing the weapon to be fired. This device clearly shared features with the early Adams safety bolt, differing in that it did not have to be manually engaged. The arbor is secured by a characteristic "S"-shaped spring.

Variations
Six basic variations are known, apart from special order or custom-made weapons.

- Holster Model: Cylinder with five chambers, in 38, 50, and 54 bore, usually with a 7½ inch barrel.
- Belt Model: Cylinder with five chambers, in 80 or 90 bore, usually with a 6 inch barrel.
- Pocket Model: Cylinder with five chambers, in 120 bore, usually with a 4½ inch barrel.

Values: Good: $1,800-2,300
(£1,100-1,350)
Fine: $4,200-4,700
(£2,500-£2,800)
Cased: $6,200-6,800
(£3,700-4,000)

Rare at UK and U.S. auctions.

TRANTER-FRAMED REVOLVERS

By 1856, Tranter had begun to produce weapons under his own name, although, at first, he appears to have made some 2nd Model revolvers with his remaining stock of Adams frames. Later examples feature a heavier frame of Tranter's own design.

TRANTER 2ND MODEL (PRODUCTION BEGUN: 1853-1856)

Frame number range (including 2nd, 3rd, and 4th Models, with considerable overlap between models): 100T–55000T, probably not reflecting production.

These weapons were made on both conventional Adams frames and the more massive Tranter type. They are fitted with Tranter's double trigger, "hesitating" mechanism, and 1st Model safety, although a small number of revolvers with Adams's mechanism are also known to have been built on the Tranter frame.

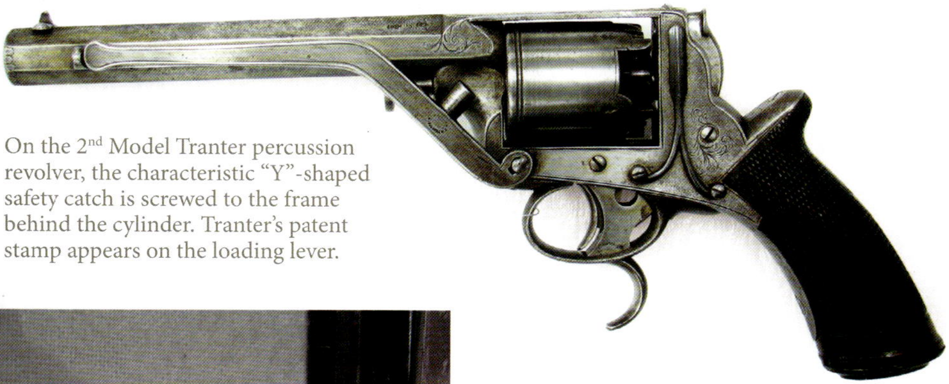

On the 2nd Model Tranter percussion revolver, the characteristic "Y"-shaped safety catch is screwed to the frame behind the cylinder. Tranter's patent stamp appears on the loading lever.

2nd Model Tranter percussion revolver showing detail of the loading lever.

All models bear a "T"-suffixed number on the right side of the frame below the cylinder, which is inscribed:

TRANTER'S PATENT

This is followed by the frame or serial number.

An oval "TRANTER'S PATENT" mark is also sometimes found on the left side of the frame, below the cylinder, in 2nd, 3rd, and 4th Models.

Tranter's 2nd Model is found in 54, 80, and 120 bore, with barrels varying in length from 6 inches to 4½ inches. Larger caliber weapons tend to have longer barrels, although large caliber, short-barreled examples are known.

Its loading lever forms one of the characteristic features of the 2nd Model. In one piece, it is mounted on the left side of the frame by means of a round lug bearing two projections on its opposing sides. The lever itself has a "keyhole" at its lower end that fits over this lug and is then turned to secure it in place; the other end is secured to the barrel by means of a hook. These loading levers were usually carried on the revolver, although they could be easily removed if necessary.

Variations
Three basic variations are known, apart from special order or custom-made weapons.

- Holster Model: Cylinder with five chambers, in 54 bore, usually with a 6 inch barrel.
- Belt Model: Cylinder with five chambers, in 80 bore, usually with a 6 inch barrel.
- Pocket Model: Cylinder with five chambers, in 120 bore, usually with a 4½ inch barrel.

Values: Good: $1,800-2,300
(£1,100-£1,350)
Fine: $4,200-4,700
(£2,500-2,800)
Cased: $6,200-6,800
(£3,700-4,000)
Rare at UK and U.S. auctions.

TRANTER 3RD MODEL (PRODUCTION BEGUN: CIRCA 1860)

Bearing a "T"-suffixed frame number on the right side below the cylinder, these revolvers are built on Tranter's frame, with a more angled (and awkward) butt, 1st Model safety, and Tranter's double trigger "hesitating" action fitted. Loading levers were permanently fixed to the

3rd Model Tranter percussion revolver from the right, showing the position of the frame number. Courtesy of James D. Julia Auctioneers, Fairfield, Maine (www.jamesdjulia.com).

3rd Model Tranter percussion revolver from the left, showing the characteristic loading lever. Courtesy of James D. Julia Auctioneers, Fairfield, Maine (www.jamesdjulia.com).

frame and covered by Tranter's previous British patent, although they shared characteristics with Kerr's device. The main difference was the position of the retaining screw, which was sited on the frame below and forward of the cylinder in the Tranter, rather than below the barrel, as in the Beaumont-Adams and Webley 3rd Model Longspur, which both used the Kerr loading lever.

Most commonly found in 54, 80, and 120 bore with barrels between 4½ to 6 inches, although there is also a rarely seen 38 bore.

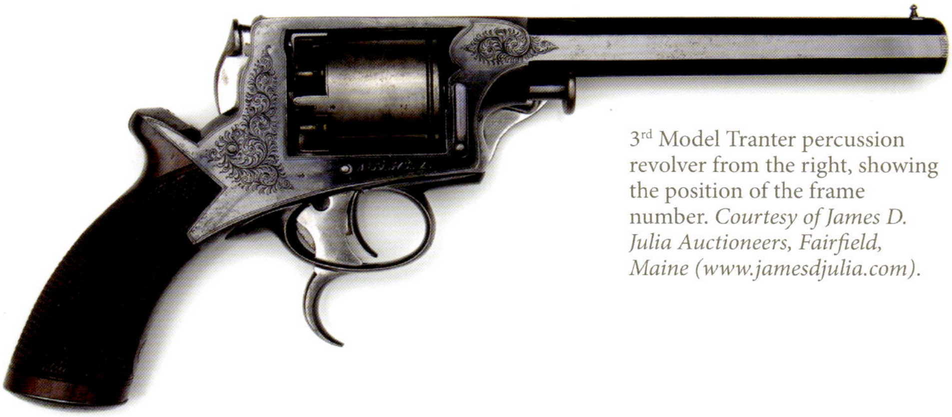

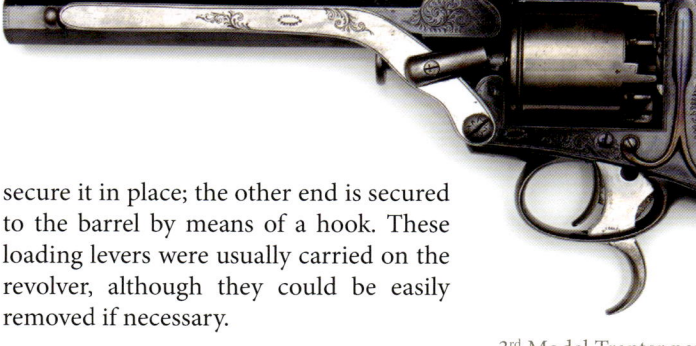

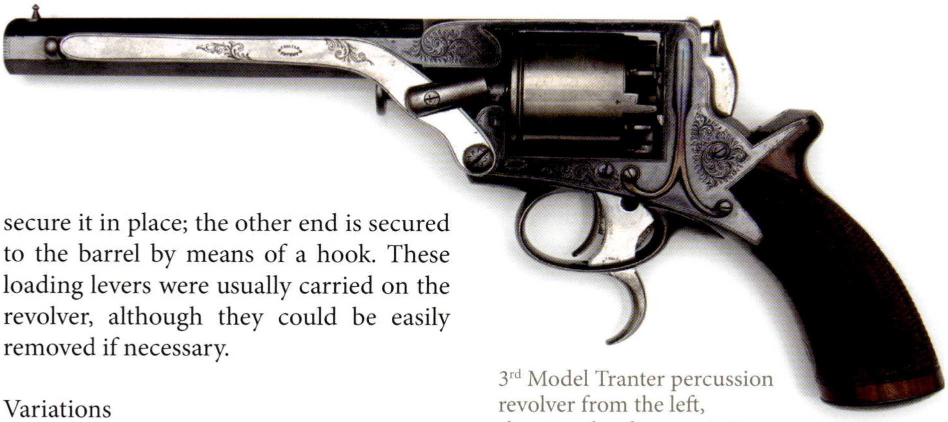

3rd Model Tranter percussion revolver showing cylinder detail, the loading lever head, and the safety bolt. *Courtesy of James D. Julia Auctioneers, Fairfield, Maine (www.jamesdjulia.com).*

3rd Model Tranter percussion revolver in a case with accessories. The short barrel indicates this is possibly a 90 bore weapon. *Courtesy of Thomas del Mar Ltd.*

4TH MODEL TRANTER REVOLVER (PRODUCTION BEGUN CIRCA 1860)

The first of the Tranter percussion revolvers not fitted with the "hesitating" action, this was also the first model fitted with a single trigger, which allowed it to be operated as a conventional double-action revolver. Its most striking difference from the early models is the hammer spur, and it is also characterized by the 3rd Model loading lever and a large lug on the rear of the trigger that served to disengage the sear and drop the hammer.

4th Model Tranter percussion revolver from the right side, showing the position of the frame number, the characteristic safety catch, and the "S"-shaped arbor spring. *Courtesy of James D. Julia Auctioneers, Fairfield, Maine (www.jamesdjulia.com).*

Variations

Four basic variations are known apart from special order or custom-made weapons.

- Holster Model: Cylinder with five chambers, in 38 (rare) or 54 bore, usually with a 6 inch barrel.
- Belt Model: Produced in 80 or 90 bore, usually with a 6 inch barrel.
- Pocket Model: Produced in 120 bore, usually a 4½ inch barrel.

Values: Good: $1,800-2,100 (£1,100-1,250)
Fine: $3,500-3,900 (£2,100-2,300)
Cased: $4,500-5,000 (£2,700-3,000)

Common at UK and U.S. auctions.

TRANTER REVOLVERS

4th Model Tranter percussion revolver from the left side, showing the Tranter Patent loading lever. The earlier "Y"-shaped safety bolt is absent and the trigger features the large lug on the rear of the trigger characteristic of these 4th Models, which were fitted with Tranter's double-action mechanism. *Courtesy of James D. Julia Auctioneers, Fairfield, Maine (www.jamesdjulia.com).*

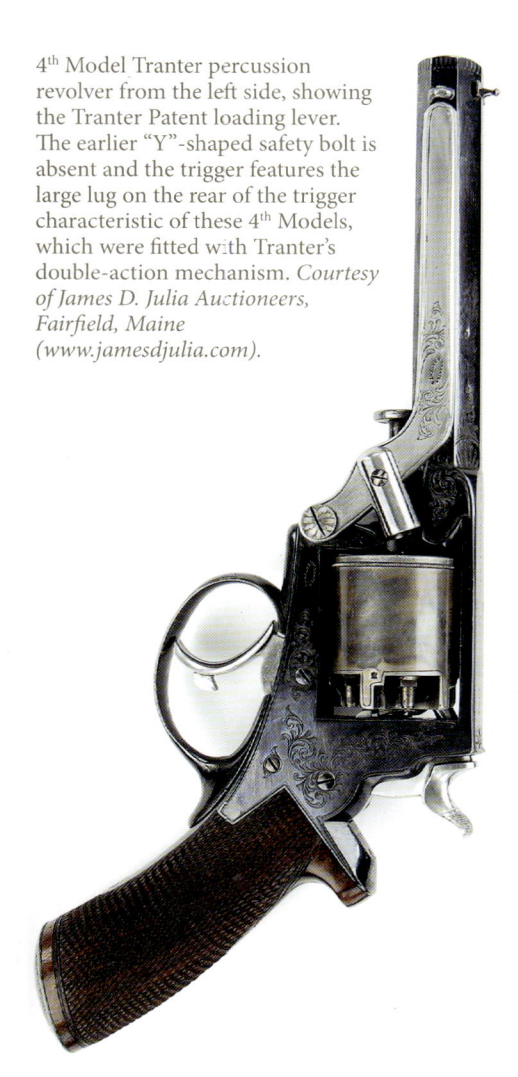

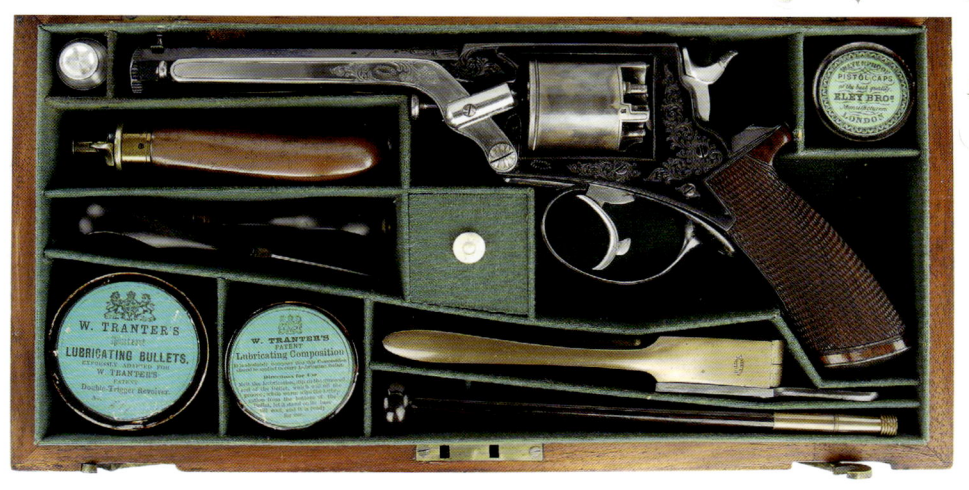

4th Model Tranter percussion revolver in case with accessories, which include a tin of "W. Tranter's Patent Lubricating Bullets" and "Lubricating Composition," both with well preserved labels. *Courtesy of James D. Julia Auctioneers, Fairfield, Maine (www.jamesdjulia.com).*

4th Model Tranter percussion revolver showing the top-strap and its engraved address: "THOS WILLIAMS. SOUTH CASTLE ST LIVERPOOL". *Courtesy of James D. Julia Auctioneers, Fairfield, Maine (www.jamesdjulia.com).*

These revolvers could now be set at "half-cock" for loading, but they also had an additional safety device in the form of a pivoted, "L"-shaped catch. This was screwed to the frame on the lower right side, from where it could be pushed forward to engage one of the holes drilled in the cone partitions, locking the cylinder with the hammer adjacent to the cone partition, rather than the percussion cone itself.[4] A few 4th Models will also be found with a sliding catch similar to the later Adams safety device.

Bore, barrel length, and other characteristics correspond to the earlier models.

These revolvers appear to have enjoyed a good reputation amongst those who used them and were known to be well made, robust weapons. They were a favorite with Allan Pinkerton, who carried a pair of the 4th Model and even bought them for use by members of his Agency. Despite their mechanical quality, a 4th Model must have suffered from a lack of accuracy, even in single-action operation,

4th Model Tranter percussion revolver showing the safety bolt, frame number, trigger, and arbor spring. *Courtesy of James D. Julia Auctioneers, Fairfield, Maine (www.jamesdjulia.com).*

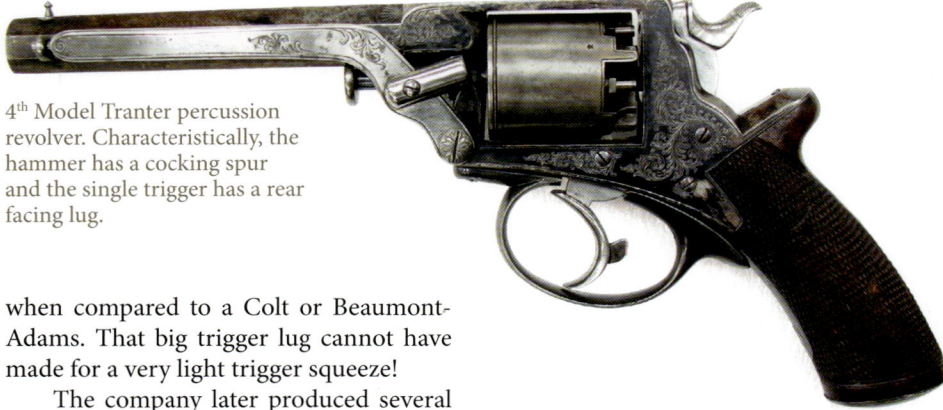

4th Model Tranter percussion revolver. Characteristically, the hammer has a cocking spur and the single trigger has a rear facing lug.

when compared to a Colt or Beaumont-Adams. That big trigger lug cannot have made for a very light trigger squeeze!

The company later produced several other percussion revolvers, although these are much less common than the four previously described.

Variations

Three basic variations are known, apart from special order or custom-made weapons.

- Holster Model: Cylinder with five chambers, in 38 (rare) or 54 bore, usually with a 6 inch barrel.
- Belt Model: Usually in 80 bore, with a 6 inch barrel.
- Pocket Model: Usually in 120 bore, with a 4½ inch barrel.

Values: Good: $2,400-2,800
(£1,500- £1,750)
Fine: $4,300-4,980
(£2,700 - £3,100)
Cased: $5,900-6,900
(£3,700 -4,300)
Very common at UK and U.S. auctions.

TRIPLE-ACTION, DOUBLE-TRIGGER OR "EXPORT" MODEL

Frame numbers: Most frequently found in Tranter's 15000T series, although there may be a number of these revolvers scattered through the other Tranter frame number series.

This revolver could be fired like a conventional Tranter or cocked to operate as a single-action weapon. They were always double triggered, with a hammer spur, and may be distinguished by a sear on the upper trigger, similar in construction to the 4th Model. Other features are also similar to Tranter's 4th Model.

Variations

Only one is recorded, although there may be others:

- Holster Model: Cylinder with five chambers, in 54 bore, with a 6 inch barrel.

Very rare at UK and U.S. auctions.

TRANTER, ADAMS, KERR MODEL

Frame numbers: Recorded in Tranter's 15000T and 17000T series, although there may be a number of these revolvers scattered through the other Tranter frame number series.

Adams-Tranter, Kerr revolver in case with accessories. *Courtesy of James D. Julia Auctioneers, Fairfield, Maine (www.jamesdjulia.com).*

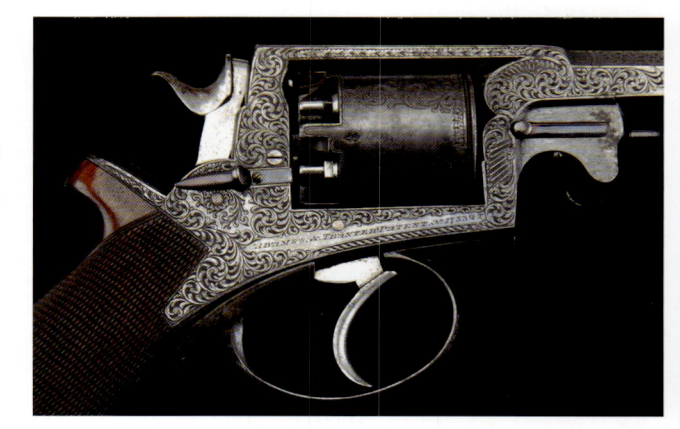

Frame of the Adams-Tranter, Kerr revolver. Details, such as the safety catch and absence of the lug from the rear of the trigger, correspond to a normal Beaumont-Adams, but it is differentiated from that model by the characteristically massive Tranter frame, with a more acutely angled butt and the patent inscription "ADAMS'S. & TRANTERS PATENT", followed by a "T"-suffixed frame number. *Courtesy of James D. Julia Auctioneers, Fairfield, Maine (www.jamesdjulia.com).*

This revolver looks like a conventional Beaumont-Adams, except for a slightly more angled butt, and is a copy of the London-made revolver.

Available as a single- or double trigger weapon, this model is always fitted with a conventional Kerr loading lever characterized by the position of its retaining screw, which inserts into the frame just below the barrel. They are distinguished from a very similar Beaumont-Adams revolver by a "T"-suffixed serial number. Examples have been found bearing the following inscription, on the right side of the frame:

ADAMS-TRANTER PATENT

This is followed by the "T"-suffixed frame number. The butt is in one piece and of walnut.

Variations

Only one variation is known, although there may be others:

- Holster Model: Cylinder with five chambers, in 54 bore with a 6 inch barrel.

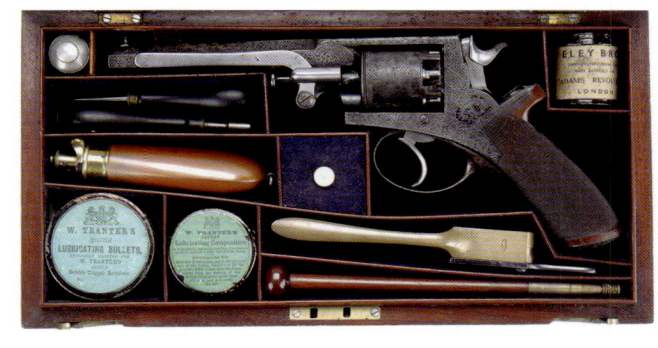

TRANTER REVOLVERS

Retail address found on Adams-Tranter, Kerr revolver. The tiny notched rear sight is shown on the left. *Courtesy of James D. Julia Auctioneers, Fairfield, Maine (www.jamesdjulia.com).*

Values: Good: $3,500-5,000
(£2,100-3,000)
Fine: $5,900-6,900
(£3,500-4,100)
Cased: $8,400-10,100
(£5,000-6,000)
Rare at UK and U.S. auctions.

DUAL IGNITION OR "TRANSITIONAL" MODEL

Just prior to beginning production of cartridge revolvers, Tranter produced this revolver, supplied with both percussion and cartridge cylinders, which were fully interchangeable.

Very rare at UK and U.S. auctions.

SERIAL NUMBERS ASSOCIATED WITH TRANTER'S PERCUSSION REVOLVERS

The classification provided above should certainly not be regarded as a definitive account of Tranter's percussion revolvers. There are a number of discrepancies and exceptions, particularly in the early models. To cite just one example, in the "T" frame number range, there are 3rd Models with numbers earlier than those found on some 1st Models.

This clearly makes determining the actual figures for factory production difficult, to say the least, although details of these frame number anomalies will be found at the Firearms Technology Museum website.[5]

CONFEDERATE TRANTERS

Tranter's "hesitating action" revolvers were imported to the Confederate States through New Orleans, and although the company did not have a government contract, Hyde & Goodrich reached an agreement with Tranter to import and sell these weapons before the war began in 1861. They were popular with the Confederacy; General J.E.B. Stuart himself owned and used one.

Tranter revolvers with a Confederate history are most often either 3rd or 4th Models, although privately owned 1st and 2nd Models may have been used in the war. Both 3rd and 4th Models usually bear some

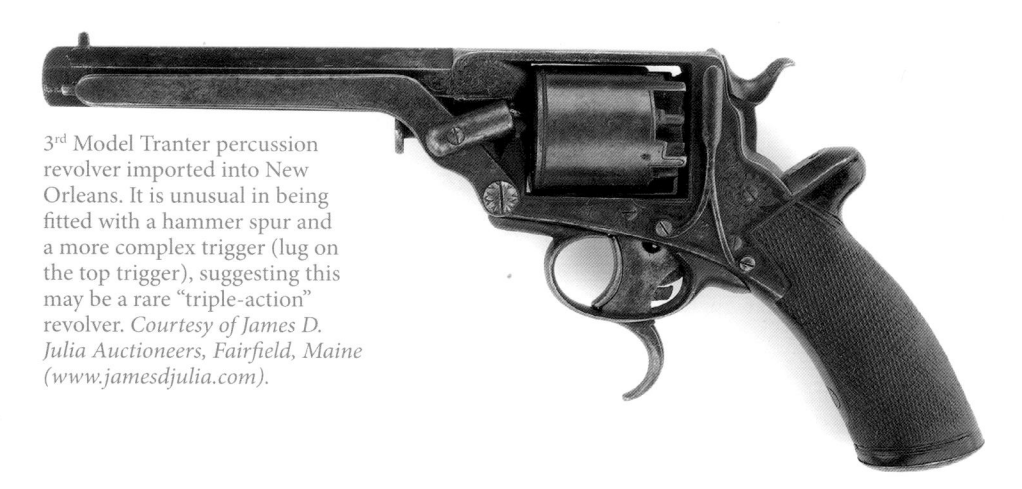

3rd Model Tranter percussion revolver imported into New Orleans. It is unusual in being fitted with a hammer spur and a more complex trigger (lug on the top trigger), suggesting this may be a rare "triple-action" revolver. *Courtesy of James D. Julia Auctioneers, Fairfield, Maine (www.jamesdjulia.com).*

New Orleans 3rd Model Tranter showing the barrel address: "MADE BY W M TRANTER FOR A.B GRISWOLD & CO NEW. ORLEANS". *Courtesy of James D. Julia Auctioneers, Fairfield, Maine (www.jamesdjulia.com).*

3rd Model Tranter percussion revolver imported into New Orleans, with the characteristic barrel address found on these weapons. *Courtesy of James D. Julia Auctioneers, Fairfield, Maine (www.jamesdjulia.com).*

Another form of the barrel address found inscribed on the top-strap of Tranter revolvers imported into New Orleans. *Courtesy of James D. Julia Auctioneers, Fairfield, Maine (www.jamesdjulia.com).*

form of "T"-suffixed frame (or serial) number. They are usually from the New Orleans retail source and marked on the top-strap with the names:

Hyde & Goodrich

or one of their successors,

Thomas, Griswold & Company
or
A.B.Griswold & Company.

This top-strap legend will show variations dependent on the agents at the time of importation. These imported Tranters do not usually differ significantly from the guns made for retail sale in Britain. The most common variation is in the front sight, which takes the form of what modern shooters refer to as a "peppercorn," rather than the blade sight of Birmingham guns. Occasionally, examples may also be found with a butt less sharply raked than the English guns.

Values: Good: $5,000-5,650
($3,000-3,350)
Fine: $8,400-9,100
(£5,000-5,400)
Common at UK and U.S. auctions.

Tranters are well made and popular amongst collectors, although they are not often seen at UK auctions. The 3rd and 4th Models seem to be most frequent, with the 1st Model particularly rare. Later models, especially the Dual-Ignition revolver, appear very rarely.

TRANTER METAL CARTRIDGE REVOLVERS

Tranter's metal cartridge revolvers are described here in the order in which they were manufactured, beginning with his British patent of 1862. Retailer names and addresses, when they are present, will be found on the top-strap of these revolvers, while patent information is inscribed on the right side of the frame below the cylinder, although it is not unusual for Tranter revolvers to be without such markings. When present, patent marks are stamped:

TRANTER'S PATENT

This is followed by a frame or serial number. It may also appear on triggers, loading levers, and other components as an oval stamp. Proof marks may be from either the London Gunmakers or Birmingham's Proof House. Details of all these revolvers will be found on the Firearms Technology museum website.[6]

TRANTER COPIES AND WEAPONS MADE UNDER LICENSE

Tranter's larger rim-fire and center-fire revolvers exhibit a consistent standard of quality in their production; this suggests that most of these arms were produced in Tranter's Aston factory. The quality of the smaller rim-fire revolvers (No 1, No 2, and the "House Defence" revolvers) is more variable, and this has led to the suggestion that Tranter may have employed a number of the smaller Birmingham makers to produce revolvers that were subsequently sold under his name.[7]

TRANTER NO 1 SHEATH TRIGGER REVOLVERS

Three serial ranges:

1000 – 2000
6000 – 7000
10000 – 11500

Solid-frame, gate-loading, single-action rim-fire revolvers with a sheathed trigger, in .230 rim-fire. They have cylinders with seven chambers, and on some examples notches were cut into the outer edge of the rear face to allow spent cartridges to be pried out. Frames are either brass or gunmetal, with a 2½ inch iron barrel screwed into the breech piece. The cylinder arbor latch may be button or see-saw type. An inspection plate was fitted, with a single screw fixing into the hammer pivot, allowing access to the lock mechanism.

Tranter No. 1 Model sheath trigger revolver. The No. 2 is of similar conformation. This one shows the arbor spring on the frame.

Cased example of a Tranter No. 1 Model sheath trigger revolver. *Courtesy of James D. Julia Auctioneers, Fairfield, Maine (www.jamesdjulia.com)*.

TRANTER REVOLVERS

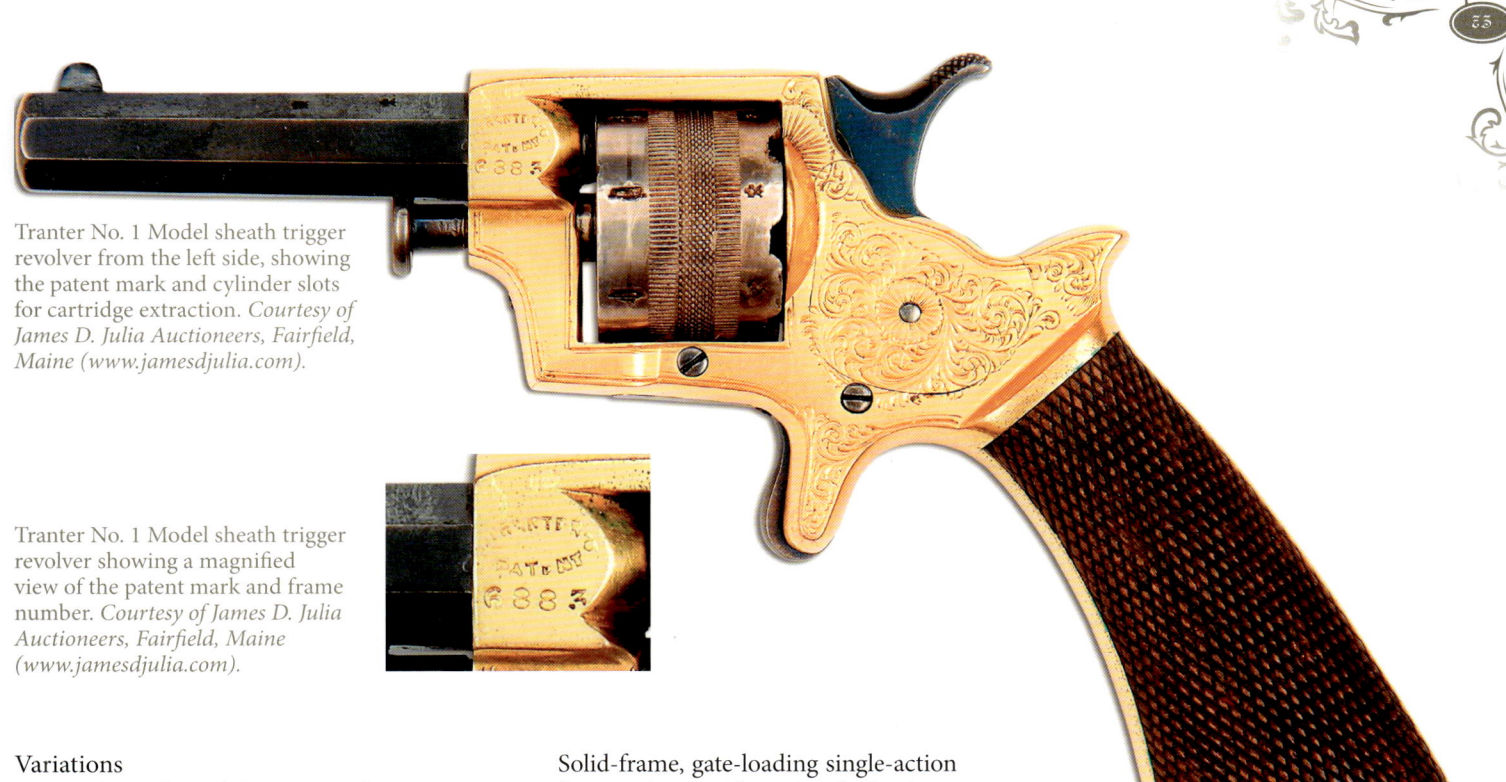

Tranter No. 1 Model sheath trigger revolver from the left side, showing the patent mark and cylinder slots for cartridge extraction. *Courtesy of James D. Julia Auctioneers, Fairfield, Maine (www.jamesdjulia.com).*

Tranter No. 1 Model sheath trigger revolver showing a magnified view of the patent mark and frame number. *Courtesy of James D. Julia Auctioneers, Fairfield, Maine (www.jamesdjulia.com).*

Variations

- Brass framed Model: Frame in brass, 2½ inch iron barrel, chambered for seven cartridges in .230 caliber rim-fire.

    Values: Good: $1,800-2,200
    (£1,100-1,300)
    Fine: $2,800-3,400
    (£1,700-2,000)
    Cased: $6,700-6,740
    (£3,700-4,000)

- Gunmetal framed Model: As before, except in this model the frame is made from gunmetal and exhibits a grey patina.

    Values: Good: $2,100 (£1,250)
    Fine: $4,400 (£2,600)
    Rare at UK and U.S. auctions.

TRANTER NO 2 SHEATH TRIGGER REVOLVERS (BRITISH PATENT 2067/1862 AND 1863/1862)

Five serial ranges, with patent information and frame numbers on the left side of the breech:

    2000 – 4000
    8000 – 9000
    10000 – 11000
    30000 (few revolvers in this range)
    50000 (only one so far recorded)

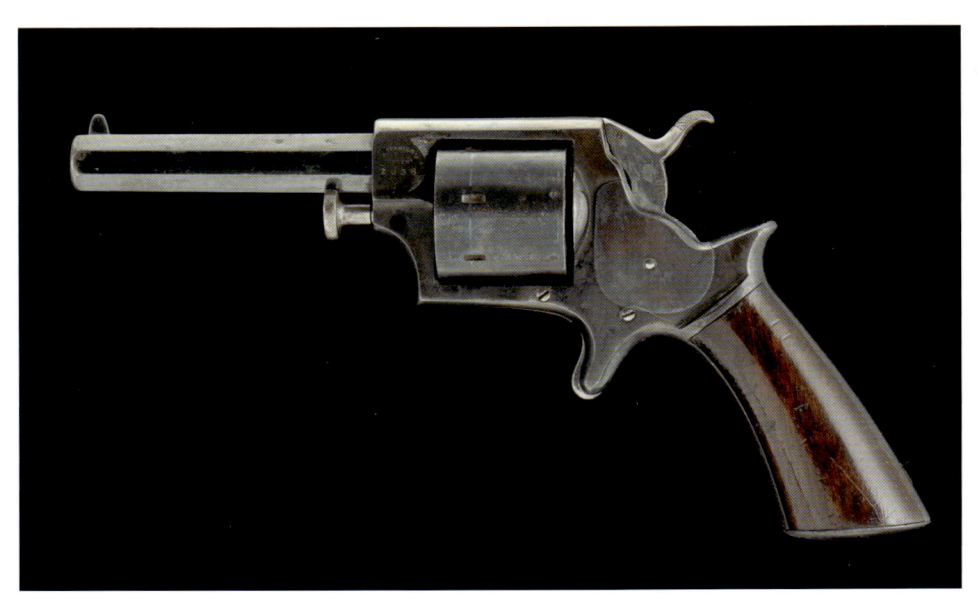

Solid-frame, gate-loading single-action rim-fire revolvers with a sheathed trigger and 3½ inch barrel in .320 rim-fire. They have ylinders with seven chambers and some examples have notches cut into the outer edge of the chambers to allow spent cartridges to be pried out. A spring loaded hammer lock may be found fitted in the frame of some weapons to facilitate loading and an inspection plate was fitted, with a single screw fixing into the hammer pivot, allowing access to the lock mechanism.

Variations

Only this single variation is known:
- Cylinder with seven chambers, in .320 rim-fire, with a 3½ inch barrel.

    Values: Good: $1,600-1,800
    (£1,000-1,100)
    Fine: $2,900-3,500
    (£1,700-2,100)

Rare at UK and U.S. auctions.

Tranter No. 2 Model sheath trigger revolver; this example is chambered in .32 rim-fire. Courtesy of Thomas Del Mar Ltd.

TRANTER HOUSE DEFENCE REVOLVERS (BRITISH PATENT 2067/1862 AND 2113/1866)

Four serial ranges:

    7000 (.380 cal)
    9000–10000 (.320 cal)
    30000 (.230 cal)
    50000–60000 (.297 cal)

Small revolvers produced, as their name suggests, for occasional use in the home against intruders.

Solid-frame, gate-loading rim-fire revolvers, with a cylinder chambered for five rounds (seven rounds in .230 cal.) in .230, .297, .320, and .380 calibers. Barrels in various lengths: 2½ inch (.230 and .297 cal), 3½ inch (.320 cal), and 5 inch (.380 cal).

An inspection plate was fitted with a single screw fixing into the hammer pivot, allowing access to the lock mechanism, as well as a spring steel friction plate that stopped free cylinder rotation. A case extractor is either absent or consists of a small device screwed into the butt cap. The cylinder arbor catch is spring loaded and similar in design to the earlier percussion revolvers.

Variations
House Defence revolvers:

- .230 caliber Model: Usually with a 2½ inch barrel, with a cylinder chambered for seven cartridges in .230 rim-fire.
- .297 caliber Model: Usually with a 2½ inch barrel, with a cylinder chambered for five cartridges in .297 rim-fire.
- .320 caliber Model: Usually with a 3½ inch barrel, with a cylinder chambered for five cartridges in .320 rim-fire.
- .380 caliber Model: Usually with a 5 inch barrel, with a cylinder chambered for five cartridges in .380 rim-fire.

Very rare at UK and U.S. auctions.

TRANTER MODEL 1863 REVOLVER (BRIT PATENTS 2067/1862 AND 1862/1863)

Serial range:

    4000–4500 (approx.) for the single-action rim-fire version
    4500–5800 (approx.) for the double-action rim-fire version
    30000 for the .450 center-fire version

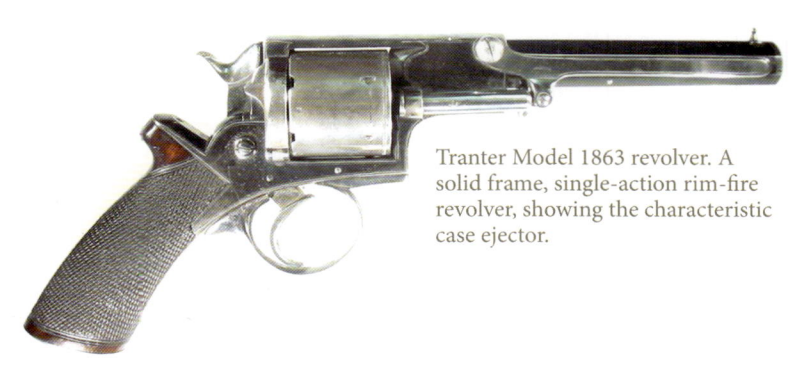

Tranter Model 1863 revolver. A solid frame, single-action rim-fire revolver, showing the characteristic case ejector.

Sometimes referred to as the "Army" revolver, although it was never adopted by any military body, this solid-framed, gate-loading revolver comes in either single- or double-action. The cylinder has six chambers in .442 rim-fire (6½ inch barrel) and there is a later, .450 center-fire version with a shrouded hammer (6 inch barrel). These revolvers also featured an inspection plate with a single screw fixing into the hammer pivot, allowing access to the lock mechanism. The compound case extractor is characteristic of this revolver (similar in appearance and action to the Kerr loading lever, except it moves downwards) and is protected by Tranter's patent of 1863 (British Patent 1862/1863). The butt is in one piece and of chequered walnut.

Variations
- Single-action Rim-fire Model: Single-action with 6½ inch barrel, cylinder with six chambers in .442 rim-fire.
- Double-action .442 Rim-fire Model: In this model, the mechanism is double-action with a 6½ inch barrel and a cylinder with six chambers in .442 rim-fire.
- Double-action .450 Center-fire Model: Double-action with a 6 inch barrel and a cylinder with six chambers in Adams .450 center-fire. This model characteristically has a floating firing pin and a shrouded hammer.

Tranter Model 1863 solid frame, double-action rim-fire revolver. The trigger bears a lug on its rear face, distinguishing it from the single-action arm.

A case ejector with a similar configuration to the 1863 Army is frequently seen on rim-fire revolvers made for the Birmingham trade by various makers, including P. Webley & Sons.

Values: Good: $2,900-3,300
(£1,700-1,950)
Fine: $3,900-4,500
(£2,300-2,700)
Rare at UK and U.S. auctions.

TRANTER MODEL 1868 REVOLVER (BRIT PATENTS 282/1868)

Most popular of Tranter's cartridge revolvers. Serial number ranges:

04000–05000
30000–60000, possibly as a continuation of the 1863 .450 center-fire range.

Solid-frame, gate-loading revolvers, all fitted with Tranter's patent double-action mechanism and bearing the characteristic lug on the rear face of the trigger.

Produced in .320 (3 inch barrel), .380, .450, and .500 center-fire, as well as .380 and .442 rim-fire, all with 4½ inch barrels (except the .320 center-fire). The cylinder has five chambers in the smaller calibers, six in the larger. An inspection plate was fitted with a single screw fixing into the hammer pivot. Early examples had what appears to be a somewhat fragile under-barrel case extractor, while later revolvers were fitted with a more robust device stored in the cylinder arbor. The butt is in one piece of walnut, with chequering.

Variations
Rim-fire Models:
- .380 caliber rim-fire Model: Barrel 4½ inches, cylinder with five chambers in .380 rim-fire.
- .442 caliber rim-fire Model: Barrel 4½ inches barrel, cylinder with six chambers in .442 rim-fire.

Center-fire Models:
- .320 caliber center-fire Model: Barrel 3 inches, cylinder with five chambers in .320 center-fire.
- .380 caliber center-fire Model: Barrel 4½ inches, cylinder with five chambers in .380 center-fire.
- .450 caliber center-fire Model: Barrel 4½ inches, cylinder with six chambers in .450 center-fire.
- .500 caliber center-fire Model: Barrel 4½ inches, cylinder with six chambers in .500 center-fire.

Values: Good: $1,800-2,300
(£1,100-1,350)
Fine: $2,800-4,200
(£1,700-2,000)
Rare at UK and U.S. auctions.

TRANTER .577 CALIBER REVOLVER

Serial number ranges:

33400- 33700
50100- 50200

Tranter Model 1868 revolver, showing the characteristic, under-barrel case ejector.

Tranter .577 Model revolver. The shape of the cylinder is characteristic and serves to identify this unique revolver. Copied by Webley, the two arms may be differentiated by the six-chambered cylinder of the Webley copy. *Courtesy of James D. Julia Auctioneers, Fairfield, Maine (www.jamesdjulia.com).*

A solid-frame, gate-loading double-action revolver in Tranter .577 center-fire caliber. The cylinder has five chambers, with characteristic deep fluting over the whole length; this is probably necessary because of the chambering for the massive .577 caliber cartridge. The barrel is characteristically short at three inches, but otherwise similar in configuration to Model 1868. A breech piece is fitted between the rear of the cylinder and frame and pierced to allow the hammer nose to strike the cartridges. It is differentiated from the very similar Webley copy by the five-chambered cylinder. The butt in one piece, walnut.

A later six-chambered variant was produced at the Braedlin factory that had its own serial number range.

Variations
Two variations are known:

- Tranter .577 Revolver: Barrel three inches, cylinder with five chambers, in .577 center-fire caliber.
- Tranter-Braedlin's .577 Revolver: Barrel three inches, cylinder with six chambers, in .577 center-fire caliber. Barrel, frame or, most usually, the breech piece bears maker's stamp: "BRAEDLIN."

Values:　Good: $2,200-2,600
　　　　　(£1,300-1,550)
　　　　　Fine: $3,300-3,900
　　　　　(£2,000-£2,300)
Rare at UK and U.S. auctions.

TRANTER MODEL 1868 "EXTRACTING TIP" REVOLVER (BRITISH PATENT 3622/1868)

Serial number range: Unknown
Similar to Smith & Wesson's early .22 and .32 caliber revolvers of 1862, it is hinged at the top of the standing breech with a catch at the front of the lower frame. Self extracting, the star-shaped extractor is operated by a toothed lever operating against a fixed, correspondingly toothed rack on the underside of the barrel. Dimensions and calibers are not available, but may have been produced as a competitor to the smaller Smith & Wesson revolvers.

Very rare at UK and U.S. auctions.

TRANTER MODEL 1868 "PIVOTED ROD EXTRACTOR" REVOLVER

Serial number range:

33000 – 34900
60000 – 69000, in a range shared with the self-extracting model.

Solid-frame, gate-loading revolver, single-action or fitted with Tranter's twin trigger, double-action mechanism, although examples of the latter are rare. The cylinder has five chambers, in calibers from .320 (3 inch barrel) to .500 center-fire. Larger calibers had correspondingly longer barrels from 4-4½ inches. The usual inspection plate is present. These are usually fitted with a one piece walnut butt, although other materials may be encountered. The case extractor in these arms lies along the side of the frame, below the cylinder, when not in use. If required to extract an empty case, the extractor rod is pulled forward and swiveled upwards before being pushed into the adjacent chamber to extract the cartridge. It seems a fragile and somewhat unsatisfactory device in common with many of the extractors fitted to gate-loading revolvers.

Variations
As described, although specific dimensions are not recorded.

Very rare at UK and U.S. auctions.

TRANTER MODEL 1878 REVOLVER

Produced to help fill John Adams's contract to Britain's War Department (see Military Pistols and Revolvers).

Tranter Model 1878. The last of Tranter's solid frame revolvers still featuring the lug on the rear of the trigger, which is characteristic of weapons fitted with his double-action mechanism and one of the few Tranter revolvers to be fitted with a fluted cylinder.

TRANTER MODEL 1879 REVOLVER (BRITISH PATENTS 2855/1879)

Detail of the Tranter 1879 hinge frame revolver, the last model made before his factory was taken over by Kynoch.

Serial number ranges:

04000 – 05000
60000 – 69000, in a range shared with the 1868 "Pivoted Rod" Extractor Model

Hinge-frame, double-action, self-extracting revolver. The cylinder has six chambers in either .380 or .450 calibers, with barrels between four and six inches (six inches was the usual length for .450 cal). The top break loading mechanism is operated by a thumb-actuated lever on the left side of the frame, adjacent to the hammer slot. The lever is retained in firing position by a substantial lug projecting from the frame. It is fitted with a rebounding hammer and button to disable the self-extractor. This model may be found with either a vertical or horizontal cylinder arbor release catch and a single piece, chequered wooden butt (usually walnut).

Variations
Model 1879 Revolver:

- .380 caliber Model: cylinder with six chambers in .380 center-fire caliber, 4 inch barrel.
- .450 caliber Model: cylinder with six chambers in .450 center-fire caliber, 4 inch or 6 inch barrel.

Very rare at UK and U.S. auctions.

TRANTER RIC REVOLVER

Tranter also made a copy of the Webley RIC revolver using his own double-action mechanism, but these are very rare.

KYNOCH REVOLVERS

When William Tranter retired in 1885, he leased his Aston factory to George Kynoch, who then operated the works as the Kynoch Gun Works, Aston, later becoming the Aston Arms Co Ltd.

British Patent 9084/1885
Serial number range: Unknown
Although these revolvers are referred to by collectors as "Kynoch revolvers," the original patents were taken out by Henry Schlund, Kynoch's works manager. There were three models, all hinge-frame, double-action, self-extracting revolvers chambered for six rounds with a concealed hammer and double triggers. The top break action was opened for loading by a small catch at the rear of the hammer cover.

Variations
- Model No 1: Cylinder with six chambers in .476, .455, .450, and .430 calibers, with a 6 inch barrel.
- Model No 2: Cylinder with six chambers in .400, .380. .360, and .320, with a 5 inch barrel.
- Model No 3: Cylinder with six chambers in .300 and .297, with a 3 inch barrel.

Tranter copy of the Webley RIC, showing the octagonal barrel, top-hinged loading gate, and the case ejector screwed to the frame. Early Webley R.I.C. revolvers had oval barrels and the case ejector was secured by a strap passing around the rear of the barrel.

Kynoch revolver showing the fully enclosed hammer and massive frame hinge.

Kynoch revolver with the breech open.

Values: Good: $2,100 (£1,250)
Fine: $4,200 (£2,500)
Rare at UK and U.S. auctions.

TRANTER SERIAL NUMBERS

There is absolutely no clear-cut divisions between serial number ranges quoted here. Model 1863 revolvers, for example, are found with numbers in a range with the Model 1879 hinge-frame revolvers—production of which began some fifteen years later—and the variation is similar for many of the other revolvers.

Any collector interested in trying to work through this confusion is directed to the "Database" section of the Firearms Technology Museum website.[8]

CHAPTER FIVE

Webley Revolvers

During the early 1850s, the gun trade was not a major factor in Birmingham's economy; nail making and even coal mining were of far greater importance, which meant gunmakers were neither influential nor, more significantly, particularly wealthy men.

Lacking the money for mechanization of the sort practiced by Sam Colt and Robert Adams, the Birmingham trade continued with their usual, albeit antiquated, system—arranging for the manufacture of guns, including revolvers, with independent craftsmen. These men made the parts and assembled (or "set up") guns in either their own homes or a rented workshop, being paid a fixed price by the gunmaker for each item they produced. This system was seen as perfectly adequate by the majority in the Birmingham trade; demand for revolvers in Britain was not high, being almost totally confined to the military, unlike in America, where many still needed such weapons for personal defense, a factor which seems to have fueled much of the firearm development there.

The Webley brothers—James and Philip—were apprenticed into this close-knit community of Birmingham gunmakers and, having "served their time," went into business together in a retail premises and workshop on Weaman Street, in the Birmingham Gun Quarter. Phillip's marriage appears to have put an end to the brothers' partnership and from that time forward, until James's early death, they pursued separate business interests.

James Webley took out his first patent for a revolver in 1853. He called it an "Improved Patent Repeating Pistol," but it is more commonly known to modern collectors as the Webley "Longspur," because of the spoon-shaped spur or thumb piece projecting from the rear of the hammer. These and some of the subsequent Webley revolvers differ from Sam Colt's products in that, because they are completely hand-made, parts are not usually interchangeable, even between the same model revolver.

After his brother's death in 1856, Phillip combined the revolver companies, retaining his brother's name while he continued to make and retail the single-action "Longspur" revolvers at his own premises at 84, Weaman Street, Birmingham. Some time in the period between 1860 and 1870, Phillip was joined in his business by his two sons, Thomas and Henry, and the firm was then registered as "P. Webley & Son," at the same time adopting the "Winged Bullet" trademark. By 1864, Webley had largely abandoned percussion weapons in favor of copies of the Smith & Wesson breech loading revolvers and Tranter's massive .577 caliber revolver. Even then, however, plans must have been going forward for the production of a new revolver—the RIC No 1, chambered for a .442 caliber centerfire cartridge. This was a well designed, ultra-reliable weapon adopted in 1868 by the Royal Irish Constabulary. It sold so well that many gunmakers produced copies, including William Tranter.

Philip Webley died in 1888, only a year after the company was awarded their first government contract for the MkI Government Model revolver, and the business continued under the direction of his sons Thomas and Henry until its amalgamation, in 1897, with Richard Ellis & Son and W.C Scott & Sons. This new conglomerate was registered on 21 October 1897 as "The Webley & Scott Revolver & Arms Company Limited" of Birmingham and London, with a London outlet at 78, Shaftesbury Avenue. Manufacturing operations were carried on at Webley's old Weaman Street premises (81-91, Weaman Street) after some changes and enlargement. In 1906, there was a final name change to "Webley & Scott Limited." The Weaman Street factory was the subject of a compulsory purchase order in 1957, and Webley & Scott moved into a new, purpose-built factory in Park Lane, Handsworth, in 1958. In October of that year, Webley & Scott Limited was acquired by R.H Windsor Limited. Subsequent manufacturing operations are described in Bruce and Renhard.[1]

Later Webley revolvers are well known to many as the issue weapon of the British Army, which included the Webley Mk1 and its subsequent improved models, as well as the excellent Enfield-made copies of the MkIV. The British Army had replaced most of its Webley revolvers with the Browning Hi-Power semi-automatic pistol by 1963, but many examples of the later Webley models are still in use with both military and police forces worldwide. Not too bad for a weapon based on a design introduced well over a century ago.

WEBLEY SINGLE-ACTION PERCUSSION REVOLVERS

WEBLEY'S "LONGSPUR" REVOLVER (PRODUCTION BEGUN 1853)

British Patent 743/1853
Hand-made revolvers.

Although Philip Webley registered a patent for a revolver (Brit. Pat. 305/ 1853), no examples of this arm are known to exist, so the "Longspur" is considered the first Webley revolver.

Four distinct models of this weapon are usually recognized—all single-action

1st Model Longspur from the right side, showing the frame securing wedge, frame hinge, and loading lever pivot screw on the barrel. Courtesy of James D. Julia Auctioneers, Fairfield, Maine (www.jamesdjulia.com).

percussion revolvers. The descriptions offered here are generally applicable, although Webley revolvers, like those of Robert Adams, were often supplied to a specific customer's requirements and were also occasionally fitted with the early Adams pattern external safety device.

Proof marks are usually those of the Birmingham House, although a small but significant number bear London stamps, possibly indicating their retail origin. Retail marks also show significant variation and include some smaller, rural gunsmiths, saddlers, and suppliers of military uniforms.

WEBLEY 1ST MODEL LONGSPUR (PRODUCTION: 1853-1855)

Frame numbers range: 100 – 300.

This model is open-framed and has an inspection plate fitted on the left side, behind and below the hammer, which allows access to the single-action lock mechanism after removal of a single screw. Safety bolts are not usually fitted, although exceptions are known.

Frame numbers are inscribed on the top of the butt strap, with corresponding numbers on most of the other major components. The barrel is hinged to the frame and secured to the arbor by a wedge. The removable lock plate is inscribed:

JAMES WEBLEY, PATENTEE

The butt strap is normally inscribed:

BY HER MAJESTY'S ROYAL LETTERS PATENT

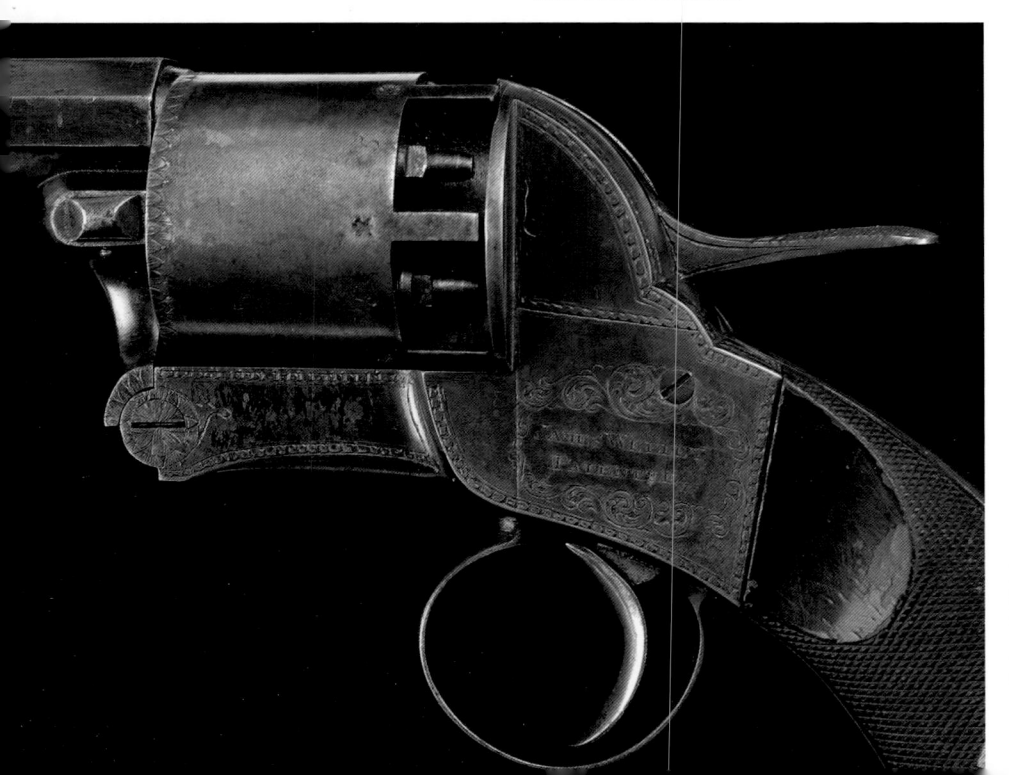

Early guns that were of James Webley's manufacture have the top flat inscribed:

JAMES WEBLEY, ST MARYS SQUARE, BIRMINGHAM.

The octagonal barrel has right twist, relatively shallow, sixteen groove rifling and is found most frequently in 48 and 54 bore, with barrels in lengths varying between 7 and 5¼ inches, respectively.

The six-chambered cylinders rotate clockwise, with the chambers often numbered counterclockwise. The flash shields between chambers were too narrow to bear either safety studs or milled safety notches, hence a "safe carry" was achieved either by leaving the hammer on an empty chamber or carrying the revolver at half-cock. Unfortunately, that meant this model became a "five-shooter," with the later models becoming "four-shooters."

All Longspurs have both front and rear sights, the rear sight consisting of a notch in the top of the hammer similar to an open-framed Colt revolver. An Adams pattern loading lever was supplied with 1st Model Longspurs and this was slipped over a peg on the side of the barrel, thus allowing the load to be rammed home securely. All models are decorated with shallow, foliate engraving. The barrel and frame are usually blued, with the cylinder, hammer, trigger, and loading lever color case hardened, although a few fully nickel plated examples are known. Butts in all models are most often formed from two chequered wooden pieces secured on either side of the frame by a cross pin, although examples have been recorded with a butt constructed in one piece.

1st Model Longspur from the left side, showing the removable lock plate with the inscription "JAMES WEBLEY PATENTEE". Courtesy of James D. Julia Auctioneers, Fairfield, Maine (www.jamesdjulia.com).

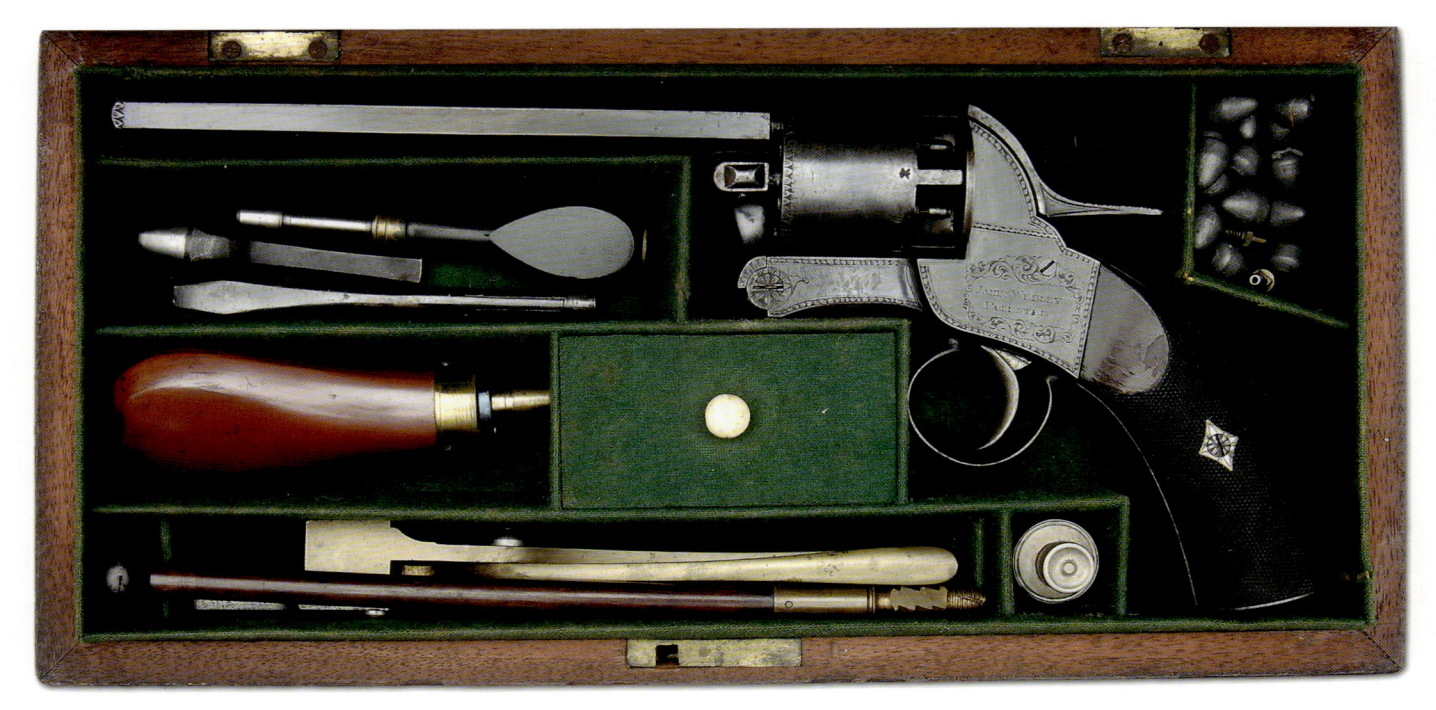

1st Model Longspur in case with accessories. The case includes a number of pre-cast conoidal bullets, rather than the more usual spherical loads. *Courtesy of James D. Julia Auctioneers, Fairfield, Maine (www.jamesdjulia.com).*

Webley 1st Model Webley Longspur in case with accessories—probably a 48 bore—with a seven inch barrel. *By kind permission of Bonhams.*

1st Model Webley Longspur showing the early "JAMES WEBLEY" barrel address. *Courtesy of James D. Julia Auctioneers, Fairfield, Maine (www.jamesdjulia.com).*

WEBLEY REVOLVERS

1st Model Longspur showing Birmingham proof marks. Courtesy of James D. Julia Auctioneers, Fairfield, Maine (www.jamesdjulia.com).

1st Model Longspur showing operation of the detachable loading lever. Courtesy of James D. Julia Auctioneers, Fairfield, Maine (www.jamesdjulia.com).

WEBLEY 2ND MODEL LONGSPUR (PRODUCTION: 1855-1857)

Frame number range: 100 – 900. These numbers may reflect production and are in a series apparently separate from the 1st Model.

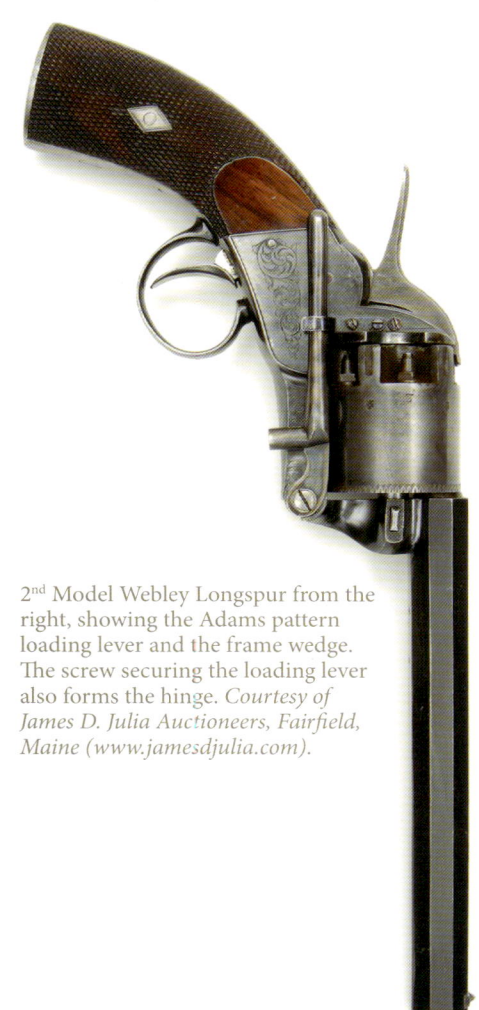

2nd Model Webley Longspur from the right, showing the Adams pattern loading lever and the frame wedge. The screw securing the loading lever also forms the hinge. Courtesy of James D. Julia Auctioneers, Fairfield, Maine (www.jamesdjulia.com).

Variations

Three basic variations are known, apart from special order or custom-made weapons.

- Holster Model: Cylinder with six chambers, in 38, 48, or 54 bore. Barrels were 3, 4, 5, 6, or 7 inches in length.
- Belt Model: Cylinder with six chambers, in 60 bore with barrels 4 or 5 inches in length.
- Pocket Model: Cylinder with six chambers in 120 bore, with barrels between 2½ and 4 inches.
- A self-cocking 1st Model is also recorded.[2]

Values: Good: $2,100-2,500 (£1,250-1,500)
Fine: $4,200-5,000 (£2,500-3,000)
Cased: $10,000-11,800 (£6,000-7,000)

Rare at UK and U.S. auctions.

2nd Model Webley Longspur revolvers differ from the 1st Model, having a permanently attached loading lever and a five-chambered cylinder, although examples with six chambers are recorded. Chambers are frequently numbered.

This model is open-framed and has an inspection plate fitted on the left side, behind and below the hammer, which allows access to the single-action lock mechanism after removal of a single screw. Frame numbers were inscribed on the top of the butt strap, with corresponding numbers on most of the other major

2nd Model Longspur from the right, showing the Adams pattern loading lever, its retaining spring clip, a "1" designating the chamber number, and an unusually clear Birmingham proof mark on the cylinder. Courtesy of James D. Julia Auctioneers, Fairfield, Maine (www.jamesdjulia.com).

components. The barrel and frame are hinged and secured together by a cylinder arbor wedge. The butt strap is normally inscribed near the top:

BY HER MAJESTY'S ROYAL LETTERS PATENT

In revolvers numbered up to 573, the removable lock plate is inscribed:

JAMES WEBLEY, PATENTEE

After this number, the inspection plate is inscribed:

WEBLEY'S PATENT

A barrel inscription is often present on the top flat:

WEBLEY'S PATENT . LONDON .

Conformation is similar to the 1st Model, except cylinders fitted to the larger arms are five-chambered, while all

2nd Model Longspur showing the patent mark on the top flat of the barrel. Courtesy of James D. Julia Auctioneers, Fairfield, Maine (www.jamesdjulia.com).

2nd Model Longspur showing the frame hinge and an unusually clear pair of Birmingham proof marks on the lower flat of the barrel. Courtesy of James D. Julia Auctioneers, Fairfield, Maine (www.jamesdjulia.com).

WEBLEY REVOLVERS

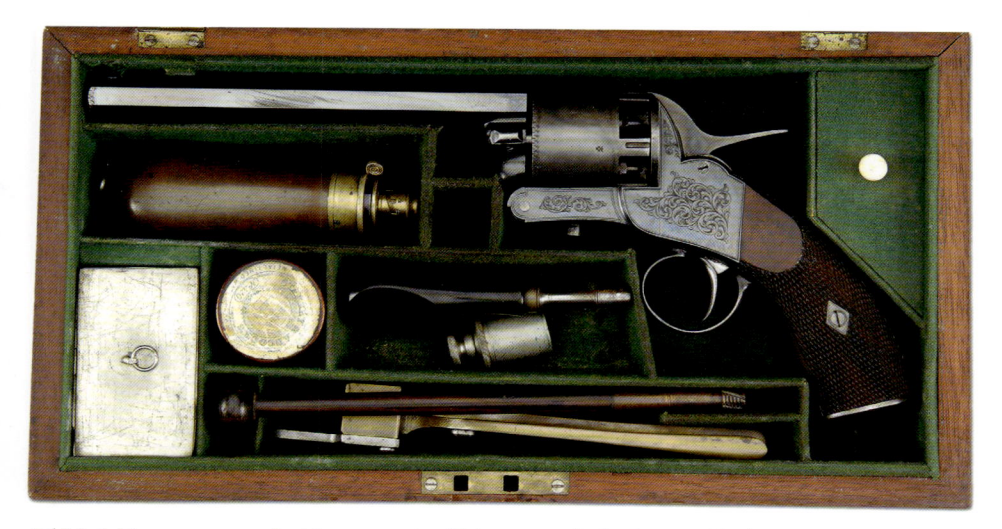

2nd Model Longspur cased with accessories. This weapon lacks the usual lock plate inscription. *Courtesy of James D. Julia Auctioneers, Fairfield, Maine (www.jamesdjulia.com).*

examples of the 120 bore Pocket version so far described are six-chambered, both versions rotating clockwise.

In this model, the Adams pattern loading lever was permanently attached, usually to the right side of the frame, although a few examples are known with left-mounted loading levers. This device consisted of a straight lever, with the rammer head attached at right angles close to the end nearest the cylinder and pivoting on the screw that secured the barrel hinge, then being turned back and secured along the frame by a spring clip when not in use.

Variations
Four basic variations are known, apart from special order or custom-made weapons:

- Holster Model: Cylinder with five chambers, in either 48 bore with a 7 inch barrel or 54 bore with a 5 ¼ inch barrel.
- Belt Model: Cylinder with five chambers, in 60 bore, 4 inch barrel.
- Pocket Model: Cylinder with six chambers, in 120 bore. Barrels between 3 and 4 inches.

Values: Good: $3,800-5,000
          (£2,250-3,000)
          Fine: $7,600-8,400
          (£4,500-5,000)
          Cased: $16,800-21,000
          (£10,000-12,500)

Rare at UK and U.S. auctions.

WEBLEY 3RD MODEL LONGSPUR
PRODUCTION: 1857-1859

Frame number range: 900–1600.

3rd Model Webley Longspur revolvers differ from the 1st and 2nd Models in having the barrel screwed on to the threaded end of the cylinder arbor and secured by a large-headed screw, often with a "butterfly" head, passing through the bottom of the barrel lug and into the lower front end of the frame. This modification was covered by a patent assigned to James Bentley, a Liverpool gunmaker and retailer, in 1852 (Brit. Pat. 960/1852). Webley presumably came to some satisfactory financial arrangement with the patentee, because Bentley found it unnecessary to go to the expense of renewing his patent protection in 1861.[3]

A transition version between the 2nd and 3rd Model is also recorded.[4] This weapon is fitted with the 3rd Model's characteristic Kerr loading lever, but has the barrel secured to the lock frame by a wedge through the cylinder arbor, as well as a screw passing through the barrel lug and into the frame.

3rd Model Longspur from the right, showing the frame conformation and frame securing bolt. *Courtesy of James D. Julia Auctioneers, Fairfield, Maine (www.jamesdjulia.com).*

3rd Model Longspur from the left, showing the Kerr pattern loading lever and lock plate secured by a single screw. *Courtesy of James D. Julia Auctioneers, Fairfield, Maine (www.jamesdjulia.com).*

3rd Model Longspur from the left, showing the cylinder numbering and the lock plate inscribed "WEBLEY'S PATENT". *Courtesy of James D. Julia Auctioneers, Fairfield, Maine (www.jamesdjulia.com).*

3rd Model Longspur showing the cylinder numbering and conformation of the hammer rear sight. *Courtesy of James D. Julia Auctioneers, Fairfield, Maine (www.jamesdjulia.com).*

3rd Model Longspur showing the butt strap inscription "BY HER MAJESTY'S ROYAL LETTERS PATENT". *Courtesy of James D. Julia Auctioneers, Fairfield, Maine (www.jamesdjulia.com).*

3rd Model Longspur from the right, showing the cylinder numbering and engraving. *Courtesy of James D. Julia Auctioneers, Fairfield, Maine (www.jamesdjulia.com).*

3rd Model Longspur cased with accessories. *Courtesy of James D. Julia Auctioneers, Fairfield, Maine (www.jamesdjulia.com).*

3rd Model Longspur cased with accessories. Both case and revolver show signs of heavy use. *Courtesy of Thomas Del Mar Ltd.*

Apart from the system for securing the barrel to the lock frame, 3rd Models are similar in conformation to the 1st and 2nd Models, although all 3rd Models are five-chambered, even the Pocket Model. Lock plates are usually inscribed:

WEBLEY'S PATENT

The butt strap is normally inscribed:

BY HER MAJESTY'S ROYAL LETTERS PATENT

Webley 3rd Model Longspur revolvers seem to have been invariably fitted with Kerr patent loading levers, similar in conformation to those supplied with Beaumont-Adams revolvers.

Variations
Five basic variations are known, apart from special order or custom-made weapons.

- Holster Model: Cylinder with five chambers. Produced in 48 bore with a 7 inch barrel and 54 bore with a 5 ¼ inch barrel.
- Belt Model: Cylinder with five chambers, in 60 bore with a 4 inch barrel (rare).
- Pocket Model: Cylinder with five chambers, in either 86 or 120 bore. Barrels between 3 and 4 inches.

Values: Good: $2,100-2,500
(£1,250-1,500)
Fine: $4,200-5,000
(£2,500-3,000)
Cased: $10,100-11,800
(£6,000-7,000)

Rare at UK and U.S. auctions.

WEBLEY 4TH MODEL LONGSPUR

These arms are very rare and appear to have been a development of the successful 3rd Model, sharing most of that weapon's characteristics. The main point of difference is a strengthening top-strap between the barrel and the lock. Only two 54 bore examples, with 4¾ inch barrels rifled and three grooves of right hand twist, are known. They are both unnumbered and unsigned.

Very rare at UK and U.S. auctions.
Upon the death of his brother, Philip Webley not only continued manufacturing "Longspur" revolvers, but also produced a single-action design of his own (Brit. Pat. 2127/1853).

WEBLEY'S MODEL 1853 REVOLVER

Frame number range: 100 – 200 (numbers may not reflect production)

These revolvers were made in small numbers and consequently are extremely rare. Most are museum pieces, so auction prices, if one ever appeared, would be correspondingly high.

This is an open-frame, single-action revolver, similar to the 3rd Model "Longspur," in that the barrel is fixed to the lock frame by a screw thread on the cylinder arbor. This assembly is secured by a bolt that passes through the barrel lug and into the end of the lock frame. The securing bolt is squared off to fit the percussion cone key supplied with these weapons, unlike the "butterfly" screw of the 3rd model. A lock plate is fitted to the left side, behind the hammer, giving access to the single-action lock mechanism. The rear sight is fixed to the top of the frame, not a hammer notch as in the open-frame Longspur models. The hammer spur is similar to the Longspur pattern. Frames are usually inscribed on the left:

P. WEBLEY'S PATENT.
or
P. WEBLEY'S PATENT NO.

Barrels are octagonal, with a brass pin serving as the front sight. Only weapons in 48 bore with 5½ inch barrels are recorded, all with 9-groove, right twist rifling. So far, all recorded have five-chambered cylinders, with thick partitions between the chambers that are drilled to accept the hammer-nose and thus ensure a "safe carry," incidentally making them true "five shooters." Tranter pattern, fixed-head loading levers are fitted, screwed to the frame below the cylinder.

Butts are usually in one piece, which is unusual in Birmingham-made revolvers of this period. They often have a cap box in the base and sometimes a prawl or protuberance behind the hammer for an improved grip. The trigger guards are quite characteristic, being large and round.

They may have a "spur" fitted for use as a finger rest when firing, although not every revolver had this modification.

Variations
Only the model described is known.

- Holster Model: Cylinder with five chambers, in 48 bore, with a 5½ inch barrel and 9-groove, right twist rifling.

Very rare at UK and U.S. auctions.

These revolvers were subsequently followed by a range of more robust solid- and wedge-framed weapons. Although Philip Webley secured a British patent protecting a design of a self-cocking revolver (Brit Pat. No 305/1853),[4] he never appears to have manufactured it in large numbers.

WEBLEY SELF-COCKING PERCUSSION REVOLVERS

The only self-cocking percussion revolver the Webley brothers were ever extensively involved with is the pattern known to collectors as the "Webley-Bentley." This is based on Joseph Bentley's original, patented design, and was produced by Bentley and a number of other makers. Retail marks clearly show that both James and Philip Webley were certainly amongst the suppliers of such weapons, although they do not appear to have been involved in manufacturing them, even under license.[5]

BENTLEY AND WEBLEY-BENTLEY SELF-COCKING REVOLVERS

Joseph Bentley was a Birmingham gunsmith who registered a number of revolver patents during the 1850s, most importantly, for a safety catch and a method of barrel attachment—both used by Webley—as well as two revolver patents. Confusion sometimes arises when trying to differentiate between Bentley and Webley-Bentley revolvers, although the two types are quite dissimilar and Bentley's arms, at least, are usually clearly marked as such on either the frame or the barrel.

Bentley's excellent revolvers are described here in order to allow a comparison between the two types.

BENTLEY REVOLVERS

Both models differ from Webley-Bentley revolvers in not being fitted with a lock plate; this characteristic feature serves to differentiate the two groups.

BENTLEY MODEL 1852 REVOLVER

British Patent No 960/1852
Frame number range: 1 – 1200
Hand-made revolvers, often produced by other gunmakers under license.

This is a self-cocking, solid-frame revolver without hammer spur, usually chambered for five rounds. Well made weapons and often heavily engraved. Frame numbers are generally preceded either by:

BENTLEY'S PATENT NO....
or
PATENT NO .

Weapons with a frame number above 200 are sometimes prefixed with an "A" and there may be other ranges (a weapon numbered 80C is known).

A safety catch was fitted to the right side and is spring operated, similar to Adams's first type. The barrels are octagonal, and found as 54/56, 70, 80, and 100 bore; they are secured to the arbor by a wedge, entering from the left. The barrel is inscribed on the top barrel flat:

J. Bentley & Sons, Liverpool.

Examples may also be encountered inscribed only with the name of the retailer and with the maker's name absent.

Cylinders were engraved, unfluted, and chambered for five rounds. Loading levers were usually similar to the Colt 1851 Navy pattern, but examples may be found fitted with Bentley's patent loading lever (British Patent 768/1854). The butts are always in two pieces with a central, fixing screw, although the shape is variable.

Variations
Five basic variations are recorded, apart from special order or custom-made weapons, although there may be others.

- Holster Model: Cylinder with five chambers, in 54 or 56 bore, with a 7 inch barrel.
- Belt Model: Cylinder with five chambers, in 70 bore, with a 7½ inch barrel.
- There is also a rare second Belt Model with a 4 inch barrel, chambered in 80 bore.
- Pocket Model: Cylinder with five chambers, in 100 bore, with a 4½ inch barrel.

Values: Good: $1,600-2,000
(£1,000-1,200)
Fine: $3,300-3,950
(£2,000-2,350)
Cased: $5,400-6,900
(£3,250-4,100)
Rare at UK and U.S. auctions.

BENTLEY MODEL 1857 DOUBLE-ACTION REVOLVER

British Patent No. 2657/1857.
Frame number range: 1-50
Hand-made revolver.

Cased double-action Bentley revolver. The lock plate characteristic of the Webley-Bentley arms is absent. Courtesy of Thomas Del Mar, Ltd.

Although no weapon with a number above 50 is recorded in the relevant literature,[6] an example is recorded numbered "625" and others may subsequently appear. Bentley himself appears to have made few double-action revolvers under this patent, with most being manufactured by other Birmingham makers who he licensed.

These are characterized by the presence of a hammer spur and are often fitted with a plate across the front of the cylinder to prevent loads falling from the cylinder during firing.

These revolvers are open-framed, with a frame number on the left side, usually preceded by a stamped or inscribed marking, depending on the maker:

Bentley's Patent No.

The octagonal barrels were usually heavily engraved, fitted with a front sight and secured to the arbor by means of a wedge entering from the left with a securing screw above. Examples in 74 and 140 bore are recorded. The barrels are inscribed on the top barrel flat:

J. Bentley & Sons, Liverpool
or
J. Bentley & Son, 6, South Castle Street, Liverpool

This may be missing in authentic weapons.

Cylinders are plain, chambered for five rounds, and may be highly engraved. Bentley's safety device is often found fitted to the hammer nose. This consisted of a tiny lever pivoted on the top of the hammer, which could be pushed up to rest on top of the frame for a "safe carry." Pulling the trigger caused this "nose piece" to drop either under its own weight or by the action of a spring when the trigger was squeezed. Loading levers were similar to those fitted to the Colt 1851 Navy revolver, with the lever extending the full length of the barrel. Examples may also be found fitted with a Kerr loading lever. Butt shapes differ; some examples have the smooth outer curve of the Longspur, while others are more angular.

Variations
Two basic variations are known, apart from special order or custom-made weapons.

- Belt Model: Cylinder with five chambers, in 70 bore, with a 5 inch barrel.
- Pocket Model: Cylinders with five chambers in 140 bore, with a 5 inch barrel.

Values: Good: $2,000-2,500
(£1,250-1,500)
Fine: $3,300-3,900
(£2,000-2,300)
Cased: $5,400-6,200
(£3,250-3,700)
Rare at UK auctions
Very rare at U.S. auctions.

WEBLEY-BENTLEY REVOLVERS

(Perhaps more correctly referred to as Bentley "Pattern" or Bentley "Licensed" revolvers, since Webley never made revolvers of this type.[7])

Hand-made revolvers.
Frame number range: 111-73200

Their numbers almost certainly do not correspond to production, since different licensees will probably have assigned their own number series, although the purpose of these numbers remains a mystery.[8] They do not appear to be serial

Webley-Bentley self-cocking revolver with an unusual "plunger type" loading lever showing the characteristic safety catch on the hammer. *By kind permission of Bonhams.*

Cased self-cocking revolver of the Webley-Bentley type. *By kind permission of Bonhams.*

Cased double-action revolver of the Webley-Bentley type. *By kind permission of Bonhams.*

numbers and may be production numbers stamped on the frame to allow the licensee to calculate his royalty payments. Philip Webley's company never made any of these revolvers, and those weapons with the "Webley" name on the frame or barrel were weapons sold by that company from their retail outlet.

These so-called Webley-Bentley revolvers are a good example of the confusion that can arise when trying to identify an English revolver. They were produced by hand, from the workshops of a number of gunsmiths, and are of varying quality. Nor do they conform to any particular type. Barrel lengths, calibers, and other characteristics are so variable that only the general term "Webley-Bentley type, self-cocking revolver" may be safely applied.

These are self-cocking or, rarely, single-action revolvers. The majority were open-framed, although some had a top-strap that fitted into a recess in the top of the lock. Frames were of malleable cast iron with integral butt straps and a removable side plate. Bentley's safety device is often found fitted to the hammer nose, although some weapons were fitted with a more conventional spring steel safety catch, similar to the Adams pattern. A few have an Adams pattern, side-mounted safety.

Barrels are octagonal and found in 54, 80, 90, and 120 bore with 6 inch, 4¾ inch, and 4½ inch barrels, respectively (120 bore weapons are rare). Rifling is variable, with a few examples being smooth bore. Barrels were fixed to the lock by either a screw thread on the arbor—in a manner exactly similar to the Longspurs—or by a wedge, with both open-frame and top-strap variants being found with the arbor wedge. Retailers' names, including Webley's, may occasionally be found on the top barrel flat. More commonly, patent information is inscribed on the frame:

Improved Patent
or
Patent No.
or
London Patent No.

This inscription may be followed by a number.

Cylinders are plain and usually five-chambered, although six-chambered examples are known, with horizontal percussion cones.

A number of these arms were produced without loading levers. When fitted, two types of loading levers are encountered: the left-mounted, Kerr loading lever predominates, while some weapons may have the Colt under-barrel pattern. There is a third type, similar to the Colt but more fragile in appearance, although this is more rarely seen. Butts were made in two pieces with a single screw fixing, often described as characteristic of Birmingham-made revolvers of the period. They may include a butt case for percussion caps, although this feature is very rare.

Variations

So many variations are recorded that these weapons are best described as "Webley-Bentley type" revolvers, followed by basic information on the mechanism, caliber, and barrel length. Given the number of individual gunmakers who produced these weapons, any designation into model types would be problematic at best.

Some examples have been recorded as chambered for rim-fire or center-fire cartridges, but in every weapon so far examined these are percussion weapons converted to metal cartridge, rather than originally manufactured.

Values: Good: $1,090-1,260
(£650-750)
Fine: $3,000-3,350
(£1,800-2,000)
Common at UK and U.S. auctions.

WEBLEY DOUBLE-ACTION PERCUSSION REVOLVERS

Frame number range: 1015–36649.

These were machine-made revolvers, although probably with significant hand finishing and produced from around 1861.

Wedge frame and solid-frame revolvers are distributed arbitrarily through this range, which is suggested are true serial numbers.[9]

WEDGE-FRAMED DOUBLE-ACTION WEBLEYS (PRODUCTION BEGUN: 1857 - 1859)

These are the much more common of the two types. Frames are of malleable cast iron and without a lock plate. The barrel and frame are secured together by a wedge through the cylinder arbor. In addition, the top-strap locates into a slot in the top of the lock and a stud on the front of the frame enters a corresponding hole in the back of the barrel lug, thus holding the barrel and cylinder in alignment. Frames bear, on the left side, the stamp:

PATENT NO.
or, much more rarely
LONDON.

This precedes the frame number. Both wedge-framed and solid-framed weapons may be found inscribed with the names of a number of retailers, usually on the top-strap.

A Webley wedge frame double-action revolver; this example is fitted with a Colt pattern loading lever. By kind permission of Bonhams.

Webley wedge-framed double-action revolver fitted with the Kerr loading lever and the more angled design of the butt, with its emphasized prawl. By kind permission of Bonhams.

Webley wedge-framed, double-action revolver fitted with a Colt pattern loading lever and showing the junction between the top-strap and the lock frame. By kind permission of Bonhams.

Produced in 54, 90, 100, and 120 bore versions, with barrels lengths of between 6¼ and 4½ inches, with the shorter barrels, as usual, having correspondingly smaller bores, although there are apparently custom-made exceptions. Rifling is usually three groove, although occasionally examples with fourteen groove rifling are encountered. The groove width and depth is variable. Cylinders are plain, with five or six chambers. Loading levers are either Kerr or Colt pattern. Colt pattern loading levers are not fitted to either type of weapon with serial no. 4000 and above. Two butt shapes were used, one of which has a significant prawl or hump near the hammer, while in the second this feature is absent.

Variations
Six basic variations are known, apart from special order or custom-made weapons.

- Holster Model: Cylinders with five or six chambers, in 54 bore with a 6¼ inch barrel.
- Belt Model: Cylinders with five or six chambers in either 90 or 100 bore and having either 6¼ or 4½ inch barrels. Bore and barrel length combinations were variable.
- Pocket Model: Cylinders with five or six chambers, in 120 bore with a 4½ inch barrel.

Values: Good: $1,500–1,700
(£900–1,000)
Fine: $2,500–2,900
(£1,500–1,700)
Cased: $3,300–4,700
(£2,000–2,800)
Common at UK and U.S. auctions.

SOLID-FRAME DOUBLE-ACTION WEBLEY REVOLVERS (PRODUCTION: 1859)

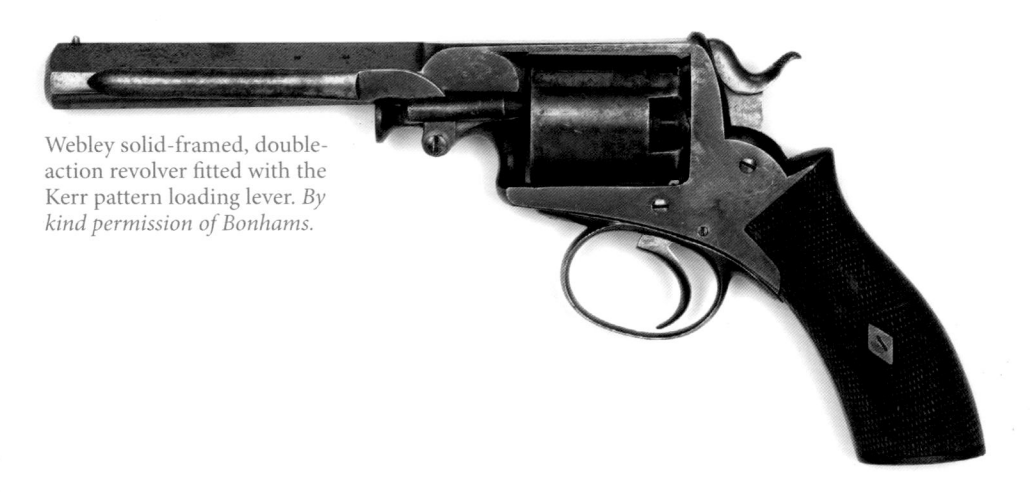

Webley solid-framed, double-action revolver fitted with the Kerr pattern loading lever. By kind permission of Bonhams.

Produced as a development of the wedge-framed revolver, this was a better, stronger design than its fore-runner. Unfortunately, by the time this revolver came into production, the market had shifted towards the newer, metal cartridge revolvers, so few of these excellent revolvers were made.

The frames are in malleable cast iron and without a lock plate. The barrel is permanently screwed into the frame, thus not infringing Adams's patent. A cylinder arbor latch is fitted either as a thumb screw or spring-loaded stud. Frames are stamped on the left side:

PATENT NO.
or
LONDON

The stamp precedes the frame number.

Produced in 54, 60, 80, 90, 100, and 120 bore versions, with barrel lengths between 6¼ and 4½ inches, the shorter-barreled weapons usually having correspondingly smaller bores, although there are apparently custom-made exceptions. Rifling is usually three-groove or five-groove in the Holster, fourteen-groove in the Belt (80 bore) and Pocket arms. The cylinder is plain and may be found chambered for five or six shots. The loading lever is either the Kerr or Colt pattern. As in the wedge-framed revolver, two butt shapes were again used, one of which has a significant prawl or hump near the hammer; the other is without this feature.

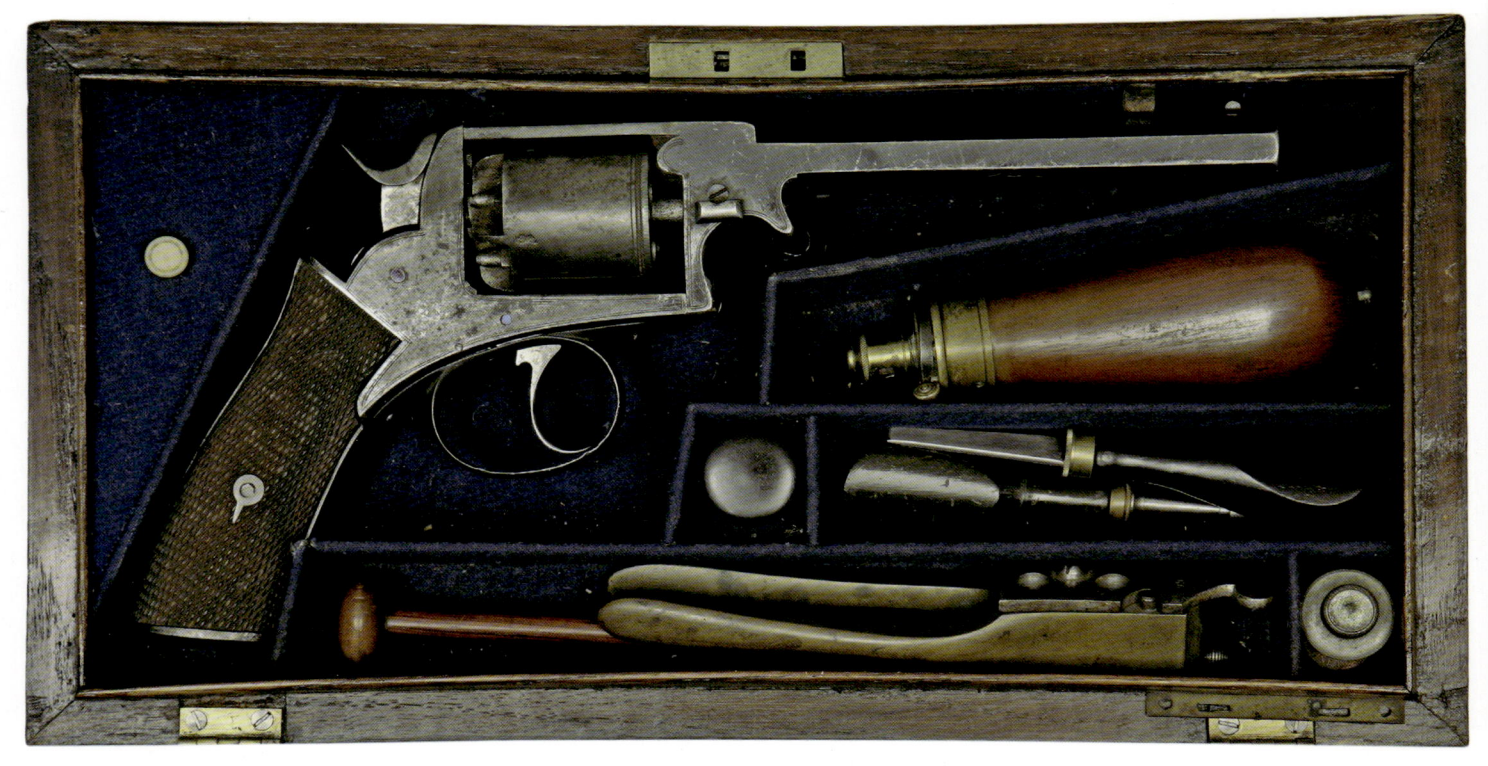

Webley wedge-framed, double-action revolver cased with accessories. *By kind permission of Bonhams.*

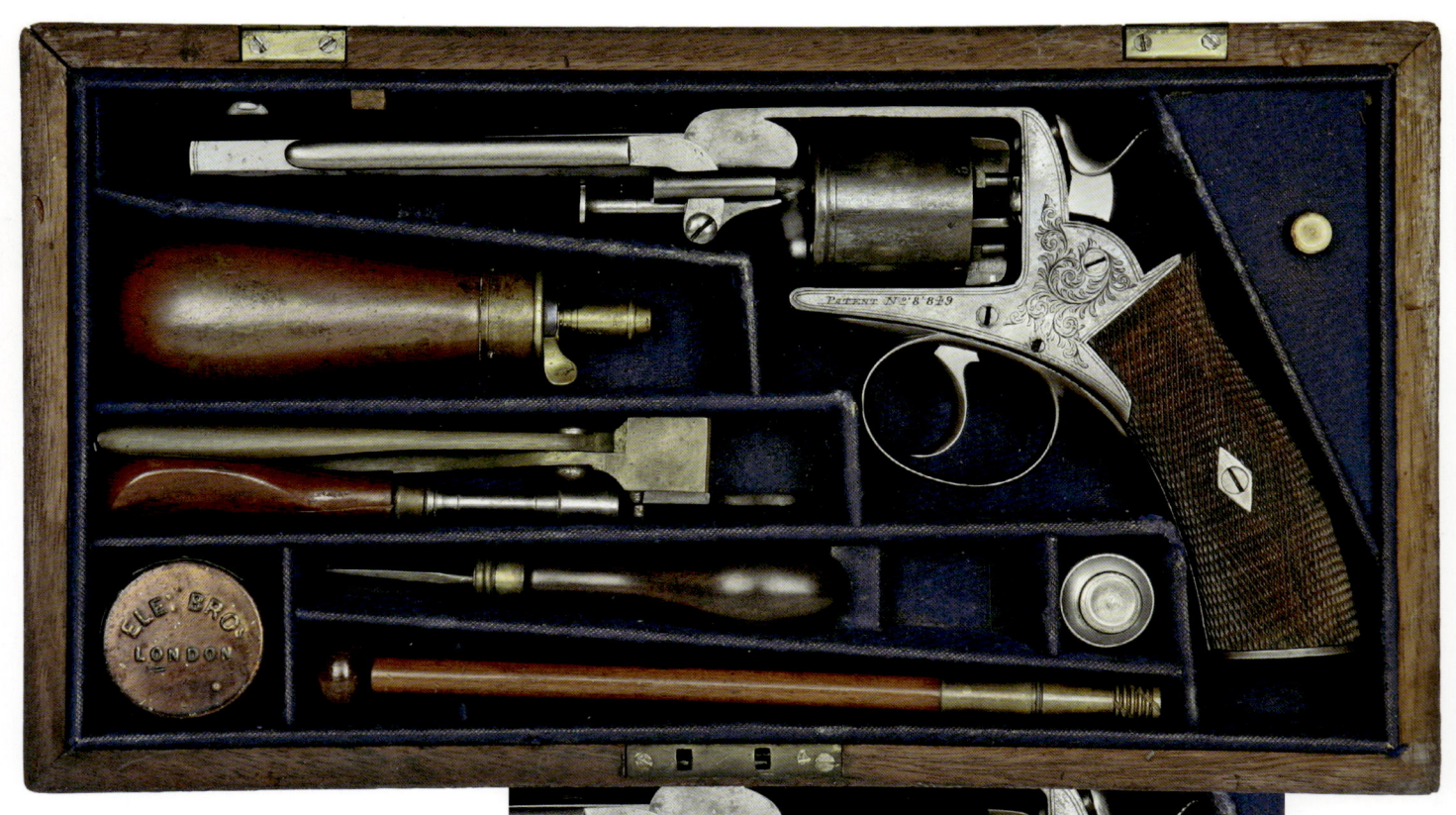

Webley solid frame double-action revolver fitted with a Kerr pattern loading lever and cased with accessories. *By kind permission of Bonhams.*

Webley solid frame double-action revolver showing the frame number and superior casting of the cylinder. *By kind permission of Bonhams.*

Variations

Six basic variations are known, apart from special order or custom-made weapons.

- Holster Model: Cylinders with five or six chambers, in 54 bore with a 6 inch barrel and three-groove, clockwise rifling. Also cylinders with five or six chambers, in 60 bore with a 6 inch barrel and five groove, clockwise rifling.
- Belt Model: Cylinders with five or six chambers in 90 bore or 100 bore and with 6¼ or 4½ inch barrels with fourteen-groove, clockwise rifling.
- Pocket Model: Cylinders with five or six chambers, in 120 bore. Usually with a 4½ inch barrel and fourteen-groove, clockwise rifling, although shorter variations are known.

Both models of the double-action revolver were converted to take metal cartridges in rim-fire and center-fire, although these are less common than percussion weapons.

Values: Good: $2,000-2,500
(£1,200-1,500)
Fine: $3,200-3,900
(£1,900-2,300)
Cased: $4,200-5,500
(£2,500-3,300)
Common at UK and U.S. auctions.

WEBLEY DUAL IGNITION REVOLVER (PRODUCED IN SMALL NUMBERS: 1865-1866)

Frame number series: Unknown

Webley marketed a revolver from 1865-1866 that was sold with a six-chambered percussion cylinder in 54 bore and a second cylinder that had six chambers designed for the .422 center-fire cartridge, probably as a development of their solid-frame percussion arm.

Solid-frame, gate-loading double-action revolver, having a 5½ inch barrel with eleven-groove, clockwise rifling. It was supplied with two cylinders, both having six chambers in either 54 bore or for Webley, .442 center-fire caliber cartridges. A Kerr-pattern loading lever is fitted to the left and a case ejector of the sliding rod type is fitted to the right of the barrel. A loading gate hinged on the top, but opening to the rear is also fitted on the left of the frame. On the left side of the frame, in front of the cylinder, is stamped:

WEBLEY'S
PATENT

Proof marks may be either London or Birmingham. The butt is chequered walnut, in one piece.

Very rare at UK and U.S. auctions.

THE HISTORY OF WEBLEY'S METAL CARTRIDGE REVOLVERS

Webley's first metal cartridge revolver was the Royal Irish Constabulary Model, chambered for Webley's own .442 center-fire cartridge. This first appeared in 1867 (Patent date 1867), although the company had been making good copies of the Smith & Wesson .22 and .32 caliber rim-fire revolvers since 1862 and Tranter's "Boxer" revolver since 1866.

The RIC proved a popular weapon, and it is said that General George Custer was carrying a pair at the Battle of Little Bighorn, although some authorities dispute this. Subsequent models included the short-barreled British Bulldog, Webley Express, and Webley-Pryse, as well as a range of small, hammerless revolvers. Some privately purchased Webley revolvers certainly saw service with the British armed forces during the later part of the nineteenth century, but in 1892, a Webley revolver was adopted for British military use.

This was the Webley Mk I Government Model (accepted into the British Army as Pistol, Webley Mk I), and it began a long association between the British Army and Webley's robust, reliable revolvers. Replacing the unpopular, unreliable Enfield Mk I and Mk II, Webley's first contract called for 10,000 Mk I revolvers, at £3 1s 1d each (about £3.06, or $5.14). This revolver subsequently went through a series of minor changes and improvements, culminating in the Mk VI, introduced in 1915. An excellent weapon, it remained in service with the British Army until 1947, although another Webley—the Mk IV, this time chambered in .38/200—was still in service until 1963, when it was finally replaced by the Browning Hi-Power semi-automatic pistol.

P. Webley & Son became The Webley and Scott Revolver and Arms Company Ltd of Birmingham, after amalgamation with W & C Scott and Sons in 1897, so revolvers made after this date should strictly be referred to as "Webley & Scott" revolvers. The name was changed again in 1906 to Webley and Scott Ltd.

Webley & Co remained in business long after the last of their competitors in the revolver market had disappeared, mainly because of their willingness to produce what their customers wanted: well made, cheap, reliable revolvers, chambered in a wide variety of calibers. Most importantly, they did not make the mistake of trying to compete with the big American firms, adapting their manufacturing methods to produce small numbers of a wide variety of models and calibers that satisfied their customers' requirements while keeping their production overheads minimal. These factors, as well as their diversification into other areas, ensured their survival long after their UK rivals had disappeared. Details of the Webley Company's activities and their revolvers are found in Bruce and Reinhart.[10]

IDENTIFICATION AND DISTINGUISHING MARKS

Revolvers made under one of the patents registered to either the Webley company or a member of the family are usually stamped on the frame:

WEBLEY
or
WEBLEY PATENTS

This appears in a characteristic oval format, frequently with a stamp specifying the cartridge the weapon was chambered for, together with the company's "Winged Bullet" trademark. The form of the "Winged Bullet" was retained on the later revolvers made by Webley & Scott, so it is of little use when trying to date a particular weapon, and both marks may be missing from earlier weapons made by Webley, since it was only after 1889 that revolvers from their factory always received these stamps.

Serial numbers are usually stamped on the frame below the cylinder, but their position is variable, and they may also be found on the right side of the frame, as well as the cylinder. Additional stamps on the top-strap or butt straps include:

P. WEBLEY & SON, BIRMINGHAM
P. WEBLEY & SON, LONDON & BIRMINGHAM.
WEBLEY & SCOTT, LONDON & BIRMINGHAM.

Frames may also occasionally be stamped:

W & S

WEBLEY CARTRIDGE REVOLVERS

Models described here are those a collector most commonly encounters, although there are some rare models and a number of variations on the more common Webley models that will also be found listed in more detailed works by other authors.[11]

Webley's "Winged Bullet" trademark usually found stamped on the frame of Webley-made guns. *Courtesy of Joel Black.*

WEBLEY PIN-FIRE REVOLVERS

Pin-fire revolvers are shown in catalogs from P. Webley and P. Webley & Son from 1860-1865, but none are of original Webley design under British patents registered to any member of the company. They were either revolvers made on the Continent and retailed by Webley or arms copied by the company. Alternatively, they may have been assembled and finished in the company's workshops from imported parts.

RIM-FIRE REVOLVERS

The first metal cartridge revolvers produced by P. Webley and P. Webley & Son were copies of Smith & Wesson's .22 caliber and .32 caliber hinge-frame revolvers, although they also made a number of cheaper trade guns in larger calibers.

WEBLEY SMITH & WESSON COPIES (1862 - 1866)

Serial number series: 1-1000 (probably higher, but records are not available)

Hinged frame, double-action, "Tip-up" rim-fire revolvers in .22 and .32 caliber made under license from Smith & Wesson. The frame is hinged between the top-strap and the barrel and the cylinder must be removed for loading, with empty cases being ejected by the rod on the front of the barrel lug. Plain cylinders have seven chambers in the .22 caliber arm, six in the .32 caliber weapon, with barrels of just over 3 inches and five-groove clockwise rifling being fitted to both types.

This Manhattan .22 caliber revolver is a copy of a Smith & Wesson No 1. Webley also retailed copies of this revolver, beginning manufacture in 1862. *Courtesy of Mike Meuwly.*

Early Webley "Tip-up" revolvers may be differentiated from the similar Smith & Wesson arm by the position of the cylinder bolt slots, which are at the front of the cylinder in the early Webley copy, although later guns have slots at the rear of the cylinder and are similar to the Smith & Wesson revolvers in this respect. They are usually stamped with a serial number and London or Birmingham proof marks, but no patent information. The butts are two-piece, in chequered walnut.

Variations
Webley "Tip-up" revolvers.

- .22 caliber revolver: Chambered in .22 caliber rim-fire, cylinder with seven chambers, 3 inch barrel.
- .32 caliber revolver: Chambered in .32 caliber rim-fire, cylinder with six chambers, 3 inch barrel.

Webley also made a solid-framed revolver virtually identical to the "Tip-up" revolvers chambered in .30 caliber, with the cylinder having six chambers and a barrel of approximately 3¼ inches.

Very rare at UK and U.S. auctions.

WEBLEY SOLID-FRAME .44 CALIBER RIM-FIRE REVOLVER, MODEL 1864

Frame number range: Unknown; numbers are often missing.

Solid-frame, single-action or double-action revolver, chambered for a .44 caliber rim-fire cartridge with a barrel 6-6½ inches long, with fourteen-groove clockwise rifling. The case ejector is either the powerful device registered to P. Webley & Son (British Patent 4634/1864) or a less robust spring-loaded, side barrel ejector rod.

Frames are sometimes stamped in the usual oval format:

WEBLEY'S
PATENT

This appears along with the trademark, although both are frequently omitted.

The loading gates are in two forms: an early device hinged at the top, which opened to the rear and is usually found fitted to arms with the Webley patent ejector; and a later type, hinged at the base and opening outwards, usually fitted to arms with the side barrel ejector. An inspection plate is fitted to the left side of the frame and secured by a single screw, the removal of which, together with the butt plate, allows access to the mechanism. Front and rear sights were fitted, with the conformation of the front sight either blade or "peppercorn." Butts are in the form of two plates of finely chequered walnut held by a single screw entering from the left and engaging a diamond-shaped nut recessed in the right plate.

Variations
Webley .44 caliber rim-fire revolvers.

- Webley Compound Case-Ejector Model: Cylinder with six chambers, in .44 caliber rim-fire, with Webley compound case ejector and loading gate hinged at the top and opening to the rear. Barrel between 6 and 6½ inches in length.
- Side-Barrel Case-Ejector Model: Cylinder with six chambers, in .44 caliber rim-fire, with a spring-loaded side barrel case ejector and the loading gate hinged at the bottom and opening to the side. Barrel between 6 and 6½ inches in length.

Very rare at UK and U.S. auctions.

"TRADE" REVOLVERS

Webley also made a substantial number of "Trade" revolvers chambered for rim-fire cartridges in a variety of calibers, such as .320 and .380. These revolvers are often not stamped with the Webley patent mark, but simply bear the name of the retailer. They are also sometimes fitted with devices copied from other manufacturers' patents, most notably Tranter's case ejector (British Patent 1862/1863), which was fitted to his Model 1863 revolver.

WEBLEY CENTER-FIRE REVOLVERS

Solid-frame, gate-loading revolvers. The first revolver using a center-fire cartridge to be produced by P. Webley & Son was a copy of Tranter's .577 Boxer revolver, with production beginning in 1866. The first revolver wholly designed by them—the RIC No 1—was introduced in 1867, and was adopted by the Royal Irish Constabulary in 1868.

WEBLEY .577 BOXER CENTER-FIRE REVOLVER

Serial number range: 1–10000 (Manufacture 1866–1870)
Number stamped on left of frame.

Solid-frame, gate-loading, double-action revolver with a four inch octagonal barrel in .577 caliber and five-groove, clockwise rifling. The cylinders are deeply fluted over their whole length—with six chambers for the .577 Boxer cartridge—resembling a collection of tubes joined along their length, rather than a conventional cylinder. These revolvers were made under license from William Tranter and incorporate Tranter's double-action mechanism and revolving recoil shield. The side of the barrel may be stamped:

1 INCH .577 BOXER

They may be differentiated from Tranter's very similar weapon by the cylinder chambering (the original Tranter cylinder has five chambers, while the Webley copy has six chambers). Proof marks, usually of the Birmingham Proof House, are stamped on both barrel and cylinders. The butt is one piece and of finely chequered walnut.

Webley .577 caliber revolver from the left side, showing the lug of its Tranter double-action mechanism on the trigger. Courtesy of Joel Black.

Webley .577 caliber revolver from the right side, showing the lug of its Tranter double-action mechanism on the trigger. Courtesy of Joel Black.

Webley .577 caliber revolver showing the backing plate, cylinder with cartridge, and the cylinder arbor. Courtesy of Joel Black.

Variations
- Webley .577 caliber "Boxer" revolver: Chambered for Tranter's .577 caliber cartridge, the cylinder has the six characteristic, nearly spherical chambers, along with a 4 inch barrel.

Values: Good: $2,000-2,500
(£1,200-1,500)
Fine: $3,100-3,900
(£1,900-£2,300)
Rare at UK and U.S. auctions.

WEBLEY R.I.C. REVOLVERS

Webley Model 1867 Constabulary revolver or R.I.C. No 1, First Pattern.
Serial number range: 1-17400 (Manufacture: 1867-1885, possibly later.) The serial number is usually stamped on the left hand side of the frame in front of the cylinder.

Solid-frame, gate-loading double-action revolver, in a variety of calibers with a slightly oval, tapered 4½ inch barrel, rifled with five clockwise grooves. Characteristically, the separate trigger sear projects below the frame into the rear of the trigger guard.

The cylinder is plain with six chambers, and was first chambered for Webley's .442 center-fire cartridge, with the cylinder bolt slots at the front and a case-ejector fitted below the barrel. In use, the ejector rod was pulled forward to clear the frame; the whole assembly then being swung out on a loose collar fitted around the rear section of the barrel, so that the rod could be pushed into the cylinder, ejecting the case via the aperture left after the loading gate was opened. When not in use, the ejector rod was housed inside the hollow cylinder arbor and retained there by a flat spring.

The frame is stamped, along with the trademark, with model and cartridge information forward of the cylinder in the usual oval format:

WEBLEY'S
R.I.C
No1 .450 CF

Proof marks, usually of the Birmingham Proof House, are stamped on both barrel and cylinder. Some very early examples are fitted with a different mechanism from the later weapons and may be identified by having four large screw heads showing on the left side of the frame, instead of the more usual three slotted heads. The butt is conventional in shape, one piece, and of finely chequered walnut secured by two screws.

Engraved R.I.C. No. 1, First Pattern revolver. The cylinder has bolt slots at the front, and the case ejector is secured by a band fixed around the barrel; both features are characteristic of this pattern. *Courtesy of Joel Black.*

SILVER & FLETCHER REVOLVERS

Some later First and Second Pattern R.I.C. revolvers were also fitted with a hammer and extraction system patented by Silver & Fletcher, although all these revolvers were made by Webley for that company and are stamped on top of the barrel:

SILVER & FLETCHER'S PATENT
"THE EXPERT"

Webley's patent and trademarks are not stamped on these revolvers, although there is a Webley serial number on the left side of the frame and a second production number is also stamped on the right side of the frame.

Engraved R.I.C. No. 1, First Pattern revolver cased with accessories. This weapon is slightly unusual, in that it is quite heavily engraved. *Courtesy of Joel Black.*

WEBLEY REVOLVERS

Variations
Webley R.I.C. No 1, First Pattern.
Manufactured for:

- .320 cal. center-fire cartridge, plain cylinder with six chambers, 4½ inch barrel
- .380 cal. center-fire cartridge, plain cylinder with six chambers, 4½ inch barrel.
- Webley .442 cal. center-fire cartridge, plain cylinder with six chambers, 2½ or 4½ inch barrel.
- Adams .450 cal. center-fire cartridge, plain cylinder with six chambers, 4½ inch barrel.

These were widely copied by the British and Belgian trade, in both single- and double-action, but revolvers from this source are usually stamped with either a UK or Liege proof mark, depending on their origin, and are without the Webley trademark (see: Appendix 1: Proof Marks).

Values: Good: $1,600-2,100
(£1,000-1,250)
Fine: $2,800-3,500
(£1,700-2,100)
Cased: $5,000-5,900
(£3,000-3,500)
Rare at UK and U.S. auctions.

WEBLEY "NO 3" REVOLVER, FIRST PATTERN

These Webley revolvers have a similar frame and lock mechanism to the R.I.C. First Pattern, but are fitted with a pull-out arbor, no loading gate, and have a 2½ or 4 inch barrel; they will be found stamped:

WEBLEY'S
R.I.C
No 3.

These revolvers may have a case ejection rod screwed into the butt. Later revolvers may have cylinder bolt slots on the surface at the rear of the cylinder and a second series of slots in the middle of that component, although the mechanism is different from that fitted to the R.I.C. Second Pattern.[11]

Very rare at UK and U.S. auctions.

WEBLEY R.I.C. NO 1 REVOLVER, SECOND PATTERN

Serial number range (in a sequence from the R.I.C. First Pattern): 17000–91567 (Manufacture: 1868-1881).

A revolver sharing most of the design features of the First Pattern RIC, but was later marketed with a number of improvements. The chief difference between the two weapons was the changes to the lock mechanism of the Second Pattern. This modification meant the cylinder was locked by a lever that engaged a series of projections at the rear of that component and, consequently, R.I.C. Second Pattern revolvers may be identified by these projections on the rear circumference of the cylinder. Later, Second Pattern revolvers were also fitted with an improved case ejector pivoted to the frame.

Webley Royal Irish Constabulary (R.I.C) No. 1, Second Pattern revolver. Courtesy of Joel Black.

This is a solid-frame, gate-loading double-action revolver with a slightly oval barrel rifled with five, clockwise grooves, a plain cylinder with six chambers, and a 4 inch barrel.

The frame is stamped on the left of the breech lug with model and caliber information, along with the trademark:

WEBLEY'S
RIC
No1 .450 CF

The case ejector is fixed to the frame and is reminiscent of the device patented by John Adams used in the Adams Model 1872 center-fire revolver. Proof marks, usually of the Birmingham Proof House, are stamped on both barrel and cylinder.

The butt is conventional in shape and constructed of two plates held by a single screw entering from the left.
Variations

Webley R.I.C. No. 1, Second Pattern revolver from the right, showing its early case ejector and unfluted cylinder with projections from its rear circumference that "bolt" the cylinder. Courtesy of Joel Black.

Webley R.I.C. No. 1, Second Pattern revolver high-power (view from the right) showing the cylinder bolt projections. Courtesy of Joel Black.

Webley Model 1868 RIC No 1, Second Pattern.
Manufactured for:
- 320 cal. center-fire cartridge, plain cylinder with six chambers, 4 inch barrel
- .380 cal. center-fire cartridge, plain cylinder with six chambers, 4 inch barrel.
- Webley .442 cal. center-fire cartridge, plain cylinder with six chambers, 4 inch barrel.
- Adams .450 cal. center-fire cartridge, plain cylinder with six chambers, 4 inch barrel. Some .450 caliber revolvers were made with a 2½ inch barrel for a number of British police forces. They bear a police number, as well as the more usual serial number.

Values: Good: $1,600-2,100
(£1,000-1,250)
Fine: $2,800-3,500
(£1,700-2,100)
Cased: $5,000-5,900
(£3,000-3,500)
Rare at UK and U.S. auctions.

WEBLEY "NO 3" REVOLVER (SECOND PATTERN)

These are Webley revolvers with a similar frame and lock mechanism to the R.I.C. Second Pattern, but fitted with a pull-out arbor (used as a case ejector) and no loading gate. They will be found stamped:

WEBLEY'S
R.I.C
No 3.

These revolvers sometimes have a case ejector rod in the butt and may be fitted with a 2½ inch barrel.

This revolver and the Webley No 3, based on the R.I.C. First Pattern, may have been produced as economy revolvers for customers who wanted either a cheaper gun or preferred a weapon without the under-barrel case ejector. Both weapons could only be loaded after the cylinder was removed from the frame.

Very rare at UK and U.S. auctions.

R.I.C. NO 1 "NEW MODEL"

Serial number range: 1–102000
(Manufacture 1881-1914)
A solid-frame, gate-loading, double-action revolver. Cylinders are fluted, with six chambers and a 4½ inch barrel rifled with seven clockwise grooves. The mechanism is the same as the Second Pattern R.I.C, although instead of projections from the rear circumference of the cylinder, this revolver has recessed cylinder bolt slots on the rear surface designed to engage the cylinder bolt. The ejector rod has an ovoid or "acorn"-shaped head and is similar to that fitted to the R.I.C. Second Pattern revolvers.

Frames are stamped with model and cartridge information, along with the trademark, in the usual oval format:

WEBLEY'S
RIC
NO1 .475 C.F
NEW MODEL

R.I.C. No. 1, New Model revolver from the left, showing its characteristic fluted cylinder and the "acorn" head of the case ejector. Courtesy of Joel Black.

R.I.C. No. 1, New Model revolver from the right, showing the loading gate and the fixing point of the improved case ejector mechanism. Courtesy of Joel Black.

WEBLEY REVOLVERS

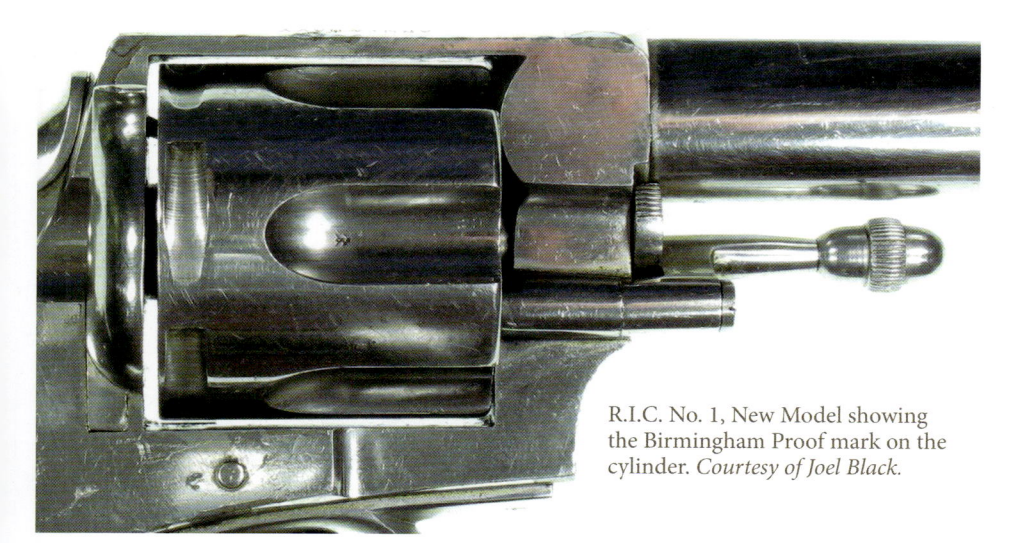

R.I.C. No. 1, New Model showing the Birmingham Proof mark on the cylinder. Courtesy of Joel Black.

Frame stamps on the New Model RIC revolver. Courtesy of Joel Black.

Proof marks, usually of the Birmingham Proof House, are stamped on both barrel and cylinder. The butt is conventional in shape and made from one piece of finely chequered walnut.

Variations
• Webley R.I.C. No 1 "New Model": Fluted cylinder with six chambers, 4½ inch barrel. Manufactured for:

Adams .450 cartridge.
Adams .450 "Man-Stopper" cartridge
Webley .455 cartridge
Webley .455 "Man-Stopper" cartridge
Enfield Mk II .455 cartridge
Enfield Mk III .476 cartridge

R.I.C. "New Model" revolvers would use all of these cartridges without modification. R.I.C. "New Model" revolvers were also made to chamber American cartridges:

Colt .45 (.45/40/250)
RM .44 (.44/23/256)
UMC .44 (.44/40/217)

Values: Good: $1,800-2,100
(£1,100-1,250)
Fine: $3,000-3,600
(£1,800-2,150)
Cased: $5,300-6,200
(£3,200-3,700)

Rare at UK and U.S. auctions.

WEBLEY R.I.C. NO 2 REVOLVER

Frame number series: 1-100000
(Manufacture: 1870-1914)
This revolver was based on the R.I.C. No I, Second Pattern and shared many of its characteristics.

A solid-frame, gate-loading, double-action revolver with a slightly oval, tapering 2¼, 3, or 4 inch barrel and a plain cylinder with five or six chambers, depending on chambering. R.I.C. Second Pattern lockwork was fitted, so in early weapons, the cylinder bears projections from the rear circumference designed to engage the cylinder bolt, while later arms have recessed cylinder bolt slots on the rear surface of the cylinder. The case ejector is of the later type, mounted on the frame, but with a flat plate at its head, instead of the more usual acorn-shaped device.

Frames are stamped with model and caliber information, along with the trademark, in the usual oval format:

WEBLEY'S
RIC
No 2 .450 CF

Proof marks, usually of the Birmingham Proof House, are stamped on both barrel and cylinder. The butts on larger caliber revolvers are one piece, held by two screws, while smaller revolvers had two butt plates; both types are in chequered walnut.

Variations
R.I.C. No 2 revolver:

• Chambered for .320 caliber cartridge, plain cylinder with five chambers, 2¼ inch barrel, rifled with five clockwise grooves. The butt is constructed with two butt plates, in walnut. Later versions may have a fluted cylinder.
• Chambered for .380 caliber cartridge, plain cylinder with five chambers, 3 inch barrel, rifled with seven clockwise grooves. The butt is constructed with two butt plates in walnut.
• Chambered for .442 caliber cartridge, plain cylinder with six chambers, 3 ½ or 4 inch barrel, rifled with seven clockwise grooves. The butt is one piece, walnut.

R.I.C. Model 1882:

• Chambered for an Eley .430 or Adams .450 caliber cartridge, plain cylinder with recessed stop slots and six chambers, 2½ inch barrel. The butt is one piece. It was advertised in the Army & Navy Cooperative stores catalog in January 1884: "as adopted by the Metropolitan Police."[12]

Values: Good: $1,500-1,800
(£900-1,050)
Fine: $2,300-2,900
(£1,400-£1,750)
Cased: $5,000-5,400
(£3,000-3,200)

Rare at UK and U.S. auctions.

R.I.C. MODEL 83

Serial number range: 1–102634
(Manufacture, 1884-1939)

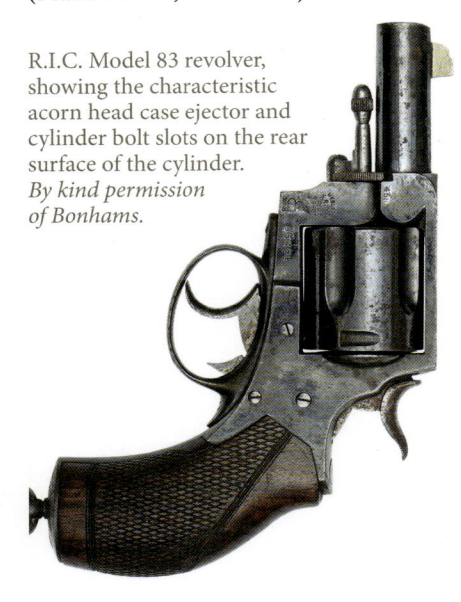

R.I.C. Model 83 revolver, showing the characteristic acorn head case ejector and cylinder bolt slots on the rear surface of the cylinder. By kind permission of Bonhams.

Solid-frame, double-action, gate-loading revolver with a 2½ or 4 inch round barrel, rifled with seven clockwise grooves. The cylinder is fluted, with five chambers, and manufactured in .455, .450, .380, and .320 calibers. The usual Adams pattern case ejector with the acorn head was fitted. The top of frame is stamped with caliber information:

.455

The frame in front of the cylinder is stamped in the usual oval format:

WEBLEY'S
RIC
MODEL/ 83

Beneath that mark is stamped:

5 SHOT

The butt is "Birds-head" in configuration, one piece, and walnut. A lanyard ring is usually fitted.

Variations
- R.I.C. Model 83: Cylinder with five chambers, 2½ or 4 inch barrel.

Chambered for:

- .320 cartridge
- .380 cartridge
- Adams .450 cartridge
- Enfield .476 cartridge
- Enfield .455 cartridge
- Webley .455 cartridges.

Revolvers chambered for either of the .455 cartridges had a larger frame, longer cylinder, and a broader butt.

Values: Good: $330-580
(£200-350)
Fine: $800-1,000
(£500-600)
Cased: $1,600-2,000
(£1,000-1,200)

Webley also produced a brass-framed Naval service RIC Model 1884, with blackened steel components and a 2⅝ inch barrel.
Rare at UK and U.S. auctions.

The R.I.C. revolver served as the basis for several later arms, including the Webley Metropolitan Police revolver (double-action, six shot in .450 caliber, with a 2½ inch barrel) and the Webley "British Bull Dog" range.

WEBLEY METROPOLITAN POLICE REVOLVER

This is really a short-barreled variant of the New Model RIC, made to the order of London's Metropolitan Police.
Serial number range: 500–98000
(Manufacture: 1883-1911)

A solid-framed, double-action, gate-loading revolver in .450 caliber with a 2½ inch round barrel rifled with seven clockwise grooves. The cylinder has six chambers and may be plain or fluted; both types have recessed cylinder bolt slots. The swing-out, under-barrel case ejector is pushed into the arbor when not in use and resembles the Adams pattern device fitted to the New Model RIC and later Webley revolvers; those revolvers with plain cylinders have a flat plate instead of the acorn head fitted to those "M.P" revolvers with fluted cylinders. Frames are stamped on the left side "POLICE" above "WEBLEY'S," which is, in turn, above a stamp of a pair of hands in manacles; all of these are above a stamped "M.P". A number is often found stamped above

R.I.C. Model 83 revolver showing the frame stamps. By kind permission of Bonhams.

Webley Metropolitan Police revolver showing the distinctive frame stamps, including the "Manacled Hands." Courtesy of the National Firearms Museum (NRAmuseum.com).

MODEL NO 1½ REVOLVER

Webley Metropolitan Police revolver from the left side. (NRAmuseum.com).

Webley Metropolitan Police revolver from the right side, showing the case ejector, which is similar to that fitted to both the New Model RIC and the Bulldog revolvers. (NRAmuseum.com).

Serial number series: 1–60000 (may not reflect production).

A solid-frame, double-action, gate-loading revolver with an octagonal 4¼ inch barrel. The cylinder is plain, with projections from its rear circumference to engage the cylinder bolt. The lock mechanism has no intermediate sear and consequently, there is no projection through the frame into the trigger guard, which serves to differentiate this revolver from earlier Webley models and the No 2 Bull Dog.

A loading gate is fitted on the right, hinged at the lower end and opening outwards, with a case ejector rod screwed into the butt. When loading, the hammer is locked at half-cock by a spring lever safety. The butt is reminiscent of the "Birds-head" configuration, but with a flat base made of chequered walnut in two pieces.

Variations
• Model No 1½ revolver: Cylinder with six chambers, 4¼ inch barrel.

Manufactured for:
• Webley .442 cartridge.
• Adams .450 cartridge.

Very rare at UK and U.S. auctions.

WEBLEY "BRITISH BULL DOG" REVOLVER (1872-1914)

Serial numbers form a complex series:[12]

20000 – 25000
(manufactured 1872-1876)
50000 – 55000
(manufactured 1877-1888)
600 – 1600
(manufactured 1881-1884)
4000 – 4600
(manufactured 1881-1884; this and the previous series are considered concurrent)
60000 – 100000
(manufactured 1884-1914)

Serial numbers are inscribed on the front of the frame, below the cylinder, or occasionally on the breech.

A solid-frame, gate-loading, double-action revolver with a 2½ inch round barrel, rifled with either five or seven

and separate from this collection on the breech lug and is probably an identifying number stamped on the weapon when it was accepted into service. The serial number is stamped on the left side below the cylinder.

The top-strap is often stamped:

P. Webley & Son, Birmingham

Proof marks, usually of the Birmingham Proof House, are stamped on both the barrel and cylinder. The butts are conventional in shape, one piece, and made of walnut.

Variations
Metropolitan Police (M.P) revolver.

• Plain cylinder Model (earlier Model): Chambered in .450 caliber, plain cylinder with six chambers, 2½ inch barrel. Case ejector rod with a flat head.
• Fluted cylinder Model: Chambered in .450 caliber, fluted cylinder with six chambers, and a 2½ inch barrel. Case ejector rod with an "acorn" head.

Values: Good: $2,000-2,250
(£1,200-1,350)
Fine: $2,500-2,800
(£1,500-1,700)
Rare at UK and U.S. auctions.

Early Webley Bull Dog revolver showing the caliber stamp on the breech and the Webley & Scott "Flying Bullet" trademark. *Courtesy of Joel Black.*

A good nickel-plated example of a Webley "Pug" showing the cylinder bolt projections around the rear circumference of the cylinder. Caliber (.41 rimfire) is stamped on the barrel lug. *Courtesy of Joel Black.*

WEBLEY REVOLVERS

A later Webley Bull Dog. Courtesy of Joel Black.

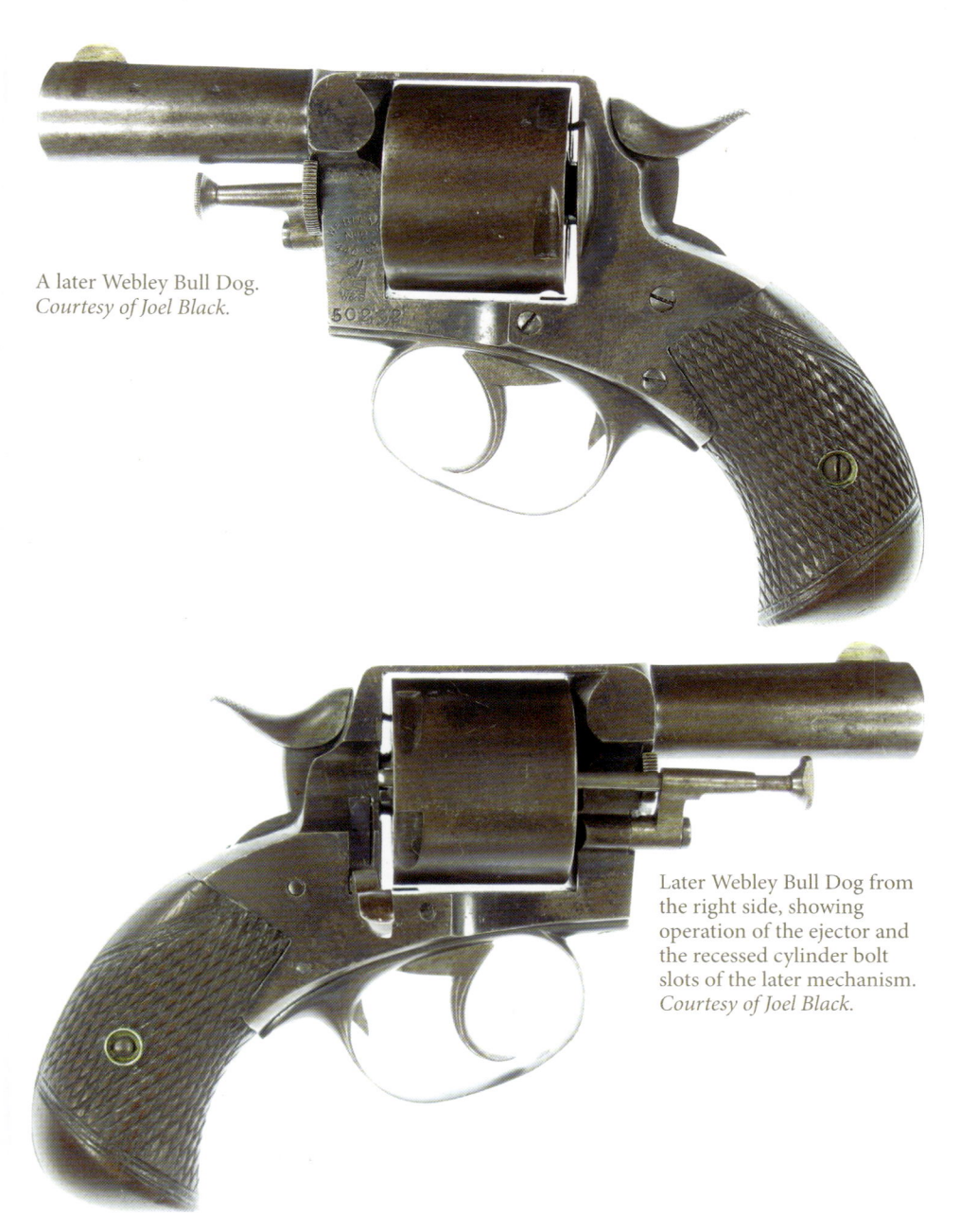

Later Webley Bull Dog from the right side, showing operation of the ejector and the recessed cylinder bolt slots of the later mechanism. Courtesy of Joel Black.

clockwise grooves depending on the chambering. The cylinder has five chambers for a variety of cartridges. The cylinders are usually plain, although they may be fluted in the weapons in the higher serial number ranges, as well as some of the many copies. The lock mechanism has an intermediate sear that projects through the frame into the trigger guard.

Subsequently, revolvers of this type. retailed by Webley. were chambered for six cartridges in .32 and .38 center-fire, but these weapons were not marked "THE BRITISH BULL DOG".

FRAME MARKINGS

Early revolvers (serial no. 20000) have the caliber marked on the barrel and are stamped on the left frame in the usual oval format:

WEBLEY'S
PATENT

Later revolvers (serial no. approximately 22300) are stamped on the left side of the frame in front of the cylinder:

WEBLEY'S
No 2
.450 CF.

This stamp corresponds to the size and type of cartridge for which the revolver is chambered. A few early weapons bear London proof marks, but marks of the Birmingham Proof House predominate.

A small, rare group of revolvers called "The Pug" were also produced (serial number range approximately 26000-29000); these revolvers bear the oval frame stamp on the left side of the breech frame:

WEBLEY'S
No 1
.442 CF

Caliber stamps again correspond to the cartridge size for which the revolver was designed. Most of the Pug "No 1" revolvers were made for a rim-fire cartridge, with a few later revolvers chambered for the early Webley .442 center-fire cartridge. Most of these Pug revolvers have a mechanism similar to the R.I.C. Second Pattern, with projections for engaging the cylinder bolt on the rear circumference of the cylinder and cartridge ejector rods screwed into the butt, although some later examples are fitted with the early, under-barrel case ejector.

Large caliber Bull Dog revolvers (Webley .442 and Adams .45 center-fire) made by Webley have the top-strap of the frame stamped:

THE BRITISH BULL DOG .

With the exception of the Pug revolvers, Webley Bull Dog revolvers are fitted with an under-barrel case ejector hinged to the front part of the frame that is swung out and pushed into the cylinder adjacent to the loading gate when required to eject a cartridge; they have either a flat or "acorn" head. The butts are usually two piece, "Birds-head" configuration and secured by a single screw, entering from the left. Later models occasionally have butts slightly longer than the earlier revolvers.

WEBLEY "BULL DOG" COPIES

These revolvers were widely copied by both the Birmingham and Belgian trade, with revolvers from the latter source always being stamped with a Liege proof mark (see Appendix: Proof marks). American copies were manufactured by the firms

Later, British-made Webley Bull Dog revolver manufactured by the Kynoch Gun Works and showing the company stamp on the barrel. *By kind permission of Bonhams.*

Belgian-made copy of the Webley Bull dog revolver. Frame marks are absent, which differentiates this weapon from the English guns. (NRAmuseum.com)

Detail of the Webley Bull Dog breech stamp. This form is typical for all Webley metal cartridge revolvers, although the wording is changed to correspond to the particular model. *Courtesy of Joel Black.*

Forehand & Wadsworth, Iver Johnson, and Harrington & Richardson. British, Belgian, and American versions were produced in all the standard Webley calibers, except the large caliber American copies, which, so far, have only been recorded chambered for the Webley .442 cartridge. Such weapons could also use the American-made, low-powered, short .44 Bulldog cartridge offered as a cheaper option to the Webley .442 center-fire round.

These copies, which are often very well made, will sometimes bear barrel, frame, or top-strap marks to indicate their place of manufacture, but do not bear either the Webley trademark or that company's top-strap legend.

Variations
Bull dog revolvers No 1 and No 2:

- "PUG" No 1 revolvers: cylinder with five chambers, 2½ inch barrel, and an extractor rod screwed into the butt.

  Chambered for:
  - .41 rim-fire cartridge.
  - .44 rim-fire cartridge.
  - Webley .442 center-fire cartridge

Bull dog No 2 revolvers, top-strap stamped:

THE BRITISH BULL DOG

Chambered for:

- Webley .442 cartridge: Cylinder with five chambers, 2½ inch barrel with seven clockwise grooves, and either a flat or acorn head extractor.
- Adams .450 center-fire cartridge: Cylinder with five chambers, 2½ inch barrel with seven clockwise grooves and either of the two types of extractor.

WEBLEY REVOLVERS

- Adams .450 center-fire cartridge: Cylinder with six chambers, 2½ inch barrel with seven clockwise grooves and either of the two types of extractor. The butt is one piece and walnut.

Smaller caliber Bull dog revolvers, not stamped on top-strap.

Chambered for:

- .32 caliber center-fire: Cylinder with six chambers, 2¼ inch barrel with five clockwise grooves and either of the two types of extractor.
- .38 caliber center-fire: Cylinder with six chambers, 2 inch barrel, and either of the two types of extractor.

Variations and copies of this revolver are numerous and ensure that any system describing them is, of necessity, complex. With that in mind, it is recommended that those interested in these revolvers consult the excellent work by Black, Ficken and Michaels (2008) listed in the Bibliography.

Values: Good: $2,000-2,250
(£1,200-1,350)
Fine: $2,500-2,800
(£1,500-1,700)
Rare at UK and U.S. auctions.

WEBLEY NO 5 EXPRESS REVOLVERS

Serial number range: 300–73000.
(Manufactured 1881-1897)
Produced to compete with Colt's double-action Model 1878 "Lightning" revolver.

A solid-frame, gate-loading, single- or double-action revolver with a rebounding hammer (M. Kaufmann's Br. Pt. 3913/1881). The barrels are roughly oval and of varying lengths, depending on the chambering, with seven groove clockwise rifling. The cylinder is fluted, with six chambers; later, small caliber weapons have "church steeple" fluting.

Case ejectors are of two types: either a spring-loaded rod housed in a tube on the right side of the barrel or an Adams pattern ejector with either a flat or acorn head. Early models were fitted with Kaufmann's loading gate safety[13] and had a square, walnut butt in one piece. On the later New Model, the safety device was not fitted and butts were changed to a Birds-head configuration, with two separate butt plates.

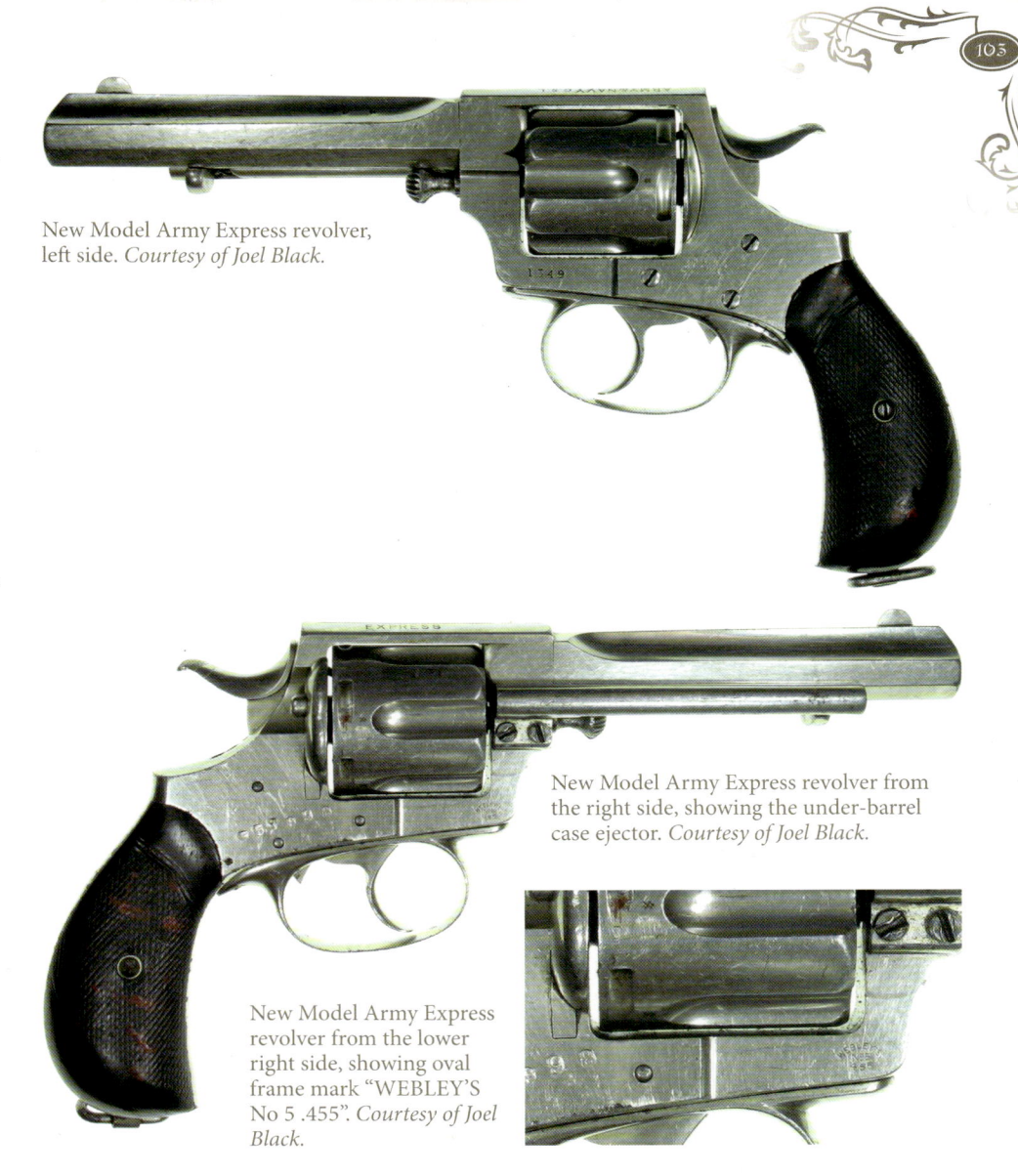

New Model Army Express revolver, left side. *Courtesy of Joel Black.*

New Model Army Express revolver from the right side, showing the under-barrel case ejector. *Courtesy of Joel Black.*

New Model Army Express revolver from the lower right side, showing oval frame mark "WEBLEY'S No 5 .455". *Courtesy of Joel Black.*

New Model Army Express revolver showing the "ARMY & NAVY' STORES, C.S.L EXPRESS" retail mark on the top-strap. The rear sight on this revolver is a V-shaped groove running the full length of the top-strap, a similar conformation to Colt's SAA. *Courtesy of Joel Black.*

The frames are stamped on the left side with a serial number, Webley trademark, and the cartridge stamp, in the usual oval format:

.455 C.F
&
.45 LONG.

The right, lower side of the frame may be found stamped in the usual oval format:

WEBLEY'S
No5
.455

Proof marks, usually of the Birmingham Proof House, are stamped on both barrel and cylinder. A lanyard ring was often fitted, and these revolvers were usually given a blue finish, although nickel-plated examples are common.

SILVER & FLETCHER REVOLVERS

Some later New Model No 5 Army Express revolvers were also fitted with a hammer and extraction system patented by Silver & Fletcher, although all these revolvers were made by Webley for that company and are stamped on top of the barrel:

SILVER & FLETCHER'S PATENT "THE EXPERT"

Webley's patent and trademarks are not stamped on these revolvers, although there is a Webley serial number on the left side of the frame and a second production number is also stamped on the right side of the frame.

Variations
No 5 Express revolvers.

- Single-action Army Express revolver (Manufactured in 1881 as the issue weapon for Cape Mounted Rifles): Single-action; cylinder with six chambers for the Enfield .476 cartridge, side barrel ejector, and conventional one-piece butt with prawl and a 5½ inch barrel. The loading gate is safety fitted.
- Double-action Army Express revolver: Double-action, cylinder with six chambers for the Adams .450 or Enfield .455 cartridges, side barrel ejector, conventional one-piece butt with prawl and a 6 inch barrel. The loading gate is safety fitted.
- New Model No 5 Army Express revolver: Double-action, cylinder with six chambers, side barrel ejector, and "Birds-head" butt.

Chambered for:

- Adams .450 cartridge, 5½ inch barrel.
- Enfield .455 cartridge, 5½ inch barrel.
- Enfield .476 cartridge, 5½ inch barrel.

New Model No 5 revolvers would accept all of these cartridges without modification.

American cartridge variations:

- Colt .45 caliber cartridge, 5½ inch barrel
- Smith & Wesson .44 caliber "Russian" cartridge, 12 inch barrel with three leaf sights and a detachable shoulder stock.

- No 5 .360 Express revolver: Double-action, cylinder with six chambers, 3 or 4½ inch barrel and Adams pattern extractor.

Chambered for:

- Webley No 5 "ROOK RIFLE" cartridge
- Smith & Wesson .38 cartridge
- Webley .380
- Webley .380 "Man stopper" cartridge
- Webley .455 MkII Government cartridges
- Colt .45 "Long Colt" cartridge

Values: Good: $3,600-3,900
(£2,200-2,350)
Fine: $4,100-4,500
(£2,500-£2,700)
Rare at UK and U.S. auctions.

THE WEBLEY HINGE-FRAME, SELF-EXTRACTING REVOLVERS

Webley's hinge-frame, self-extracting, double-action revolvers made for the civilian market form a roughly chronological, developmental series, beginning with the early revolvers constructed using the mechanisms generally attributed to Charles Pryse and ending with the small concealed hammer (Hammerless) revolvers developed for the civilian market and retailed between 1901 and 1923.

The larger revolvers all bear names such as 'British Army," "Government," and "Service," because during the period of their manufacture, British Army officers could purchase their own revolvers, provided such weapons were chambered to accept the government-issue revolver cartridge, and the Webley brothers clearly named their revolvers with this considerable and very lucrative market in mind. Manufacturing dates are included here, but may be found to be somewhat arbitrary.

Revolvers are described here under the names most familiar to the collector, with the Webley factory designation also included. Details of the development of the lock and cylinder bolting mechanisms of these revolvers are discussed in Bruce and Reinhart.[14]

WEBLEY-PRYSE REVOLVER (BRITISH ARMY EXTRACTOR, NO. 4 PATTERN, REVOLVER)

Although known universally to collectors as the "Webley-Pryse" revolver, the only contribution Charles Pryse (the younger) made to the design of this revolver was a modification to prevent the rotation of the cylinder after the trigger was released and a rebounding hammer mechanism. The lock mechanism of the revolvers made in Britain by Webley and others was that used on all the earlier solid-frame revolvers and featured an intermediate sear that projected through the frame into the trigger guard, while revolvers of Continental manufacture may be readily identified by the absence of this feature.[15]

The most characteristic feature of these Pryse-pattern revolvers is the frame catch with its twin levers, and the patent for this device, albeit with only a single lever, was registered by M. P. Counet of Liege, Belgium, in May, 1871 (Belgium Patent 28817/1871). This mechanism was extensively copied by members of the Belgian and British gun trades, including Webley, and this may be why Webley-Pryse revolvers do not usually bear "WEBLEY PATENT" stamps.

Serial number range: 300–81000 (Manufactured 1876-1896)

Webley-Pryse No. 4 Model revolver showing the frame mark "WEBLEY's No 4 .450 CF" and the cylinder release pin. The arrow marked on the broad head of the pin and the adjacent stamp on the frame point in the same direction when the cylinder is correctly secured. *By kind permission of Bonhams.*

Webley-Pryse No. 4 Model revolver (left side) with blue finish. *By kind permission of Bonhams.*

Hinge-frame, self-extracting, double-action revolver fitted with a rebounding hammer and self-locking cylinder, with both devices protected by British patents registered to Charles Pryse. They are easily differentiated from the later Webley-Kaufman and MksI-VI by the earlier frame catch, which consists of two levers instead of the button or thumb operated lever mounted on the left side that is fitted to the later revolvers. The lock mechanism is also characteristic, featuring a lug that protrudes into the rear of the trigger guard. Some later revolvers may be fitted with a device beneath the frame hinge for disengaging the extractor, allowing the frame to be opened without displacing the cartridges in the cylinder.

Barrels were made in a variety of lengths, from 3½ to 5½ inches. They are octagonal in section; the top flat is ribbed and the two upper faces are concave, while the others are flat. The cylinders may be plain or fluted, with six chambers in a variety of calibers. The frame has a cylinder release device fitted on the right side, characteristic of Webley-Pryse revolvers, and consists externally of a pin with a large milled head bearing an arrow on its upper surface, with a second arrow stamped on the frame adjacent to the pin. The cylinder is released by turning the milled pin so the two arrows face in opposite directions, indicating when the cylinder assembly may be removed from the frame. It is secured by returning the whole assembly to the frame and turning the milled pin so that the arrows point in the same direction. Cylinder bolt recesses are present on the rear surface of that component and there is also a second series of small rectangular slots near the middle of the cylinder associated with the cylinder locking mechanism (Br. Pat. 4421/1876).

An oval cartridge stamp is usually found on the left of the barrel or frame:

WEBLEY'S
No 4
.450 CF

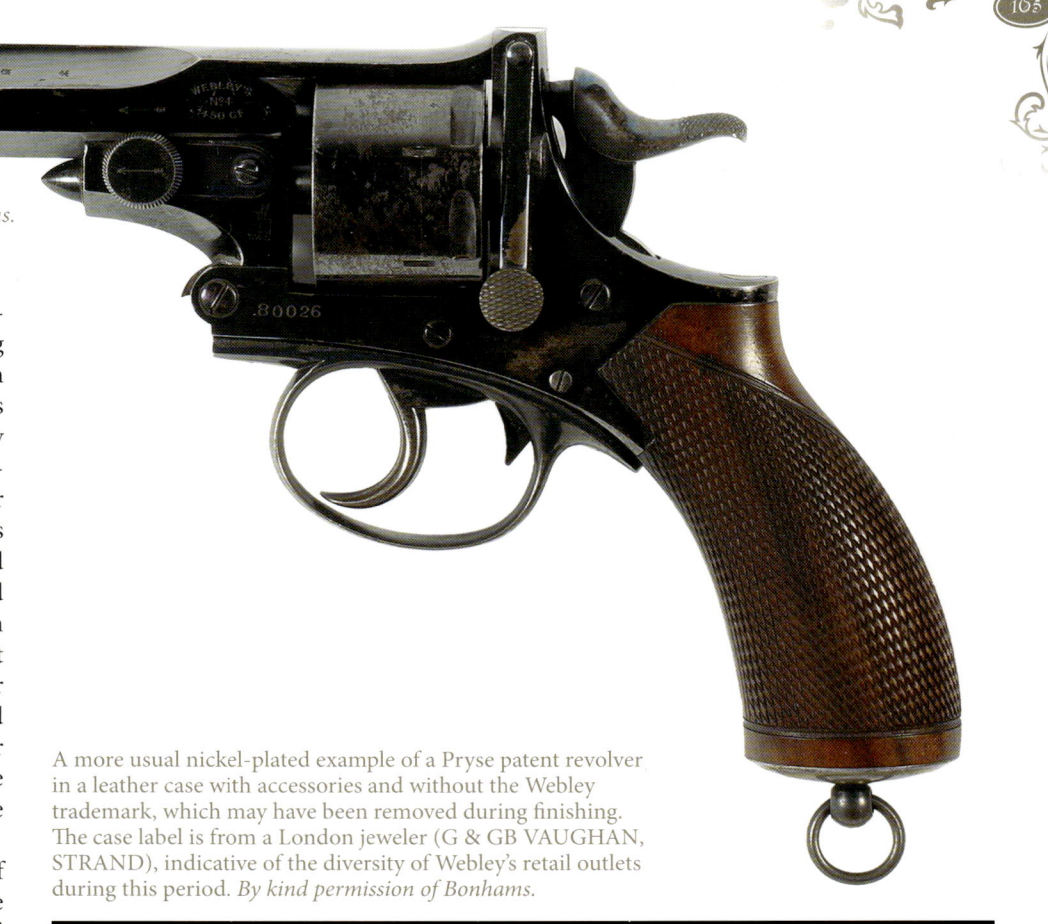

A more usual nickel-plated example of a Pryse patent revolver in a leather case with accessories and without the Webley trademark, which may have been removed during finishing. The case label is from a London jeweler (G & GB VAUGHAN, STRAND), indicative of the diversity of Webley's retail outlets during this period. *By kind permission of Bonhams.*

Webley-Pryse No. 4 Model revolver; a superb, gold-plated example with a plain cylinder in a case with a label from "Manton & Co," including accessories. It has the characteristic frame catch, and the lug projecting into the rear of the trigger guard shows the weapon to be of British manufacture. This revolver was made by Webley & Scott, as it bears the "Flying Bullet" trademark, but was finished by Manton & Co. *By kind permission of Bonhams.*

Webley-Pryse No. 4 Model revolver in a wooden case with accessories and bearing the Webley trademark. The case label shows this weapon to have been retailed by P. Webley. *Courtesy of James D. Julia Auctioneers, Fairfield, Maine (www.jamesdjulia.com).*

Webley-Pryse No. 4 Model revolver from the right side. *Courtesy of James D. Julia Auctioneers, Fairfield, Maine (www.jamesdjulia.com).*

The "Flying Bullet" trademark may also be found stamped on the frame somewhere in the vicinity of the caliber stamp on those revolvers manufactured by Webley. Proof marks, usually of the Birmingham Proof House, are stamped on both barrel and cylinder. Webley patent stamps are not usually found on this revolver. The butts are in one piece, conventional in shape, and secured by two screws. A lanyard ring is usually fitted.

Variations
Webley-Pryse No 4 revolver.
  Chambered for:
- Adams .450 caliber: Plain cylinder with six chambers and either a 4 or 5 ½ inch barrel.
- Adams .450 caliber: Semi-fluted cylinder with six chambers and either a 4 or 5 ½ inch barrel.
- Enfield Mk II .455 caliber cartridge: Semi-fluted cylinder with six chambers and a 5¾ inch barrel.
- Enfield Mk II .455 caliber cartridge: Semi-fluted cylinder with five chambers and a 4½ inch barrel.
- Enfield Mk III .476 caliber cartridge: Semi-fluted cylinder with six chambers and a 5 ½ inch barrel.

Webley-Pryse No. 4 Model revolver from the left side, showing the frame stamps and characteristic loading lever. The Webley trademark is present, although the company "WEBLEY PATENTS" stamp is absent. *Courtesy of James D. Julia Auctioneers, Fairfield, Maine (www.jamesdjulia.com).*

Webley-Pryse No. 4 Model revolver showing the barrel address. *Courtesy of James D. Julia Auctioneers, Fairfield, Maine (www.jamesdjulia.com).*

- Enfield Mk III .476 caliber cartridge: Semi-fluted cylinder with six chambers and a 3 ½ inch barrel. (Sold by Army & Navy stores as the "BULLDOG" EXTRACTOR.").

All calibers were manufactured with various barrel lengths (4 inch was a common variation) by Webley & Scott, who also supplied complete revolvers to gunmakers for finishing, such as Manton & Son and Joseph Lang & Sons.

The frame lever catch and lock mechanism fitted to these revolvers was also used by a number of London, Birmingham, and European manufacturers, including Bonehill, Francotte, and Horseley. Revolvers from these manufacturers are similar in conformation to those made by Webley.

Values: Good: $3,600-3,900 (£2,200-2,350)
Fine: $4,100-4,500 (£2,500-£2,700)
Cased: $5,800-7,000 (£3,500-£4,200)
Common at UK and U.S. auctions.

WEBLEY-KAUFMAN OR WEBLEY IMPROVED GOVERNMENT MODEL 1884 REVOLVER

Webley produced another revolver in 1880, known to collectors as the Webley-Kaufmann, although the factory designation was the "Improved Government Model." This revolver featured a new lock mechanism (British Patent 4302/1880) and an improved frame catch (British Patent 3313/1881), with both British patents registered to Michael Kaufmann, one of Webley's designers.

Webley-Kaufmann Second Pattern revolver from the right, showing the stud that operates the cylinder release mechanism. *Courtesy of James D. Julia Auctioneers, Fairfield, Maine (www.jamesdjulia.com).*

Serial number range: 1-1300
(Manufactured: 1882-1886)

Top-break, double-action, self-extracting revolver in a variety of calibers, with a 5¾ inch ribbed octagonal barrel similar in conformation to that fitted to the Webley-Pryse revolver and rifled with seven, clockwise grooves. The frame is similar in conformation to the No 4 revolver, except an inspection plate is fitted over the lock components on the left side and secured by two screws.

The cylinder is fluted with six chambers, and secured in the frame by a metal stud with a serrated face mounted on the right,

WEBLEY REVOLVERS

Webley-Kaufmann Third Pattern revolver showing the Kaufmann patent barrel latch, differentiated from the later Webley patented device by the position of the screw fixing, which is nearer the top of the lever in this weapon. The cylinder bears slots in the area of the fluting, showing it is fitted with Carter's cylinder locking mechanism. This is an expertly engraved presentation example cased with the usual accessories. By kind permission of Bonhams.

which was pushed into the frame to release the cylinder and its associated mechanism. Cylinder bolt recesses are present on the rear surface of that component and there is also a second series of small rectangular slots near the middle of the cylinder that are associated with Carter's cylinder locking mechanism (Br. Pat. 2555/ 1884). Carter's breech safety device is also fitted to later revolvers (British Patent 1820/ 1884).

In First Pattern revolvers, the frame latch takes the form of a stud with a serrated face on the upper lock frame. Pressing this releases the frame for loading. Second and Third Pattern revolvers were both fitted with a lever to operate the frame catch, which in the Third Pattern was the robust "stirrup" fastener that would be fitted to Webley's later Mk I-Mk VI Government revolvers (Webley and Carter: British Patent 4070/1885).

The barrel lug or frame is stamped on the left in the usual oval format:

WEBLEY'S
PATENTS

The frame is also stamped with the Webley trademark and an "MK" enclosed within a triangle on the right side above the production number. This acknowledges the use of Michael Kaufmann's patent, and the number was used to calculate his royalties. The Webley serial number is stamped on the rear face of the barrel lug below the cylinder arbor hole, on the left side of the butt strap, and inside each butt plate. Proof marks, usually of the Birmingham Proof House, are stamped on both barrel and cylinder. The butt has a "Birds-head" configuration, with separate butt plates secured by a screw entering from the left.

Variations
Webley-Kaufman revolver.
First Pattern: Serial number series 1-121. The frame latch is in the form of a stud.

Chambered for:
- Enfield .455 cartridge: Fluted cylinder with six chambers and a 5¾ inch barrel.

Second Pattern:
Serial number series: 160-1200. The frame latch is in the form of a lever, operating a cammed pin and bolt system.

Chambered for:
- Enfield .455 cartridge: Fluted cylinder with six chambers and a 5¾ inch barrel.

Third Pattern: Serial number series: 1200-1300. The frame latch is in the form of a lever operating a Webley "stirrup" catch.

Chambered for:
- Enfield .455 cartridge: Fluted cylinder with six chambers and a 5¾ inch barrel.

Webley-Kaufmann Second Pattern revolver showing the characteristic frame-locking mechanism. Courtesy of James D. Julia Auctioneers, Fairfield, Maine (www.jamesdjulia.com).

Values: Good: $4,800-5,600
(£2,900-3,350)
Fine: $5,800-6,200
(£3,500-£3,700)
Cased: $5,800-8,200
(£3,500-£4,900)
Rare at UK and U.S. auctions.

THE WEBLEY "W.G" MODEL REVOLVER

Known to collectors as either the "Webley Government" or "Webley Green." The claim by Edwinson Charles Green that he invented the original stirrup latch was contested by P. Webley & Son, and after an exchange of letters—and possibly some financial settlement—Green appears to have dropped the matter. These revolvers are therefore more correctly designated the Webley "Government" Model.

This revolver, which was intended for the civilian market, resembled the Webley-Kaufmann (Third Pattern) in many of its external features, the principal difference being the larger diameter frame hinge. It was fitted with the characteristic lock mechanism and barrel catch patented by Webley and Carter (British Patent 4070/1885), as well as the self extraction mechanism patented by Thomas and Henry Webley in 1881 (British Patent 5143/1881); both were used on the "Improved Government" revolver. It is interesting to note in this context that the development of this civilian revolver closely paralleled the later Government Model. In particular, later examples of the "W.G.," with correspondingly high serial numbers, were fitted with the same cylinder locking device found on the Webley Mk III to Mk VI Government revolvers.

Serial number range (in a continuous range for all models): 1-22100 (Production: 1885-1902)

This is a hinge-frame, self-extracting double-action revolver, fitted with rebounding hammer and a six inch ribbed, octagonal barrel. There is also a "Target" Model with a 7½ inch barrel. Both are rifled with seven clockwise grooves.

The cylinder is fluted—"church steeple" fluting appears on early models—with six chambers in .455 caliber, although the length of the cylinder also allowed the Enfield .476 cartridge to be used.

Cylinder bolt recesses are present on the rear surface of that component, and there is also a second series of small rectangular slots near the middle of the cylinder associated with Carter's original 1884 cylinder locking mechanism, and, in later revolvers, the double-locking mechanism patented in 1888 by Whiting and Carter (British Patent 5778/1888). Carter's breech safety device is also fitted.

Target Models are characterized by the presence of adjustable front and rear sights; these weapons may also be encountered fitted with the conventional six inch barrel.

The frame or barrel lug often bears a cartridge stamp:

.455/.476

The frame is usually also stamped below the cylinder:

WEBLEY
PATENTS

Beginning with the Model 1889, top-straps are stamped on the left side:

"W.G" MODEL

This was followed by the date. Army Models are stamped:

"WG" ARMY MODEL

Target Models are stamped:

"W G" TARGET MODEL

The butts are a "Birds-head" or Target (square) configuration, depending upon the model. They are in two pieces of "Vulcanite" secured by a single screw, entering from the left.

Webley "W.G" revolver from the right, showing the later stirrup-shaped cylinder release mechanism. Courtesy of James D. Julia Auctioneers, Fairfield, Maine (www.jamesdjulia.com).

Webley "W.G" Army Model revolver from the left side, showing the frame catch lever and the ".455/.476" cartridge stamp. The Whiting Patent cylinder retaining system with a single, stirrup-shaped lever is characteristic of these later weapons and is visible in front of the cylinder. Courtesy of James D. Julia Auctioneers, Fairfield, Maine (www.jamesdjulia.com).

Webley "W.G" Target Model revolver, right side. *Courtesy of James D. Julia Auctioneers, Fairfield, Maine (www.jamesdjulia.com).*

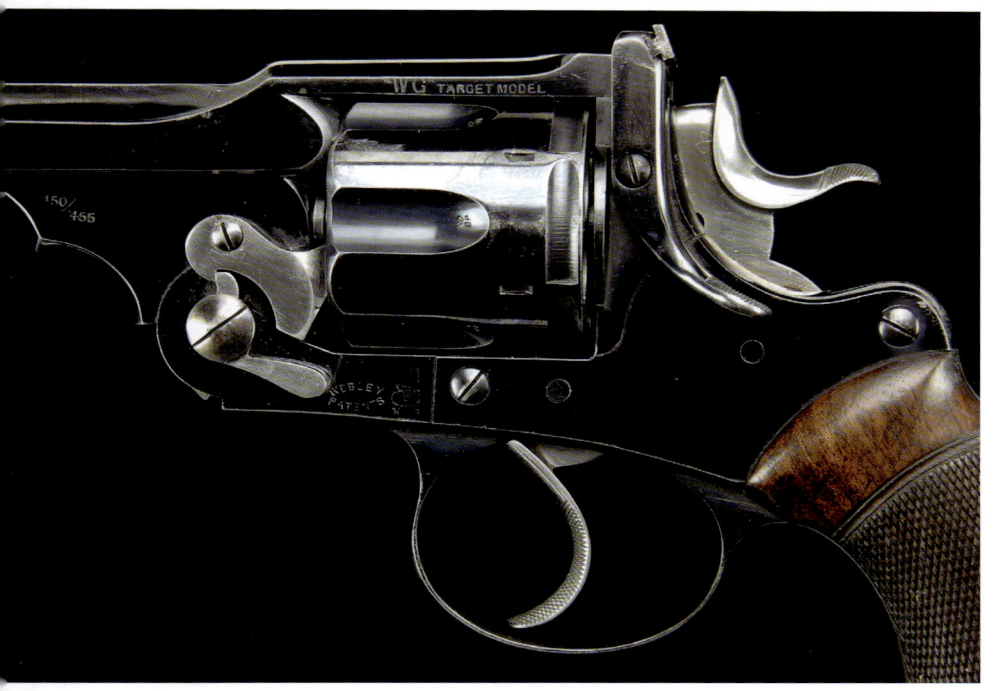

Webley "W.G" Target Model revolver, left side, showing frame stamps and the cylinder release lever. This one is stamped ".450/ .455", although the slightly increased length of the cylinder meant these revolvers would chamber Adams .450, Webley .455, Enfield .476 or commercial Eley .476 cartridges. *Courtesy of James D. Julia Auctioneers, Fairfield, Maine (www.jamesdjulia.com).*

Variations
Webley-Government "W G" Revolver.

- Model 1886: Serial number range: 1400-1870. Cylinder with "church steeple" fluting, six chambers, and a six inch barrel. The cylinder retainer is in the form of a flat-headed pin, similar to that found on the Webley-Pryse revolvers. The left side of the top-strap is stamped:

"W. G." MODEL

Chambered for:
- Enfield MkI and Mk II .455 cartridge
- Enfield Mk III .476 cartridge

- Model 1886: Serial number range: 1870-1980. Cylinder with "church steeple" fluting, six chambers, and a six inch barrel. The cylinder retainer was changed in this serial range to take the form of a broad-headed pin that passed through the frame. Externally, the head of the pin has a wide slot across the head, allowing it to be easily turned by a coin, thus improving the ease with which the cylinder could be removed. The left side of the top-strap is stamped:
"W. G." MODEL

Chambered for:
- Enfield MkI and Mk II .455 cartridge
- Enfield Mk III .476 cartridge

- Webley-Government Model 1889 Revolver: Serial number range: 1980-3930. Cylinder with "church steeple" fluting, six chambers, and a 6 or 7½ inch barrel. A Target Model was offered with improved sights and a conventional, flared walnut "target" butt. Some of these "Target" revolvers had the longer barrel, although none were stamped "TARGET MODEL". The left side of the top-strap stamped:

"W. G." MODEL 1889

Chambered for:
- Enfield Mk II .455 cartridge (the Enfield Mk I cartridge is now declared obsolete)
- Enfield Mk III .476 cartridge

- Webley-Government Model 1891 Revolver: Serial number range: 4000-4200. Cylinder with "church steeple" fluting and six chambers, a 7½ inch barrel, and a conventional, walnut butt. The cylinder retaining mechanism fitted to this revolver was entirely new and manufactured under a British patent registered to William Whiting (Brt. Pt. 3427/1891), specifically for use in the Webley Mk III Government revolver. Externally, it consists of a cam lever on the left barrel lug that engages a second cam-release lever, which is secured in place by a screw inserted in the axis pin of the hinge joint. This model also featured changes to the extractor and lock mechanisms. The left side of the top-strap is stamped:

"W. G." MODEL 1891

Chambered for:
- Eley .450 cartridge.

These models are usually stamped with the cartridge designation on the breech.

- Webley-Government Model 1892 Revolver: Serial number range: 4100-6400. Cylinder with "church steeple" fluting and six chambers, with a six inch barrel. It is fitted with Whiting's patent cylinder cam mechanism and the same lockwork and extractor as the Model 1891 revolver. The left side of the top-strap is stamped:

"W. G." MODEL 1892

Chambered for:
- Webley Mk I .455 cartridge
- Enfield Mk III .476 cartridge
- Commercial cartridges:
- Eley .450 cartridge
- Eley .455 cartridge
- Eley .476 cartridge

- Webley-Government Target Model 1892 Revolver: Serial number range: 4010-6400 (within the same range as the Model 1892 revolvers). Fluted cylinder with six chambers and a 7½ inch barrel. Adjustable front and rear sights. The left side of the top-strap is stamped:

"W. G." TARGET MODEL 1892

Chambered for:
- Enfield Mk I .455 cartridge
- Enfield Mk III .476 cartridge
- Webley Mk I .455 cartridge.

Later examples of this model may be stamped .455/.476 on the breech, indicating that the revolver can chamber either the new Webley Mk I .455 cartridge or the obsolete Enfield Mk III .476 cartridge.

A "W. G." Model 1993 is described, but this is believed to be a gun made to special order by Webley and based on a conventional "W. G." Model 1892.

- Webley-Government Army Model Revolver: Serial number range: 6400-12200. This model was produced specifically for sale to Army officers, as the name implies. It has a cylinder with conventional fluting and six chambers, with a six inch barrel. The model is fitted with Whiting's cylinder cam retaining mechanism, but it is modified in this revolver by changing the single cam lever to take the form of a stirrup that was attached to both sides of the barrel lug (Whiting's Patent 17291/1896). The lockwork and extractor are similar to those fitted to the Model 1891 revolver. The butt was a two-piece "Vulcanite" "Bird Head" configuration. Fixed front and rear sights. The left side of the top-strap is stamped:

"W. G." ARMY MODEL

Chambered for:
- Webley .455 cartridge.
- Enfield Mk III .476 cartridge
- Commercial cartridges:
- Eley .450 cartridge
- Eley .455 cartridge
- Eley .476 cartridge

This model is usually stamped .455/.476 on the breech, indicating that the revolver can chamber either the new Webley .455 cartridge or the obsolete Enfield Mk III .476 cartridge.

- Webley-Government Model 1896 Revolver: Serial number range: 10306-22126. Cylinder with conventional fluting and six chambers, with a six inch barrel. This model is fitted with Whiting's modified cylinder cam retaining mechanism, similar to that on the "W. G." Army Model. The lockwork and extractor were the same as the Model 1891 revolver. The butt was a two piece "Vulcanite" "Bird-Head" configuration. Fixed front and rear sights. The left side of the top-strap is stamped:

"W. G." MODEL
(Stamping of the year on revolvers was discontinued in 1893)

Chambered for:
- Webley .455 cartridge.
- Enfield Mk III .476 cartridge
- Commercial cartridges:
- Eley .450 cartridge
- Eley .455 cartridge
- Eley .476 cartridge

This model is usually stamped .455/.476 on the breech, indicating that the revolver can chamber either the new Webley .455 cartridge or the obsolete Enfield Mk III .476 cartridge.

Values for all models:
Good: $4,800-5,500
(£2,900-3,350)
Fine: $5,800-6,100
(£3,500-3,700)
Cased: $5,800-8,100
(£3,500-4,900)

Rare at UK and U.S. auctions.

WEBLEY-WILKINSON REVOLVERS

Revolvers supplied to the firm of Henry Wilkinson & Son, Pall Mall by P. Webley & Son—later by Webley & Scott—were usually based on their standard production models and from their normal production run. Wilkinson subsequently applied an improved finish and re-finished the mechanism, although with some models they did specify improvements to the basic design that were carried out by the Webley factory.

Serial number ranges:
The Webley serial number range is in a series of ranges corresponding to the model and stamped on the left of the frame, below the cylinder in early weapons. Soon after beginning production of the First Model 1884, the serial number was stamped on the rear face of the barrel lug, out of sight. After May 1901, the Webley serial number was stamped under the front of the barrel hinge. Webley-Wilkinson revolvers were supplied out of Webley's normal production runs, so serial numbers will reflect this.

Wilkinson Register number ranges are in a series of ranges corresponding to the model and are usually applied to the lower portion of the left butt plate.

These guns are all hinge-frame, self-extracting, double-action revolvers with a fluted cylinder with six chambers, octagonal barrels of 5¾, 6, and 7½ inches, with flat faces and a characteristic rib on the top flat running the entire length of the barrel. The self-extracting mechanism is based on Webley's 1881 Patent (British Patent 5143/1881), although with some later modifications. Cylinder bolt recesses are present on the rear surface of that component, and there is also a second series of small rectangular slots near the middle of the cylinder associated with Carter's original 1884 cylinder locking mechanism, and in later weapons, the double-locking mechanism patented in 1888 by Whiting and Carter (British Patent 5778/1888). Carter's breech safety device is also fitted. The frames were stamped with the Wilkinson trademark within a six-pointed star:

H W

Webley-Wilkinson Small-Hinge Model bright nickel-plated revolver from the left side, showing the characteristic Pryse pattern frame catch and the Wilkinson Register number stamped into the wood of the left butt plate. Courtesy of James D. Julia Auctioneers, Fairfield, Maine (www.jamesdjulia.com).

Webley-Wilkinson Small-Hinge Model bright nickel-plated revolver from the right side, showing the lug that forms part of the double-action mechanism protruding into the trigger guard. Courtesy of James D. Julia Auctioneers, Fairfield, Maine (www.jamesdjulia.com).

Webley-Wilkinson Small-Hinge Model bright nickel-plated revolver from the left side, showing the Wilkinson trademark "HW" within a six-pointed star. Courtesy of James D. Julia Auctioneers, Fairfield, Maine (www.jamesdjulia.com).

The top of the barrel rib was inscribed with the retailer's address:

WILKINSON & SON, PALL MALL, LONDON.

From December 1900, this inscription was changed to:

WILKINSON SWORD CO. PALL MALL, LONDON.

After 1909, the barrel rib was inscribed:

WILKINSON, GUNMAKERS, PALL MALL, LONDON, S. W.

The butts are either conventional in shape, with two walnut butt plates, or made in one piece, also of walnut. Both patterns are usually fitted with a lanyard ring. These revolvers were often supplied cased, with a nickel-plate finish.

Variations
Webley-Wilkinson Revolvers:

- Webley-Wilkinson First Model, Small Hinge Pattern (Manufactured 1884-1888): Included in Webley's serial number series 5000-7800. Wilkinson register number series: 7800-8301.

- Exactly similar to the Webley-Pryse No 4 revolver. Cylinder with six chambers, a 5¾ inch barrel, and rifled with seven clockwise grooves. Lockwork is of the conventional early Webley pattern, so it features a sear protruding through the frame into the rear of the trigger guard. Two forms of front sight were fitted: an early semi-circular type and a later, trapezoidal type. These later revolvers also featured changes to the self-extracting mechanism. The cylinder release pin may be of the Pryse type or the later pattern fitted to the early "W. G" revolvers. The top of the barrel rib was inscribed with the retailer's address:

WILKINSON & SON, PALL MALL, LONDON.

Webley-Wilkinson Small-Hinge Model revolver. Made by Wilkinson & Son of Pall Mall, this example is bright nickel-plated and cased with accessories. The gun bears no cartridge stamp, but the case includes a selection of .455 caliber cartridges stamped on the base "WILKINSON" and "DOMINION .455 COLT". *Courtesy of James D. Julia Auctioneers, Fairfield, Maine (www.jamesdjulia.com).*

WILKINSON & SON, PALL MALL, LONDON.

Webley-Wilkinson Small-Hinge Model revolver showing the retailer's early address inscribed on the top-strap, "WILKINSON & SON, PALL MALL, LONDON". Incidentally, Sam Colt's retail outlet was also in Pall Mall. *Courtesy of James D. Julia Auctioneers, Fairfield, Maine (www.jamesdjulia.com).*

Chambered for:
- Enfield .455 cartridge
- Enfield .476 cartridge

Commercial cartridges:
- Eley .450 cartridge
- Eley .455 cartridge
- Eley .476 cartridge

Proof marks were usually those of the London House.

- Webley-Wilkinson Second Model, Large Hinge Pattern (Manufactured 1888-1892): Included in Webley's serial number series: 7800-11000. Wilkinson register number series: 8300-8700. Made by Webley, but incorporating some amended design features that differentiate this revolver from the earlier "Small Hinge" Model and a standard production Webley No.4 revolver. Cylinder with six chambers, a six inch ribbed barrel, and rifled with seven clockwise grooves, with a two lever frame latch. The frame features a larger hinge joint than that fitted to the earlier Wilkinson First Model and the cylinder release pin is of the pattern fitted to the early "W. G" revolvers, taking the form of a bolt with a wide slot in the head. The top of the barrel rib was inscribed with the retailer's address:

WILKINSON & SON, PALL MALL, LONDON.

Proof marks were usually those of the London House. Butts were of walnut, made in one piece.

Chambered for:
- Enfield .455 cartridge
- Enfield .476 cartridge

Commercial cartridges:
- Eley .450 cartridge
- Eley .455 cartridge
- Eley .476 cartridge

- Webley-Wilkinson Model 1892 (manufactured 1892-1900): Included in Webley's serial number series: 7800. Wilkinson register number series: 8700-9300. Cylinder with six chambers, a six inch ribbed barrel, and rifled with seven clockwise grooves. The frame latch on this model is of the single lever, stirrup latch pattern patented by Carter and Webley in 1885 (British Patent 4070.1885), and the cylinder retaining mechanism is of the early Whiting pattern with a single cam lever pivoted on the left side of the frame. Cylinder release is effected by a characteristic knurled push button that was fitted to all later

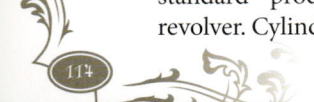

WEBLEY REVOLVERS

Webley-Wilkinson revolvers. The top of the barrel rib was inscribed with the retailer's address and model year:

"WILKINSON" MODEL 1892 PALL MALL, LONDON.

The foresight was usually of a "bead" pattern, and a laterally adjustable rear sight was available as a factory-fitted option. Proof marks were usually those of the London House. Butts were one piece, made of walnut, and secured by two screws.

Chambered for:
- Webley .455 cartridge
Commercial cartridges:
- Eley .450 cartridge
- Eley .455 cartridge
- Eley .476 cartridge

- Webley-Wilkinson "1900 Model" (Manufactured 1900-1904): Included in Webley's serial number series: 119000-120000. Wilkinson register number series: W460-W960. This is similar to the Model 1892, except this model was the first to feature Whiting's stirrup cam cylinder retaining mechanism (Br Pat 17291/1896). The top of the barrel rib was inscribed with the retailer's address:

WILKINSON SWORD CO. PALL MALL, LONDON.

No model year is included in the inscription. The foresight was usually of a "bead" pattern and a laterally adjustable rear sight was available as a factory-fitted option. Proof marks were usually those of the London House. Butts were one piece, made of walnut, and secured by two screws.

Chambered for:
- Webley .455 cartridge
- Commercial cartridges:
- Eley .450 cartridge
- Eley .455 cartridge
- Eley .476 cartridge

- Webley-Wilkinson Model 1905 (Manufactured 1905-). Webley serial number series: 120000-127000 (in later arms stamped on the right of the frame). Wilkinson register number series: W1102-2900 (in later arms they were inscribed on the underside of the trigger guard). Cylinder with six chambers, a six inch ribbed barrel, and rifled with seven clockwise grooves. This revolver retained all the features of the earlier "1900" Model, except they were fitted with the later "Webley Service" pattern frame. Rifling in later revolvers was changed to six clockwise grooves (first seen in revolver with Wilkinson register number 2976). Later revolvers also featured a strengthened frame catch. The top of the barrel rib was inscribed with the retailer's address:

WILKINSON SWORD CO. PALL MALL, LONDON.

After 1909, the barrel rib was inscribed:

WILKINSON, GUNMAKERS, PALL MALL, LONDON, S. W.

The left side of the top-strap was stamped:

WILKINSON-WEBLEY '05

The foresight was usually of a "blade" pattern and rear sights were adjustable on all 1905 Model revolvers. The butts were of conventional shape to accommodate the changes to the later frame and were fitted with two butt plates in walnut secured by a single screw entering from the left.
Proof marks on early Model 1905 revolvers were those of the London House, the last Model 1905 revolver recorded with London proof stamps having Wilkinson register no. W1301. Model 1905 revolvers made subsequently all bear proof stamps of the Birmingham House. Butts were of walnut, one piece, and secured by two screws.

Chambered for:
- Webley .455 cartridge
Commercial cartridges:
- Eley .450 cartridge
- Eley .455 cartridge
- Eley .476 cartridge

- Webley-Wilkinson Model 1910: Included in Webley's serial number series: 127000. Wilkinson register number series: 3000-3100. Very similar to the Model 1905 revolver, but fitted with the later, strengthened frame catch; six groove, clockwise rifling and also available with a 7½ inch barrel. The top of the barrel rib was inscribed with the retailer's address:

WILKINSON, GUNMAKERS, PALL MALL, LONDON, S. W.

The left side of the top-strap was stamped:

WILKINSON-WEBLEY 1910

Few of these revolvers were produced.

- Webley-Wilkinson Model 1911 (Manufactured 1911-1913): Webley serial number series: 127000-129000. Wilkinson register number series: 3100-4400. Cylinder with six chambers, a 6 or 7½ inch ribbed barrel, and rifled with six clockwise grooves. The top of the barrel rib was inscribed with the retailer's address:

WILKINSON, GUNMAKERS, PALL MALL, LONDON, S. W.

The left side of the top-strap on revolvers with a six inch barrel was stamped:

WILKINSON-WEBLEY '11

This stamp appeared on the barrel of the Target Model fitted with a 7½ inch barrel. Foresights may be blade or square conformation and the rear sight could be adjusted laterally. Butts were conventional in shape and fitted with two butt plates secured by a single screw entering from the left. In the Target model, both the butt plates and trigger bore serrations to improve grip.

Chambered for:
- Webley .455 cartridge
Commercial cartridges:
- Eley .450 cartridge
- Eley .455 cartridge
- Eley .476 cartridge

Values for all Models:
Good: $4,800-5,500
(£2,900-3,350)
Fine: $5,800-6,100
(£3,500-3,700)
Cased: $5,800-8,100
(£3,500-4,900)
Very rare at UK auctions
Rare at U.S. auctions.

Webley-Fosbery semi-automatic revolver made after 1902 and showing the rebated cylinder and frame slide. *By kind permission of Bonhams.*

WEBLEY-FOSBERY AUTOMATIC CENTER-FIRE REVOLVER

Serial number range 1-5000 (Manufactured: 1900-1918. This revolver was still included in Webley's 1939 catalog). This is a solid-frame, top break, self-extracting, semi-automatic revolver in .445 or .38 caliber, with barrel lengths varying from 4 to 7½ inches.

The cylinder is semi-fluted with six chambers, machined on the external surface with a series of zig-zag grooves, making this arm easy to recognize. A later version had a shorter cylinder with eight chambers designed for the .38 ACP (Automatic Colt Pistol) cartridge. The thumb operated frame catch lever is on the left side, exactly similar to Webley Government revolvers, but with a safety catch—also thumb operated—on the lower left side of the frame.

The frame is stamped on the left side of the top-strap:

"WEBLEY-FOSBERY AUTOMATIC"

Webley-Fosbery revolver with the frame open for reloading, showing the star-shaped ejector and the thumb-operated frame catch lever. This mechanism is similar to that fitted to Webley Mks I-VI. *(NRAmuseum.com)*

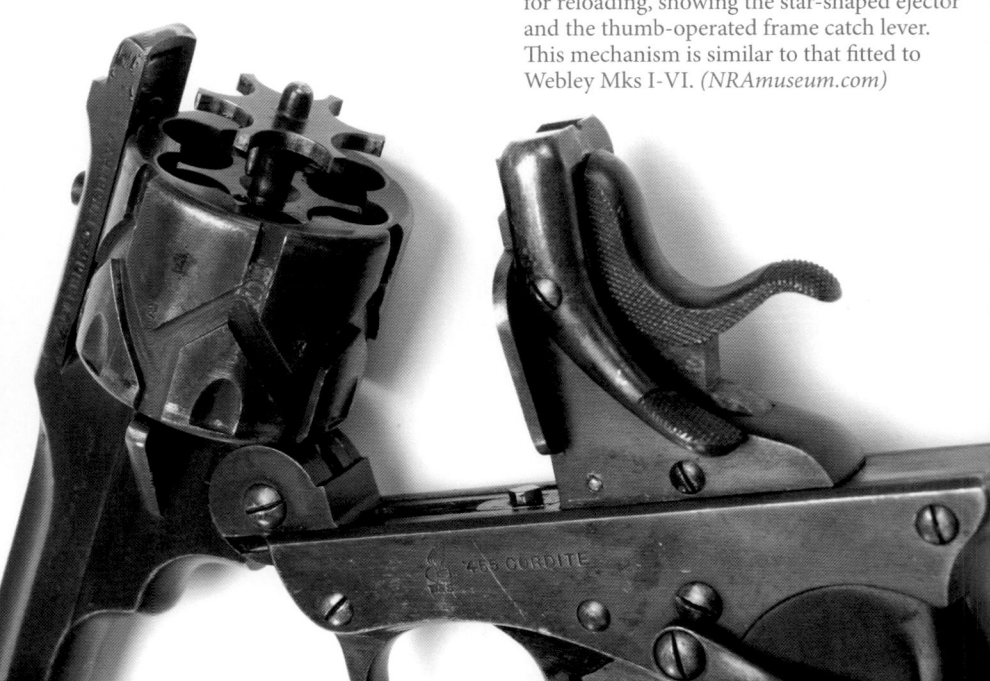

Webley-Fosbery revolver showing the frame stamps and cylinder, which bears a Birmingham House "View" mark. These are characteristic of guns made in 1902 and later. *By kind permission of Bonhams.*

which became, on arms made in 1902 and later:

"WEBLEY-FOSBERY"

On the left side of the frame below the cylinder is stamped:

.455 CORDITE ONLY

which became on weapons made in 1902 and later:
.455 CORDITE
or, on the revolvers chambered for .38ACP:
.38 AUTOMATIC"

indicating the chambering of the weapon. Proof marks, usually of the Birmingham Proof House, are stamped on both the barrel and cylinders.

The lower frame of the revolver was fixed, while the hexagonal barrel, cylinder, and upper frame assembly moved on machined rails under the force of the weapon's recoil, cocking the hammer and rotating the cylinder, so the action was analogous to a modern semi-automatic pistol. Incidentally, the weapon seems to have only functioned correctly with the higher power smokeless or cordite rounds, hence the stamp on the frames of the early weapons. Fosbery's revolver was very accurate and fast to shoot, but the precise machining of the moving surfaces meant it was expensive to produce and susceptible to stoppages in muddy conditions, which made it unsuitable for service use.

Variations
Webley-Fosbery semi-automatic revolver.

- Webley-Fosbery .445 caliber Model: This is the weapon chambered for the government issue Webley .455 cartridge. It has a cylinder with six chambers and barrel lengths between 4 and 7½ inches.

Pre-1902 revolvers: serial range 1-600. The left side of the top-strap is stamped:

"WEBLEY-FOSBERY AUTOMATIC"

The left side of the frame is stamped:

.455 CORDITE ONLY

Post-1902 revolvers: Serial range 600-5000. The top-strap is stamped:

"WEBLEY-FOSBERY"

While the left side of the frame is stamped:

.455 CORDITE

A number of further variations were produced of the 1902 Model, involving changes in barrel length and designated Mk I to Mk VI. This revolver was also produced as a "Short-Frame" Model, with a cylinder having similar dimensions to the .38 ACP Model, but with only six chambers.

- Webley-Fosbery .38 Caliber Model: Manufactured for the .38 ACP cartridge; it has a cylinder with eight chambers and various barrel lengths.

Values:
Good: $4,600-5,500
(£2,800-3,350)
Fine: $5,400-6,100
(£3,300-3,700)
Cased: $7,400-8,100
(£4,500-4,900)
Rare at UK and U.S. auctions.

WEBLEY POCKET "HAMMERLESS" CENTER-FIRE REVOLVER

Serial number range: 1-10000 (1901-1936)
Solid-frame, self-cocking, top break, self-extracting revolver; semi-fluted cylinder with six chambers and a three inch barrel rifled with seven clockwise grooves.

Early revolvers lacked a hammer spur and a sliding safety catch was fitted above the hammer shroud, with the frame being locked by a thumb-operated frame catch incorporating the rear sight, consisting of a simple notch. The lock mechanism employed a flat-faced hammer and striker mounted on the standing breech—similar in conformation to the MkI and Mk II Pocket Model revolvers—and a lock inspection plate is fitted on the left side, retained by two screws.

A later version fitted with a conventional, spurred hammer and striker was also produced, featuring a frame catch without a side-mounted lever that was operated by pulling back the catch from above. This was facilitated by chequering on its upper edges.

Webley Pocket "Hammerless" Model 1898 revolver from the left side. This example is unusual, being fitted with the later frame catch more characteristic of the 1901 revolvers, which were fitted with a spurred hammer. *Courtesy of Joel Black.*

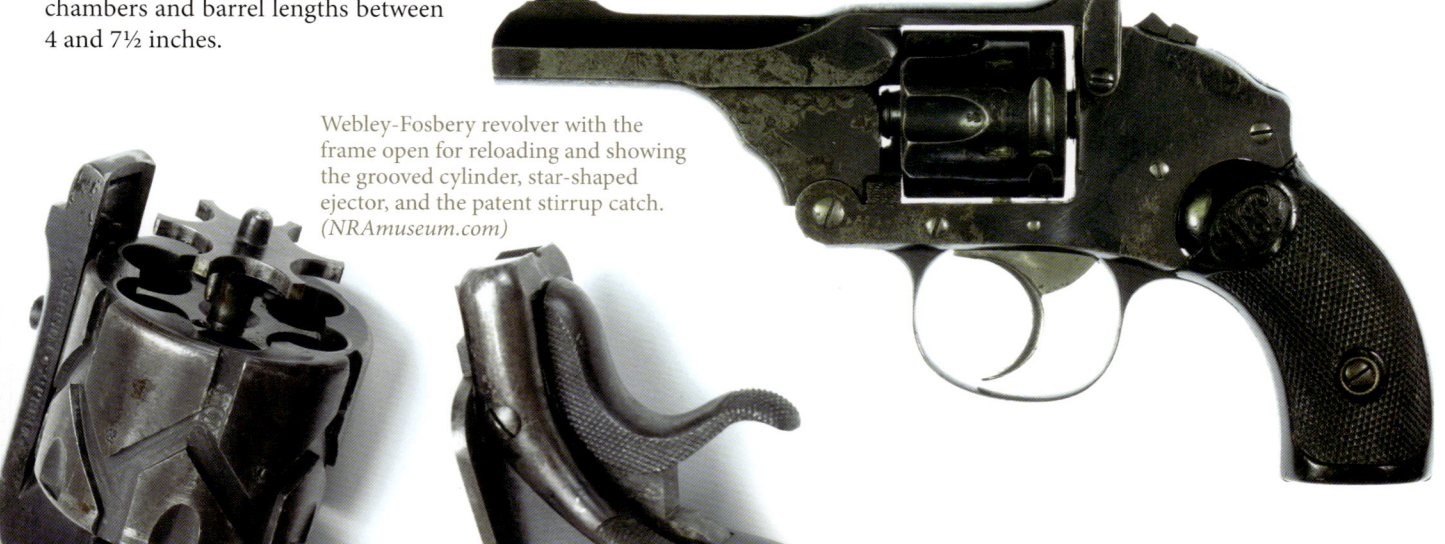

Webley-Fosbery revolver with the frame open for reloading and showing the grooved cylinder, star-shaped ejector, and the patent stirrup catch. (NRAmuseum.com)

Webley Pocket "Hammerless" revolver from the right side, showing the oval Webley Patent mark below the cylinder and the Birmingham view mark used after 1904, a crowned "BV". Courtesy of Joel Black.

Both versions were chambered for Webley .32, .32 Long Colt, .32 Short Colt, and .32 Smith and Wesson calibers, with the revolver being regulated to fire any of these cartridges without any changes to the cylinder or barrel. The frames are stamped:

WEBLEY
WR.32C.F
PATENT

They appear in the usual oval format; the cartridge stamp is dependent on the caliber of the revolver. Serial numbers are stamped on the lower right side of the frame and proof marks, usually of the Birmingham Proof House, are stamped on both barrel and cylinders.

Variations
- Webley Pocket Hammerless Model 1898 Revolver: Self-cocking revolver with a three inch barrel and a cylinder with six chambers.

Manufactured for:
- Webley .32 cartridge.
- .32 Long Colt cartridge
- .32 Short Colt cartridge
- Smith & Wesson .32 cartridge

- Webley Pocket Hammer Model 1901: Similar to the Model 1898, except in this Model the hammer is exposed and fitted with a spur. A frame catch lever was not fitted, since the frame catch had a serration on the top surface operated by the thumb.

Manufactured for:
- Webley .32 cartridge.
- .32 Long Colt cartridge
- .32 Short Colt cartridge
- Smith & Wesson .32 cartridge

Very rare at UK and U.S. auctions.

Webley Government issue metal cartridge revolvers are described under "Military pistols and revolvers."

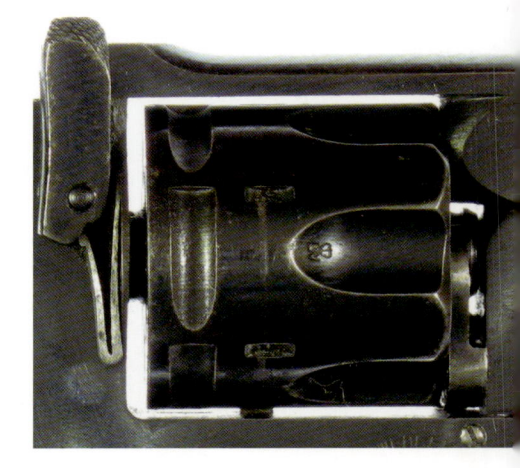

Webley Pocket "Hammerless" from the right side, showing a close-up view of the Birmingham View mark, indicating this revolver was manufactured some time after 1904. The cylinder also bears the rectangular slots characteristic of a weapon fitted with Whiting and Carter's "double-locking" cylinder mechanism. Courtesy of Joel Black.

Webley Hammerless showing the retail mark on the top-strap of the frame, "P. WEELEM & SON. LONDON & BIRMINGHAM". Courtesy of Joel Black.

WEBLEY REVOLVERS

CHAPTER SIX

English Military Pistols and Revolvers

FLINTLOCK AND PERCUSSION PISTOLS

British military single-shot pistols do not follow a very coherent pattern of production. They are usually of Dragoon pistol length, having a barrel between 10 and 12 inches, with either flintlock or percussion ignition, depending on the date of manufacture. Cruder and sturdier in construction than a corresponding weapon retailed for private use, issue weapons will all be marked with either one or two crowned initials below the lockwork. Such an inscription is termed the "cypher mark," and indicates the reign of the monarch in which the weapon entered the Ordnance system. Details of these and Ordnance proof marks will be found in the relevant literature.[1] Pistols made for

The maker's name inscribed across the tail of the lock on a Ketland pistol.

A Tower pistol originally for military issue. This weapon has the crude, heavy wood work characteristic of military weapons and is fitted with a swing-up rammer. *Courtesy of Thomas del Mar, Ltd.*

The lock of the Ketland pistol, showing the maker's name and cipher mark (a crowned GR).

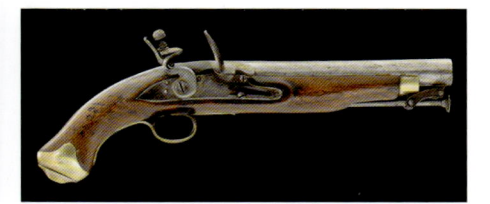

Tower pistol showing the maker's mark (BRANDON & POTTS LONDON). *Courtesy of Thomas del Mar, Ltd.*

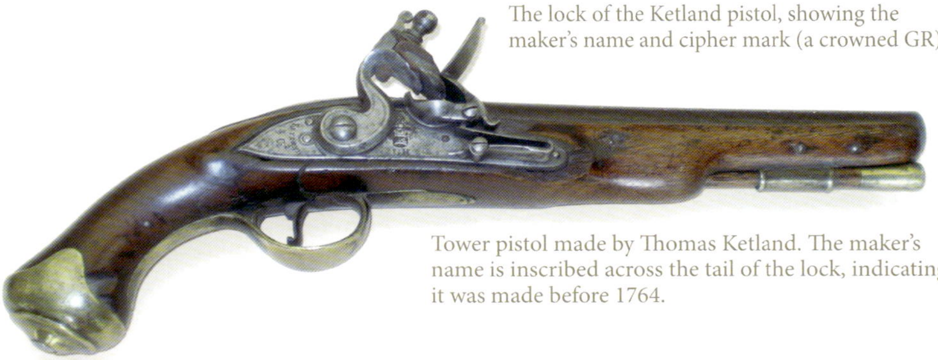

Tower pistol made by Thomas Ketland. The maker's name is inscribed across the tail of the lock, indicating it was made before 1764.

military use before 1764 will normally be inscribed with the maker's name and date across the tail of the lock. After this date, the inscription was changed to "Tower," inscribed in Roman lettering.

Their furniture frequently bears a resemblance to that used on British military muskets made during the same period, suggesting that they were produced under contract and from a sealed pattern in the same way.

Along with issue pistols, many privately retailed arms also saw military use. Private arms are not usually marked as military weapons, and the only way a collector has to follow the history of such a piece is when authentic documentation is found with the weapon.

Values: Good: $1,300-2,200
(£800-1,350)
Fine: $2,800-3,800
(£1,700-2,300)
Rare at UK and U.S. auctions.

MILITARY PERCUSSION REVOLVERS

The first trials of a percussion revolver by the British military were conducted in September 1851, although Collier's flintlock revolver was offered to the military as early as 1823. The trial took place at Woolwich, between a Colt Model 1848 Dragoon revolver and an early Adams self-cocking revolver, possibly in 54 bore. Although a contemporary leaflet published by Messrs Deane, Adams & Deane claimed superior performance for the Adams revolver, neither weapon was adopted for service use.[2] It was not until 1854 that Sam Colt secured his first order from the Board of Ordnance for 4,000 of his revolvers; presumably Model 1851 Navy revolvers, although the records are not clear on this point and the order may have included a number of Pocket Models. Thus, Colt revolvers were the first weapon of this type issued to the British Army, in this case for use in Crimea. Subsequent orders in the same year were for a further 10,500 revolvers, making a total of 14,500 revolvers for 1854, including both Hartford imports and London-made guns. The War Department ordered another 9,000 Colt revolvers in 1855; this was the last order for Colt's weapons, as Adams had now begun manufacturing his double-action Beaumont Adams revolver, which the British military authorities preferred to Colt's weapon.[3]

COLT NAVY 1851

Machine-made revolvers.

Serial Number Ranges:
British military Colt Model 1851 Navy revolvers may be found in a number of serial ranges, including:

Serial number range 1-42000: London-made revolvers based on the Hartford Third Model 1851 Navy (Manufactured: 1854-1855)
Serial number range 42000-85000: Hartford-made Third Model 1851 Navy revolvers (Manufactured: 1854-1855)
Serial number range 179000L-188000L: "Royal Manufactory" revolvers

This second (179000L-188000L) range is characterized by the inclusion of only Hartford Fourth Model 1851 Navy revolvers.[4] It is of particular interest, being associated with revolvers bearing the frame stamp:

ROYAL MANUFACTORY

and some form of American barrel address.

This stamping indicates that they were a later purchase than either the Hartford or London guns bought for use in the Crimea, and it is suggested they may have been bought for issue to the Colonial police. The "L"-suffixed serial number is often found on guns sold through Colt's Pall Mall retail outlet, from where these "Royal Manufactory" guns may have been supplied.

COLT MILITARY PERCUSSION REVOLVERS

Serial range: 1-85000
Colt British military revolvers were based on the Third Model of the Hartford 1851 Navy and were made either at Colt's London establishment or the Hartford factory.

Single-action, open-frame revolver in .36 caliber, with a 7½ inch octagonal barrel and a brass pin forming the foresight; they have the usual hammer-notch rear sight. The top flat of the barrel is stamped:

ADDRESS. COL: COLT. LONDON.
or
ADDRESS : SAM^L COLT NEW-YORK CITY.

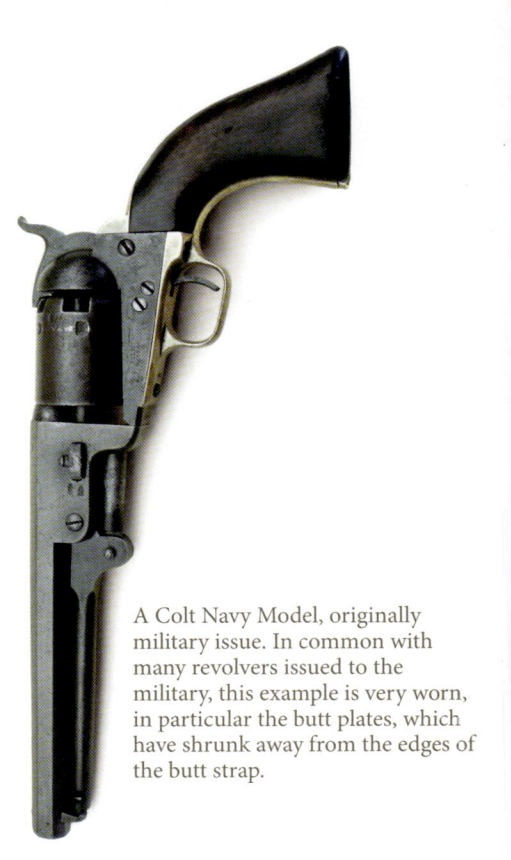

A Colt Navy Model, originally military issue. In common with many revolvers issued to the military, this example is very worn, in particular the butt plates, which have shrunk away from the edges of the butt strap.

The cylinders have six chambers, with rectangular cylinder bolt stops. Normal cylinder engraving on civilian revolvers is die-rolled, depicting the familiar naval battle with a date given as:

16 May 1843

An engraved panel contains "COLT'S PATENT", along with the serial number. Beneath this is stamped:

Engraved by W.L. Ormsby New-York

Military Colt Model Navy revolvers were issued as they were received from the Colt factory. It was only weapons returned for refurbishment that subsequently had all this cylinder decoration removed before re-issue and were inscribed or stamped on the barrel lug with the broad arrow (W /|\ D) of the War Department. Butt plates may be marked with a crowned "BR 7" or similar stamp.

Safety lugs are found on the rear of each cylinder. Cylinder wedges go through the center of the cylinder arbor, with the retaining screw above the wedge. The loading lever screws may enter from either the right or the left. Trigger guards are either iron or brass and round or square-back, with back-straps similarly in iron or brass. Butt plates are one piece, varnished walnut, and either a "Slim Jim" Hartford shape or the characteristic "bell" shape of the London-made Colt revolvers.

Values: Good: $3,800-4,500
(£2,300-2,750)
Fine: $5,400-6,100
(£3,300-3,700)
Cased: $7,400-8,100
(£4,500-4,900)

Rare at UK and U.S. auctions.

MILITARY ISSUE COLT NAVY MODEL REVOLVERS IN SERIAL RANGE 179000L-188000

Colt British military revolvers in this serial range were based on the 4th Model of the Hartford Colt Model Navy 1851 and are usually found bearing a frame stamp:

ROYAL MANUFACTORY

Weapons with this stamp do not usually bear the WD broad arrow, although there may be exceptions to this.[5]
Very rare at UK and U.S. auctions.

BEAUMONT-ADAMS REVOLVERS (1856-1860)

Although a few self-cocking Adams revolvers were bought for trials by the War Department, it was not until the development of the Beaumont-Adams that military revolver purchases really began. The War Department's first order, on 3 January 1856, was for 2,000 "Pistols Revolving, Dean & Adam's Patent, with Lieutenant Beaumont's improve't 54 gauge," and was followed by several others. It is difficult to arrive at an exact number for War Department purchases of Beaumont-Adams revolvers, although a figure of 5,000-10,000 appears to be acceptable.[6]

Frame numbers for military revolvers begin at 14000R, either with or without a "B"-prefixed serial number stamped above it. The frame numbers are in a range: 14000R-B20000/36000R.

This is a solid-frame, double-action revolver in 54/56 gauge with a 7½ inch barrel and three groove, right twist rifling, although exceptions to this (in 38 bore) may be encountered.

The frames are usually of the later "Improved" type. Adams or Kerr loading levers are usually fitted, although a Rigby or Brazier loading lever may be found occasionally on military arms.

Safety bolts are fitted, with the "New" type being the most common, although some revolvers may be encountered with both. Barrel top flats are usually inscribed:

LONDON

The butts are made in one piece of cross-hatched walnut and correspond in most features to civilian arms.

Many Beaumont-Adams revolvers with a military history will be found with the broad arrow "W /|\ D" mark stamped on the rear right side of the frame, indicating they were War Department weapons. Not all revolvers of War Department origin will be so marked, however. It has been suggested that this is because the "W /|\ D" mark was only stamped on weapons returned for repair, refinishing, or conversion to breech loading, and not on newly-issued weapons.[7]

Values: Good: $3,300-3,700
(£2,000-2,250)
Fine: $4,400-5,000
(£2,700-3,000)
Cased: $7,400-8,100
(£4,500-4,900)

Rare at UK and U.S. auctions.

GOVERNMENT-ISSUE METAL CARTRIDGE REVOLVERS

BEAUMONT-ADAMS CONVERSIONS

Beaumont-Adams revolvers will often be encountered as conversions from percussion to metal cartridge. As might be expected, those revolvers were originally chambered in 54/56 bore, with a 7½ inch barrel, and used the government-issue Adams .450 Boxer cartridge after conversion.

All military conversions were on revolvers already in military service and were carried out for the Ordnance Department by the Adams Patent Small Arms Company, which was owned by John Adams—brother of Robert—at his premises in 391, Strand, London. Civilian arms were also converted and are inscribed on the top barrel flat:

ADAM'S PATENT SMALL ARMS COMPANY, 391,STRAND, LONDON

Military Beaumont-Adams showing the "W /|\ D" stamp, early frame number, the cylinder with the gunmakers' proof mark, and the later arbor screw.

Military issue percussion Beaumont-Adams revolver, probably 54 bore, with the "W /|\ D" (War Department) stamp.

Converted Beaumont-Adams "British Army breech-loading pistol, MkI," cased and showing both John Adams's trademarks, a new serial number, and the under-barrel case ejector. The low serial number (3670) suggests this is a converted military revolver, although the short barrel is unusual on this type of weapon. *By kind permission of Bonhams.*

Revolvers converted for the Ordnance Dept. do not have this address.

Converted revolvers will not be found to differ significantly from the percussion weapons previously described, except in those features changed in conversion. A number of other, more rarely seen conversions for the civilian retail trade, including William Tranter's British Patent No 1889/1865, are discussed elsewhere.[8]

BEAUMONT-ADAMS MK1 CARTRIDGE CONVERSION

Serial number range for military arms: 1–7000
Serial number range for civilian arms: 7001–15000

Solid-framed, double-action revolver with a 7½ inch barrel and a cylinder with five chambers designed for the Adams .450 Boxer cartridge. It was accepted by the British government as "Pistol, revolver, Deane & Adams, converted breech loader, Mk1" in 1868. Conversion from percussion consisted of the following operations:[9]

1] Fitting a new breech loading cylinder—still with only five chambers—that was designed to use the original cylinder bolt.
2] Removal of the original loading lever and safety bolt.
3] Removal of the original arbor latch and replacement with a new, spring-loaded component.
4] Fitting a plate across the standing breech to take the pivot of the top-hinged loading gate, this plate having an aperture cut for the hammer nose. A loading groove was also milled or filed in the right side of the frame to fit the loading gate.
5] Fitting an ejector rod.
6] Stamping a new serial number on the right rear side of the frame, with a corresponding number on the cylinder. An acceptance date was also stamped in the corresponding position on the left side of the frame. As an example, a revolver accepted in June 1869 will bear an acceptance date in the form "6.69".
7] Refinishing and re-proofing. Refinishing removed all the former markings, including the original proof and Ordnance Department marks.

Variations
Converted civilian revolvers:
• Cylinder with five chambers in Adams .450 center-fire with a 7½ inch barrel. Barrel stamped:

ADAM'S PATENT SMALL ARMS COMPANY, 391, STRAND, LONDON

Converted military revolvers:
• Cylinder with five chambers in Adams .450 center-fire with a 7½ inch barrel. The barrel address is absent. The War Department "Broad Arrow" is sometimes found, but absence does not indicate a non-military arm.

Values:
Good: $3,100–3,900
(£1,900–2,350)
Fine: $4,100–4,800
(£2,500–2,900)
Cased: $5,800–8,100
(£3,500–4,900)
Rare at UK auctions
Very rare at U.S. auctions.

ADAMS MODEL 1861 CENTER-FIRE REVOLVER

Machine-made revolvers, although they were never purchased by the Ordnance Department. British Patent 1758/1861.

A very rare solid-framed, double-action revolver chambered for six rounds in Adams .450 caliber center-fire cartridge, with the option for use as a percussion or metal cartridge weapon.

Serial number range: Unknown.

The barrel is octagonal and 5¾ inches long, in .450 caliber. Adams designed a special .450 caliber center-fire cartridge for this revolver, which was fitted with a breech plate pierced at each chamber position for the elongated hammer nose. Loading the metal cartridges was carried out by partially withdrawing the cylinder arbor, allowing the breech piece to be swung out, exposing the rear of the cylinder to accept the cartridges. With the percussion cylinder in place, the breech piece was swung out of line in exactly the same way to allow the percussion cones to be capped. Two types of loading lever/ejector were fitted.[10]

This arm was never purchased by the military, but is logically included here with the rest of John Adams's center-fire revolvers.

Variations
The only variation known is that described. It had a cylinder with six chambers, in Adams .450 caliber, with a 5¾ inch barrel.

Very rare at UK and U.S. auctions.

ADAMS 1867 AND 1872 CENTER-FIRE REVOLVERS[11]

Manufactured under British Patent 1758/1861. (This patent also covered the frame design of the 1867 revolver, which was similar to the Model 1861. Lockwork was based on a previously developed, much-copied mechanism and so could not be the subject of a new British patent.)

British Patent 2961/1867: This patent covers the breech loading components applied to the 1861 frame, i.e., the loading groove in the right flash guard, hinged loading gate, and the early case ejector.

British Patent 2258/1872: This patent covers the new 1872 pattern case ejector.

The 1867A revolver was the first design to appear, followed closely by the 1867B, which was adopted by the British Army in 1872 as the Mk II. Soon after its

Adams 1867A center-fire revolver. This model has the more fragile ejection lever and the "turn over" ejector rod and arbor catch. *Courtesy of James D. Julia Auctioneers, Fairfield, Maine (www.jamesdjulia.com).*

Adams Model 1867A center-fire revolver. *By kind permission of Bonhams.*

Adams Model 1867A revolver and holster. *Courtesy of John R. McClean.*

adoption, the 1872 revolver was produced and adopted as the Mk III. Civilian and military arms are exactly the same mechanically; the only difference being the top-strap address inscribed on arms intended for the civilian market.

Adams Model 1867A revolver showing the military frame number, proof mark on the cylinder, and the early Adams (John) patent mark on the lower left of the frame. *Courtesy of John R. McClean.*

Frame or serial numbers:

- 1867A and 1867B (military version of the 1867B designated the Mk II): Serial number range: 500–56000
- 1872 (military version designated MkIII): Serial number range: 5600–18000

Frame numbers for all three models form a continuous series that includes both military and civilian arms randomly distributed. Final numbers are not established and the revolvers in the 17000–18000 serial range were produced by John Adams's successor, the Adams Patent Small Arms Manufacturing Company.

Although produced after the Beaumont-Adams Mk I, the Adams 1867 and later 1872 revolver did not entirely replace the Mk I, and the three weapons appear to have seen parallel use during most of their respective periods of issue.

Solid-framed, gate-loading, double-action revolver in .450 caliber. Barrel is octagonal and 5⅞ inches long, with five groove, right twist rifling, although weapons with 4 and 4½ inch barrels are recorded. They have cylinders with six chambers for the government-issue Adams .450 Boxer cartridge. The loading gate is top hinged and the ejector rod may be locked into a chamber to act as a safety device in all models.

The top flat of the barrel and the top-strap of the frame of civilian arms are stamped:

ADAM'S PATENT SMALL ARMS COMPANY, 391, STRAND, LONDON

The frames of all these revolvers bear patent information, stamped on the lower right side of the frame in the following form:

ADAM'S PATENT NO.

This is followed by what may be a frame, production, or serial number.

The trademark on early revolvers is the bi-lobed mark seen on the Model 1866 Adams revolver, but in revolvers numbered 3000 and above, a new oval mark was used. Both are found stamped on the rear right of the frame, adjacent to the butt, and weapons may be found bearing both marks. Butts are walnut, with the upper portion unchequered.

Variations
- Model 1867A (civilian) Model:
This model was never purchased by the military and was only retailed to the civilian market. It differs from the later 1867 B (Mk II), having a "turn-over" device for releasing both the arbor and

Adams Model 1867A revolver from the left side. *Courtesy of John R. McClean.*

Adams Model 1867B (MkII) revolver showing the later Adams patent mark, upper hinged loading gate, and corresponding numbers on the cylinder and frame. *Courtesy of Collectible Firearms.*

Adams Model 1867B revolver showing the upper hinged loading gate and cylinder and frame conformation. *Courtesy of Collectible Firearms.*

ENGLISH MILITARY PISTOLS

ejector rod. The ejector rod is cylindrical and mounted on the side of the barrel. The barrels are stamped:

ADAM'S PATENT SMALL ARMS COMPANY, 391, STRAND, LONDON.

Cased examples are known, but rare.

• **Model 1867B (civilian):**
Similar in both forms to the Model 1867 A, except the ejector and arbor release takes the form of a spring-loaded button. The hammers and triggers of the civilian weapons are usually bright.

Revolvers purchased from civilian retail outlets are stamped on the top flat of the barrel:

ADAM'S PATENT SMALL ARMS COMPANY, 391, STRAND, LONDON.

Cased examples are known, but rare.

• **Model 1867 Mk II (military purchase):**
Military weapons were adopted by the British military as: "Pistol, Revolver, Adams, Central Fire, Breech Loading, Interchangeable, (Mark II)" in 1872. Mechanically, they are exactly similar to the civilian arms, but may be differentiated by the presence of the "WD" broad arrow to the rear of the frame (either right or left) and the Roman numeral "II" applied to the left of the frame at the front. An acceptance date is usually found stamped on the left of the frame behind the cylinder and a "Viewer's" symbol (indicating the weapon has passed inspection) is often found on the unchequered upper portion of the butt. Hammers and triggers of military weapons (Mk IIs) are usually brown or "russeted." The top-strap address was omitted from weapons intended for military purchase.

Incidentally, the cost to the military in 1872 was $15 (£2 19 s 0d) for each Mk II revolver.

• **Model 1872 (civilian):**
Exactly similar to the two previous models in every respect, except for the new design of the case ejector. This features a shorter, more substantial rod mounted under the barrel and incorporating a tubular rod guide integral with a carrier pivoted to the lower front face of the frame. The rod itself is formed into a bulb or "acorn" at the end nearest the muzzle.

As with the Model 1867B, civilian-purchased revolver barrels are stamped:

Adam's Patent Small Arms Company, 391, Strand, London.

Cased examples are known, but rare.

• **Model 1872 Mk III (military purchase):**
Adopted by the British military as: "Pistol, Revolver, Adams, Central Fire, Breech Loading, Interchangeable, (Mark III)" in 1872. Frame marks are similar to the Mk II, except left of the frame in front of the cylinder is stamped "Mk III". The barrel address is omitted, as with the Mk II.

These are rare revolvers, with a very significant military and technological history, but this does not appear to be reflected in their popularity or value at auction.

Values:
Good: $2,400-3,300 (£1,500-2,000)
Fine: $3,900-4,400 (£2,400-2,700)
Cased: $5,300-6,800 (£3,200-4,100)
Rare at UK auctions
Very rare at U.S. auctions.

Adams Model 1872 (MK III) revolver showing the later pattern case ejector. *By kind permission of Bonhams.*

Adams Model 1872 revolver showing detail of the case ejector from the left. *Courtesy of Collectible Firearms.*

Adams Model 1872 revolver showing the barrel address. *Courtesy of Collectible Firearms.*

John Adams's oval trademark, with his earlier mark to the left. *Courtesy of Collectible Firearms.*

GOVERNMENT ISSUE TRANTER REVOLVERS

Tranter Model 1878 Center-Fire Revolver
Only one model of Tranter's revolvers was purchased for British military use: a solid-frame model produced in 1878. Fitted with Tranter's double-action and chambered for six rounds in .450 center-fire with a six inch barrel, it was produced specifically to enable John Adams to fulfill a contract with the British Army. Although it is not clear how many actually entered service with British forces, a number are recorded stamped with the initials "NZ," indicating they were issued by the New Zealand government.

Variations
- Model 1878 revolver: cylinder with six chambers for Adams's .450 government-issue cartridge, with a 6 inch barrel.

Very rare at UK and U.S. auctions.

ENFIELD MK I AND MK II REVOLVERS (1880-1889)

The Enfield Revolver Mk I and Mk II were top-break, self-extracting revolvers designed and manufactured at Enfield's Royal Small Arms Factory (RSAF) between 1880 and 1889.
Serial number range: Unknown

These were hinge-frame, self-extracting, single- or double-action revolvers.

The cylinders had six chambers, originally in .455 caliber (the later Mk II had a peculiar tapered chambering, going from 0.841 at the breech to .461 at the front of the cylinder), and the model was designated: "PISTOL, REVOLVER, B.L, ENFIELD MK I OR MK II, INTERCHANGEABLE."

Unlike the later (and far superior) Webleys, the Enfield's cylinder moved forward into the space made by the hinge as it opened, supposedly ejecting spent cartridges but leaving any live rounds in the cylinder. The weapon was then closed, latched, and loaded through a conventional loading gate in the right flash shield.

Made as either single- or double-action weapons, the extraction system and poorly designed frame hinge gave constant trouble. Both models were replaced by the Webley Mk I in 1892.

Variations
Enfield Model 1880 Revolver:
- Mk I: Cylinder with six chambers for the Enfield Mk I or Mk II .455 cartridge, or the Enfield Mk III .476 cartridge, with a 5¾ inch barrel. May be single or double-action. The right side is stamped with a crowned mark:

VR
ENFIELD
1881
I

The date is when the gun was received into service, and so will be variable.

- Mk II: Cylinder with six chambers for the Enfield Mk I or Mk II .455 cartridge, or the Enfield Mk III .476 cartridge, with a 5¾ inch barrel. This model differs from the Mk II in having a unique tapered chamber, going from 0.841 at the breech to .461 at the front of the cylinder. The right side is stamped with a crowned mark:

VR
ENFIELD
1884
II

The date is when the gun was received into service, and so will be variable.

Enfield Mk II revolver. *By kind permission of Bonhams.*

Enfield Mk II revolver showing the Ordnance stamp. *By kind permission of Bonhams.*

ENGLISH MILITARY PISTOLS

Values:
> Good: $1,100-1,500
> (£700-900)
> Fine: $2,000-2,500
> (£1,200-1,500)
> Rare at UK auctions
> Very rare at U.S. auctions.

WEBLEY GOVERNMENT-ISSUE REVOLVERS AND THEIR CIVILIAN EQUIVALENTS

Webley Government Model (Mk I-Mk VI) Center-Fire Revolver (1887-1947)
Serial number ranges and adoption dates:

Mk I – Serial number range: 679-41000. Accepted between May and July 1887, with the first order confirmed 18 July 1887 (sealed pattern approved November 1887). Officially adopted 8 November 1892 as "Pistol, Webley, Mk I, B.L Revolver," when it replaced all the older weapons. The original revolver was manufactured to use the Webley .442 center-fire cartridge and early production also included revolvers chambered to use either the Enfield .455 or Enfield .476 cartridge, although later weapons (Mk IV, Mk V, and Mk VI) were chambered only for the Webley .455 cartridge. The initial order was for 10,000 revolvers, with a total of 40,000 weapons eventually supplied.

Mk I* – A later Mk I revolver with modification to the recoil plate.

Mk II – Serial number range (continuous from the Mk I): 44000-61000. Adopted 21 May 1895.

Mk III – Serial number range: 101-80000. Adopted 5 October 1897.

Mk IV – Serial number range (possibly as a continuation of the Mk II): 77000-130000. Adopted 21 July 1899, and known to collectors as the "Boer War" Model. The initial order is unknown.

Mk V – Serial number range: 129000-214000 (higher numbers in civilian arms are recorded). Adopted 9 December 1913, with an initial order of 20,000.

Mk VI – 135000-455000 (in a range shared initially with the Mk V revolver). Approved 24 May 1915 and produced until 1939. Government figures show over 300,000 were made for WWI alone. From 1921, this model was also manufactured by the Royal Small Arms Factory, Enfield as: "Pistol, Revolver, Webley, No. 1 Mk VI."

The guns in this series are all hinge-frame, double-action, self-extracting revolvers chambered for the various government-issue revolver cartridges, featuring a rebounding hammer and fitted with the characteristic lock, frame catch, and self-extraction mechanisms based on the patents of Webley and Carter (British Patent 4070/1885) and Thomas and Henry Webley (British Patent 5143/1881).

The barrel is octagonal, with a top-strap rib, and rifled with seven clockwise grooves of the shallow, Metford type; they may be 3, 4, 5, 6, or 7½ inches in length.

The frame is hinged below the front of the cylinder and fitted with the characteristic stirrup catch, operated by a single lever on the left side of the frame near the hammer.

The cylinder is semi-fluted with six chambers and fitted with an automatic ejector that is actuated when the weapon is opened by the thumb-operated frame catch lever. Cylinder bolt recesses are present on the rear surface of that component and there is also a second series of small rectangular slots near the middle of the cylinder also associated with the cylinder locking mechanism, which is similar to that fitted to the earlier Webley revolvers.

A blade foresight and fixed rear sight are fitted, the front sight being an integral part of the barrel rib.

Webley Mk I revolver manufactured around 1887, and designed to chamber Webley .455 (Mk I) caliber ammunition. It shows the characteristic, semi-fluted cylinder.

The butts are two-piece, "Bird Head" conformation in Mks I-V, conventional in the Mk VI, and are usually of "Vulcanite" ("ebonite")—a rubber compound hardened by the inclusion of sulpher—although walnut plates were occasionally fitted to early weapons. Early weapons were designed to use black-powder cartridges, with a modification introduced during production of the Mk V to allow the use of a cordite round. A significant feature of these revolvers that assured continued government interest was that parts were largely interchangeable.

FRAME STAMPS

Military or civilian proof marks are usually stamped on the barrel or frame and every chamber of the cylinder in a form characteristic for the date. (A crowned "VR" or "GR" above crossed scepters, with a "P" beneath, are most common for government-issue revolvers: see Appendix 1: Proof marks.) Patent information, including the "Mk" of the revolver, is stamped on the left side of the barrel lug or frame and appears in a typical oval format. Government-issue revolvers produced after 1912 are found stamped on the top of the butt strap with the day and month of their year of issue (Ordnance marks) and "Corps marks" ("R.S" for Royal Scots, "R.B" for the Rifle Brigade, etc.), and after 1914 (Mk V and Mk VI revolvers), they also bear a date below the patent stamp that corresponds to the year of manufacture.

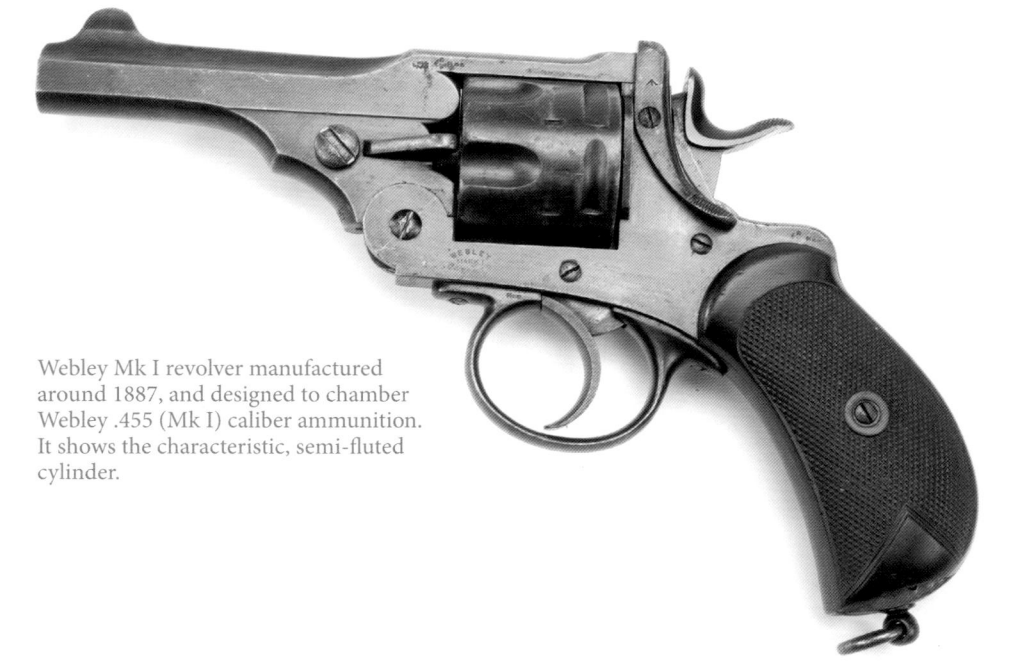

Serial number stamps may be found on either the left or right side of the frame, usually below the cylinder, although their position is variable.

Other stamps include acceptance marks, the War Department's "Broad Arrow," and Webley's "Winged Bullet" trademark. Revolvers issued to the Royal Navy were stamped on the upper surface of the prawl of the butt:

N

They also received three very deep cuts in the form of the W D "Broad Arrow." Details of all these revolvers are found in Bruce and Reinhart.[12]

WEBLEY MK I AND MK I* GOVERNMENT MODEL REVOLVER

Bird-head butt with a 4 inch barrel and chambered for the Government-issue Webley .442, Enfield .455, or Enfield .476 revolver cartridges, with a standing breech in one piece. The modification to the Mk I* revolvers consisted of the introduction of a removable recoil shield in the standing breech. This component was fixed in a dove-tailed slot and secured by a screw, allowing it to be replaced when the aperture for the firing pin showed excessive wear. The cylinder retaining mechanism was similar to the early "W.G." revolvers, taking the form of a broad-headed bolt cut with a wide slot. The left side of the frame or barrel lug is stamped in the usual oval format:

WEBLEY
MARK I
PATENTS

This may also appear as:

WEBLEY
PATENTS

The left side of the top-strap may also be stamped:

MARK " I "

The top-strap stamp may be omitted.

COMMERCIAL MK I GOVERNMENT MODEL REVOLVERS (PRODUCTION: 1890-1894)

Revolvers with the same specification as the Mk I and Mk I* Government Models were also retailed commercially.

Serial number range: 1-41000 (within the range of the Government Mk I revolver)

Chambered for:
Revolvers made from 1890 to 1894: Government-issue cartridges:
- Mk I .450 cartridge or the Mk II .455 cartridge.
- These revolvers would accept both the .450 and .455 cartridges, but not the Enfield Mk III .476 cartridge.

Revolvers made after 1904:
- MkI .450 or Mk II .455
- Mk III .476 cartridge.

Revolvers chambered for both the .450 and .455 cartridges would not accept the Enfield Mk III .476 cartridge.

WEBLEY MKII GOVERNMENT MODEL REVOLVER

Bird head butt, with a 4 inch barrel and chambered for the Government-issue Enfield .455 and Enfield .476 cartridges. The cylinder retaining mechanism was again similar to the early "W.G." revolvers, taking the form of a broad-headed screw

Webley Mk II revolver from the right, retailed by a civilian outlet (JOSEPH LANG & SON, PALL MALL). Courtesy of James D. Julia Auctioneers, Fairfield, Maine (www.jamesdjulia.com).

Webley Mk II revolver showing the retail address on the top-strap (JOSEPH LANG & SON, 10, PALL MALL, LONDON). Courtesy of James D. Julia Auctioneers, Fairfield, Maine (www.jamesdjulia.com).

Webley Mk II revolver (left side) showing the characteristic "Bird's head" butt. The cylinder locking device is a single screw with the broad slot. The frame is stamped ".455/.476" and the cartridges included with the gun are a mixture of "Colt" and "Wilkinson" retailed ammunition. *Courtesy of James D. Julia Auctioneers, Fairfield, Maine (www.jamesdjulia.com).*

Webley Mk II revolver showing frame stamps. *Courtesy of James D. Julia Auctioneers, Fairfield, Maine (www.jamesdjulia.com).*

cut with a wide slot. The butt was reshaped, excluding the prawl and necessitating adjustments to the shape of the butt plates, which were thus not interchangeable with the Mk I or Mk I*. A different pattern of hammer was also fitted with an enlarged spur, intended to improve the revolver for use by the cavalry. The left side of the frame or barrel lug was stamped in the usual oval format:

WEBLEY
MARK II
PATENTS

This may also appear as:

WEBLEY
PATENTS

The left side of the top-strap may be stamped:

MARK " II "
or
MARK " II " .455/.476.

The top-strap stamp is frequently omitted.

COMMERCIAL MK II GOVERNMENT MODEL REVOLVER (PRODUCTION: 1894-1897)

Revolvers with the same specification as the Mk II Government Model were also retailed commercially. These revolvers would accept both the Mk I .450 and Mk II .455 cartridges, but not the Enfield Mk III .476 cartridge, unless specifically designed for it.

WEBLEY MK II POCKET MODEL REVOLVER

Frame number series: 1-800 (Manufactured: 1893)
Intended for the civilian retail market and based on the Mk I Government Model, they differed only in having Whiting's strengthened cylinder release mechanism and proof marks—usually of the Birmingham Proof House—stamped on both barrel and cylinder, in place of the military stamps.

It is a hinge-frame, self-extracting double-action revolver in .38 caliber. The model has a cylinder with six chambers and a 3 or 4 inch barrel. The cylinder release is Whiting's single cam design (British Patent 3427/1891), and some early revolvers are fitted with a flat-faced hammer and a separate striker mounted in the standing breech, held away from the cartridge primer by a small spring. The left side of the top-strap is stamped:

MARK II .380

The frame is stamped with the trademark and:

WEBLEY'S
PATENT

Butts may be "Bird-Head" or conventional in conformation and fitted with either walnut or Vulcanite butt plates, secured by a screw entering from the left.

Variations.
Mk II Pocket Revolver: Cylinder with six chambers and a 3 or 4 inch barrel.

Chambered for:
Short .38 cartridge.

Very rare at UK and U.S. auctions.

Webley Mk III revolver fitted with Whiting's 1884 Patent, single cam cylinder retaining mechanism.

WEBLEY MK III GOVERNMENT MODEL REVOLVER

Birds-head butt with 4 inch barrel, although weapons with 5 and 6 inch barrels were also produced by Webley & Scott. This gun was chambered for Government-issue Enfield .476 or Webley .455 revolver cartridges. The barrel unit and cylinder assembly were improved on this pattern, so these components could

ENGLISH MILITARY PISTOLS

not be interchanged with Mk I or Mk II revolvers. They usually have Whiting's stirrup cam cylinder release mechanism, with the addition of a screw to secure the cam disengagement lever (Br. Pt. 17291/1896). Occasionally, the single lever cam will be found on early military weapons and those intended for the civilian retail market. The left side of the frame or barrel lug is stamped in the usual oval format:

WEBLEY
MARK III
PATENTS

This may also appear as:

WEBLEY
PATENTS

The left side of the top-strap may also be stamped:

MARK " III "
or
MARK " III " .455/.476

The top-strap stamp may be omitted.

COMMERCIAL MK III GOVERNMENT MODEL REVOLVER (PRODUCTION: 1897-1899)

Revolvers with the same specification as the Mk III Government Model were also retailed commercially. These revolvers would accept both the .450 and .455 cartridges, but not the Enfield Mk III .476 cartridge, unless specifically designed for it.

WEBLEY MK III POCKET MODEL REVOLVER

Serial number range continued from the Mk II Pocket: 1600–55000 (Manufactured 1896-1939)

This revolver was based on the Mk II Government Model.

Top-break, self-extracting double-action revolver in .32 or .38 caliber, with cylinders with six chambers and 3, 5, or 6 inch barrels rifled with seven, clockwise grooves. The cylinders in the .32 caliber weapons are "stepped" at the front.

Weapons in both calibers are found fitted with the flat-faced hammer and a separate striker mounted in the standing breech, although this breech-mounted striker is only found on weapons with serial numbers below 11000; conventional hammers were fitted after this number. Early revolvers with low serial numbers (below 7500) were fitted with Whiting's single cam cylinder retaining mechanism, while later guns had the later stirrup cam and a screw on the right of the frame to retain the cylinder cam release lever. Some Mk III revolvers were fitted with a safety device in the form of a horizontal slide on the right side of the frame, adjacent to the butt. Moving the slide forward blocked the action of the hammer, while at the same time exposing the word "SAFE" via a slot in the frame. The top-strap is stamped:

WEBLEY MARK " III " .38
or
WEBLEY MARK " III " .320

The frame is stamped with the trademark and in the usual oval format:

WEBLEY'S PATENTS

Proof marks, usually of the Birmingham Proof House, are stamped on both the barrel and cylinder. The butt is shorter than the military revolver and of conventional shape, with two butt plates in either walnut or Vulcanite. Target Models have a more substantial, one-piece butt.

Variations
Mk III Pocket Model Revolver: Cylinder with six chambers and a 3 or 4 inch barrel.

Manufactured for:
- Webley .320 cartridge
- Smith & Wesson .32 cartridge
- Short .380 cartridge
- Smith & Wesson .38 cartridge
- Webley & Scott .38 "Man-Stopper" cartridge
- Eley .38 cartridge
- Colt .38 cartridge

Mk III Pocket Target Model: Cylinder with six chambers and barrels any length from 6 to 10 inches supplied to the customer's order. The butt is in one piece and walnut.

Manufactured for:
- Webley .320 cartridge
- Smith & Wesson .32 cartridge
- Short .380 cartridge
- Smith & Wesson .38 cartridges
- Webley & Scott .38 "Man-Stopper" cartridge
- Eley .38 cartridge
- Colt .38 cartridge

Very rare at UK and U.S. auctions.

WEBLEY MK IV GOVERNMENT MODEL REVOLVER

This is the "Boer War" Model. This model was manufactured using better quality steel than the previous revolvers, as well as a number of case-hardened parts. These revolvers and the subsequent Mk V and Mk VI are fitted with Whiting's improved cylinder retaining mechanism, featuring the later, more robust stirrup cam and a screw on the right of the frame to prevent accidental operation of the cylinder cam release lever (British Patent 17291/1896).

They have a bird-head butt with a 4 inch barrel and are chambered for the Webley .455 cartridge. Revolvers with 5 and 6 inch barrels were also produced by Webley & Scott. The left side of the frame or barrel lug is stamped in the usual oval format:

WEBLEY
MARK IV
PATENTS

This may also appear as:

WEBLEY
PATENTS

The left side of the top-strap may also be stamped:

MARK " IV "

The top-strap stamp may be omitted. These revolvers and the later Mk V and Mk VI do not usually bear the .455/.476 stamp, as the Enfield .476 cartridge was declared obsolete in 1892 and stocks had been sufficiently depleted to render the stamp unnecessary.

Webley Mk IV revolver (left side) showing the characteristic Whiting Patent 1896 cylinder retaining system with the stirrup-shaped cam fitted to the breech lug. This device was introduced with the earlier Mk III, which is similar in conformation to this revolver.

military Mk IV revolver in having an improved butt shape and the option of better quality target sights.

Serial number range: In the same range as the Mk IV-Mk VI Government Model revolvers.

A top-break, double-action revolver made for the Government-issue .450 and Webley Mk I .455 cartridges. It has a semi-fluted cylinder with six chambers and 4, 6, or 7½ inch barrels rifled with seven clockwise grooves, although later examples (126870 and above) have six-groove rifling and an improvement to the frame catch. The frame is stamped:

WEBLEY'S
PATENTS

The left side of the top-strap is stamped:

W.S. ARMY MODEL
or
W.S. TARGET MODEL

The breech lug is stamped with chambering information:

.450/.455

Proof marks, usually of the Birmingham Proof House, are stamped on the barrel and cylinder. The butt is a conventional target shape in Vulcanite or walnut. Fixed front and rear sights were fitted as standard, but a laterally adjustable rear sight was available for both Army and Target Models from Webley & Scott.

Variations
Webley "W.S." revolver:

- "W.S." Army Model: Cylinder with six chambers for the Webley Mk I .455 cartridge. It has a 6 inch barrel and Vulcanite butt plates.
- "W.S." Target or "Bisley Target" Model: Cylinder with six chambers for the Webley Mk I .455 cartridge and a 7½ or 12 inch barrel, as well as Vulcanite butt plates.

WEBLEY MK V GOVERNMENT MODEL REVOLVER

Birds-head butt and a 4 inch barrel chambered for the Webley .455 cartridge; the frame and cylinder are enlarged

In revolvers produced after 1912, the top of the butt strap may be stamped with the day and month of their year of issue and "Corps" marks.

Revolvers with the same specification as the Mk IV Government Model were also retailed commercially, chambered for the Government-issue Webley .455 revolver cartridge and its commercial equivalents.

CIVILIAN WEBLEY MK IV GOVERNMENT MODEL, OR "W.S" REVOLVERS

These were made using the same components as the Webley Government Mk IV and produced by Webley & Scott in 1902. The guns differed from the standard

Webley Mk V revolver from the left side.

ENGLISH MILITARY PISTOLS

to allow the use of smokeless (cordite) cartridges. Weapons with 5, 6, and 7½ inch barrels were also produced by Webley & Scott in 1915. Those guns with 6 and 7½ inch barrels were designated for land service or Army issue only. The left side of the frame or barrel lug is stamped in the usual oval format:

WEBLEY
MARK V
PATENTS
1914

The year stamp signifies the date of issue and appears on revolvers produced from 1914 onwards. This may also appear as:

WEBLEY
PATENTS

The left side of the top-strap may also be stamped:

MARK " V "

The top-strap stamp may be omitted. The top of the butt strap may be stamped with the day and month of the year of issue and "Corps" marks.

Webley Mk VI showing frame stamps and a conventional butt with two ebonite butt plates. *By kind permission of Bonhams.*

COMMERCIAL MK V GOVERNMENT MODEL REVOLVERS (PRODUCTION: 1913-1939)

Revolvers with the same specification as the Mk V Government Model were also retailed commercially. They were chambered for the government-issue Webley .455 revolver cartridge and its commercial equivalents.

WEBLEY MK VI GOVERNMENT MODEL REVOLVER (1915-1947)

This revolver had a characteristically square or "Target" butt and a six inch barrel with removable foresight. It was chambered for the Government-issue Webley .455 cartridge and fitted with a strengthened frame catch similar to the

Webley Mk VI (right side) showing the serial number stamped on the cylinder and the frame catch with its characteristic "V" spring. *(NRAmuseum.com)*

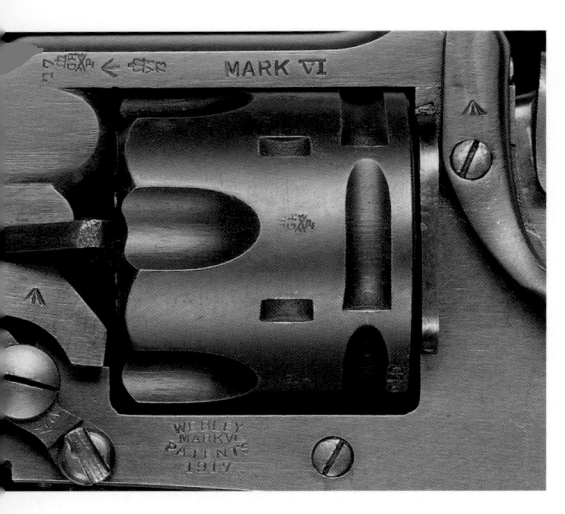

Webley Mk VI showing frame stamps. The stamp at the top left—a crowned "GR" above crossed scepters and a "P"—is a military proof mark. By kind permission of Bonhams.

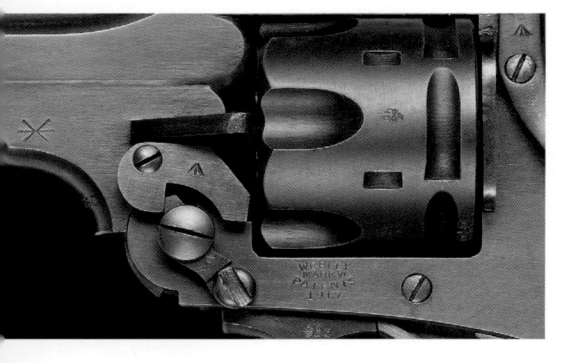

Webley Mk VI revolver showing its cylinder retaining mechanism and the cam release lever, secured by a screw in this revolver. By kind permission of Bonhams.

Webley Mk VI revolver (left side) cutaway armorer's training model.

later "W. G." models. The left side of the frame or barrel lug is stamped in the usual oval format:

WEBLEY
MARK VI
PATENTS
1918

The date indicates the year of manufacture. It may also appear as:

WEBLEY
PATENTS

The left side of the top-strap is almost invariably stamped:

MARK " V I "

The top of the butt strap may be stamped with the day and month of the year of issue (Ordnance mark) and "Corps" marks.

Variations and Additions:
- A version with a 4 inch barrel and integral foresight was made in the serial number range 453000–454000.
- A .22 caliber training model of the Webley Mk VI was also produced by Webley & Scott, featuring a shorter cylinder, round barrel that protruded through the frame and a raised foresight.
- Optional additions to the Government-issue Webley Mk VI revolver included the Pritchard revolver bayonet attachment and a shoulder stock.
- Butt plates from 1919 were made in small, medium, or large sizes and were marked "S," "M," or "L" accordingly.

ENFIELD PRODUCTION OF MK VI REVOLVERS

Serial number range: 135000-455000 (in a range shared with the Webley-made Mk VI revolver), but prefixed "A."

Manufacture of the Mk VI was transferred in 1921 to RSAF, Enfield. Revolvers produced in that factory during this period are exactly similar to the Webley arms, except they bear the crowned "ENFIELD" stamp on the right of the frame, with Mk to the left and VI to the right.

COMMERCIAL MK VI GOVERNMENT MODEL REVOLVER (PRODUCTION: 1915-1947)

Revolvers with the same specification as the Mk IV Government Model were also retailed commercially and were chambered for the Government-issue Webley .455 revolver cartridge and its commercial equivalents. Weapons with a 7½ inch barrel and "Target" Model sights were also available.

Values:
Webley Mk I-Mk VI Government Model revolvers.
   Webley Mk I-Mk V
      Government revolvers.
      Good: $2,100-2,500
         (£1,300-1,500)
      Fine: $3,000-3,300
         (£1,800–2,000)
   Common at UK auctions.
   Rare at U.S. auctions.

   Civilian Mk I-Mk V
      Government revolvers.
      Good: $2,400-2,800
         (£1,500-1,700)
      Fine: $3,100-3,500
         (£1,900-2,100)
      Cased: $5,000-6,600
         (£3,000-4,000)
   Rare at UK and U.S. auctions

   Webley Mk VI Government revolver.
      Good: $1,500-1,800
         (£900-1,100)
      Fine: $1,900-2,100
         (£1,200-1,250)
   Very common at UK auctions.
   Common at U.S. auctions.

ENGLISH MILITARY PISTOLS

Civilian Mk VI Government revolver.
Good: $2,300-2,700
(£1,400-1,600)
Fine: $2,900-3,300
(£1,800-2,000)
Cased: $4,000-6,600
(£3,000-4,000)
Rare at UK and U.S. auctions

MIXED COMPONENT VARIATIONS IN WEBLEY GOVERNMENT MODEL REVOLVERS

Due to the way parts for these revolvers could be easily interchanged, collectors may find some peculiar variations arising as the result of either repairs carried out by British Army armorers, or expediency at the Webley factory. Frames from Mk I revolvers may be found fitted with components more prone to wear from later revolvers; so, for example, it would not be unlikely to find a Mk I frame fitted with a Mk VI barrel, Mk V cylinder, and the later, broader Mk II hammer, as well as other variations of a similar nature.

WEBLEY MARK IV .38/200 CENTER-FIRE REVOLVER (1923-1963)

Officially adopted for military service in 1942, this was essentially a version of the Webley Mk III Government revolver chambered for the .380 Mk I Government-issue cartridge and developed by Webley & Scott in 1921 from the Mk III Pocket revolver.

Webley submitted an experimental version of this revolver to the War Office in 1921; following trials, the British government decided to accept a .38 caliber revolver to replace the .455 Mk VI in October 1926. Webley began preparations for manufacture—only to find that production of the new revolver, based largely on their design, had been allocated to the RSAF factory at Enfield. Webley claimed compensation for patent infringement, but received only $1,900 (£1,200), and it was not until the outbreak of war in 1939 that production of this revolver for the British government began again at the Webley & Scott factory.

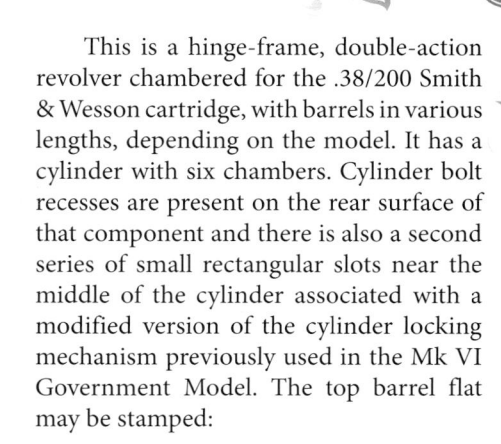

Webley Mk IV .38/200 revolver with a 5 inch barrel showing the "Webley" embossing on the butt plate. Courtesy of James D. Julia Auctioneers, Fairfield, Maine (www.jamesdjulia.com).

Webley Mk IV .38/200 revolver with a 4 inch barrel. Courtesy of James D. Julia Auctioneers, Fairfield, Maine (www.jamesdjulia.com).

This is a hinge-frame, double-action revolver chambered for the .38/200 Smith & Wesson cartridge, with barrels in various lengths, depending on the model. It has a cylinder with six chambers. Cylinder bolt recesses are present on the rear surface of that component and there is also a second series of small rectangular slots near the middle of the cylinder associated with a modified version of the cylinder locking mechanism previously used in the Mk VI Government Model. The top barrel flat may be stamped:

WEBLEY & SCOTT LTD BIRMINGHAM

The side of the top-strap is usually stamped:

Mk IV

Along with the usual military proof, serial number, and acceptance stamps, civilian models are stamped with Birmingham proof marks on the barrel and cylinder. The foresight was a fixed blade either with a round or square profile, while the rear sight was either fixed or adjustable. The butts were two pieces in either Vulcanite or walnut.

Variations
Webley Mk IV .38/200 revolver (Production 1939-1979)
Webley Mk IV Government Model .38 revolver (Production 1939-1947): Serial number range: 1–172000: Cylinder with six chambers and a 5 inch barrel.

Chambered for:
Smith & Wesson .38/200.

Commercial Models.
Serial number ranges (all models):
1923-May 1947: 1–41000
May 1947-March, 1957: A1–A100000
March 1957-September 1979: B0-B 88165

Police and Military Model (Production 1923-1939): Cylinder with six chambers and a 3, 4, or 5 inch barrel.

Chambered for:
- Webley .38 "Man-Stopper" cartridge
- Smith & Wesson .38 cartridge
- Smith & Wesson .32 Long cartridge
- Smith & Wesson .32 Standard cartridge
- Colt .32 New Police cartridge

Target Models (Production 1923-1967):

Target Model, .38 caliber (Production 1923-1967): Cylinder with six chambers, 4 inch barrel, and adjustable rear sight. Revolvers produced after 1945 had a 6 inch barrel.

Chambered for:
- Webley .38 "Man-Stopper" cartridge.
- Smith & Wesson .38 cartridge

Target Model, .22 rim-fire caliber (Production 1932-1967): Cylinder with six chambers, .22 caliber, and a 6 inch barrel.

Chambered for;
- Commercial .22 Short Rifle (SR) cartridge
- Commercial .22 Long Rifle (LR) cartridge
- I.C.I Non-Rusting .22 cartridge

American cartridges:
- High-Velocity .22 cartridge

Values:
Good: $2,300-2,600
(£1,400-1,600)
Fine: $2,900-3,300
(£1,800-2,000)
Common at UK and U.S. auctions.

ENFIELD NO.2, MKI (1932-1963)

The Webley Mk IV was copied by Royal Small Arms Factory Enfield and issued to British forces as the Enfield No.2 Mk I after slight internal changes, which means parts for the Webley and Enfield .38 revolver are not interchangeable. Enfield also produced a Mk I*, which was self-cocking, and so had no trigger spur; and a Mk I**, which was a simplified version of the earlier Mk I.

These revolvers bear the Enfield Armoury stamp, in the form of a large crown with "ENFIELD" above, the date of manufacture below, and "NO 2" and "MK 1" on the left and right of the crown, respectively.

Enfield No. 2 Mk I revolver showing the characteristic frame stamps "ENFIELD" above a crown, with "No 2" and "Mk I" to the left and right, respectively, all above the date of manufacture (1932). (NRAmuseum.com)

Enfield No. 2 Mk I revolver based on the Webley Mk IV, 38/200. (NRAmuseum.com)

Variations
Enfield No 2 revolvers.

- Enfield No.2 Mk I*: Similar to the original Webley, with slight internal changes, which mean that parts are not interchangeable between the two revolvers. Enfield revolvers with 6 inch barrels are recorded.

Values:
Good: $2,300-2,600
(£1,400-1,600)
Fine: $2,900-3,300
(£1,800-£2,000)
Rare at UK and U.S. auctions

- Enfield No.2 Mk I*: Similar externally to the Enfield No.2 Mk I, but the mechanism is self-cocking, so there is characteristically no trigger spur. Designed specifically for use by the Tank Corps, as the spur-less hammer was considered less likely to snag on the tank crews' overalls.

Enfield No. 2 Mk I revolver. This is an example of the self-cocking variant of the Mk 2, specifically designed for tank crews. The absence of the hammer spur differentiates it from the earlier revolver. (NRAmuseum.com)*

Very rare at UK and U.S. auctions.

- Enfield No2 MkI**: Similar externally to the Enfield No.2 Mk I, but the mechanism is simplified.

Very rare at UK and U.S. auctions.

The Indian Ordnance Factory (IOF) also produced a copy of this revolver, which may be differentiated from Enfield guns by the butt bearing an embossed "IOF," although they are similar in other respects.

GOVERNMENT-ISSUE REVOLVER CARTRIDGES

This list of cartridge types is based on current literature, but includes only those center-fire cartridges mentioned in the text.[12]

The cartridge size is included here in the form caliber/powder loading/bullet weight, with the last two in grains.

BLACK POWDER CARTRIDGES

.422 cartridge. (.422/10/219): Originally produced to match the caliber of the 54 bore Government-issue Adams revolver, which used a pure lead ball .442 inches in diameter. Developed for Webley's R.I.C. revolver from a rim-fire design by William Tranter, it was not approved for use until 4 June 1892 as:

CARTRIDGE, SMALL ARM, BALL, PISTOL, .442-INCH (MARK I).

It was declared obsolete by the War Department on 14 March 1921.

.450 CARTRIDGES

Adams cartridges:

Adams/ Boxer Mk I .450. (.450/13/225): approved for Naval service in December, 1868 as "CARTRIDGE, SMALL ARM, BREECH-LOADING BOXER (MARK I)" for the converted Beaumont-Adams revolvers then entering service. It was declared obsolete by the War Department on 23 August 1894.

Adams Mk II .450 (.450/13/225): Approved for service in September 1877 as "CARTRIDGE, SMALL ARM, BALL, PISTOL, REVOLVER, ADAMS, B. L. (MARK II)" for the Adams revolvers then in service. It was declared obsolete by the War Department on 23 August 1894.

Adams Mk III .450 (.450/13/225): Approved for service in September 1877 as "CARTRIDGE, SMALL ARM, BALL, PISTOL, REVOLVER, ADAMS, B. L. (MARK III)" for the Adams revolvers then in service. It was declared obsolete by the War Department on 14 March 1921.

ENFIELD CARTRIDGES

A new revolver cartridge was introduced for service use in August 1880, coinciding with the adoption of the Enfield .455 revolver.

Enfield Mk I and Mk II .455 (.455/18/265): Officially approved 30 November 1880 as "CARTRIDGE, SMALL ARM, BALL, PISTOL, REVOLVER, ENFIELD, B. L. (MARKS I & II)," it was declared obsolete by the War Department on 26 September 1892.

Enfield Mk II and Mk III .476 (.477/18/265): Officially approved 30 November 1880 as "CARTRIDGE, S A, BALL, PISTOL, REVOLVER, ENFIELD, B. L.(MARKS II & III)." The bullet had a hollow base filled with a plug of baked clay, intended to expand the ball into the rifling in a manner reminiscent of the earlier Minié bullet used in the P53 and P56 Enfield muzzle-loading and Snider breech-loading rifles. It was declared obsolete by the War Department on 26 September 1892. (Webley Mk I introduced 1891.)

WEBLEY .455 CARTRIDGES

The British Government accepted the first Webley revolver for service in 1887 and subsequently, these cartridges were introduced for those revolvers and the earlier Enfields.

Webley MkI .455 cartridge (.455/18/265): Approved 29 June 1891 as "CARTRIDGE, S A, BALL, PISTOL, WEBLEY (MARK I)." The last of the British Army's black powder revolver cartridges, it was declared obsolete on 6 August 1912.

CORDITE CARTRIDGES

Webley Mk I .455 cartridge (.455/6.5/265): Approved on 14 September 1894 as "CARTRIDGE, S A, BALL, PISTOL, WEBLEY, CORDITE (MARK I)." These cartridges bear a head stamp that includes the letter "C," indicating they differ from the earlier black powder round. It was declared obsolete on 19 March 1946.

Webley Mk II .455 cartridge (.455/ 7.5/ 265): Approved on 5 February 1898 as "CARTRIDGE, S A, BALL, PISTOL, WEBLEY, CORDITE (MARK II)." These cartridges used a Berdan Pattern primer and bear a head stamp that includes the letter "C," indicating they differ from the earlier black powder round. This cartridge was first declared obsolete in 1898, then was reintroduced on 14 March 1900. It was declared obsolete again on 20 May 1912, after the introduction of the Webley Mk IV, although some stocks of Mk II cartridges were remade to the Mk IV pattern and stamped on the head "IV." The cartridge was declared obsolete for "Land Service" 18 September 1939, Naval Service 3 November 1939, and Air Service 1 December 1939.

Webley Mk III .455 cartridge (.455/ 7/ 218.5): Approved on 5 February 1898 with the Mk II cartridge as "CARTRIDGE, S A, BALL, PISTOL, WEBLEY, CORDITE (MARK III)." This cartridge was loaded with Webley's patent "Man-stopping" pattern bullet (British Patent 14754/1897), which featured a deep cavity in the nose and a similar depression in the base. This round proved to have too violent an effect on human tissue and a more moderate round was introduced to replace it. It was declared obsolete 18 November 1902.

Webley Mk IV .455 cartridge (.455/ 7/ 220): Approved on 20 May 1912 as "CARTRIDGE, S A, BALL, PISTOL, WEBLEY, CORDITE (MARK IV)." This cartridge was also loaded with a pattern of "Man-stopping" bullet, but although retaining the hollow base, it was now flat-nosed, giving it a less extreme effect. It was declared obsolete in 1914.

Webley Mk V .455 cartridge (.455/ 7/ 220): Approved on 9 April 1914 as "CARTRIDGE, S A, BALL, PISTOL, WEBLEY, CORDITE (MARK V)." This cartridge was loaded with the same pattern of "Man-stopping" bullet as the Mk IV, but instead of being cast of 1:12 tin and lead/alloy as all the previous Webley bullets were, this was cast as a 99:1 lead/ antimony alloy. It was declared obsolete on 9 November 1914.

Webley Mk VI .455 cartridge (.455/ 7.5/ 265): This final design, designated "CARTRIDGE, S A, BALL, REVOLVER, .455 inch, Mk VI," was a metal-jacketed cartridge introduced in 1939 and declared obsolete for Land Services on 26 March 1946, marking the end of the British Army's association with the .455 revolver cartridge.

MK I AND MK 2 .380 REVOLVER CARTRIDGES (.38/ 3.7/200)

Mk I .380 revolver cartridge: Introduced on 6 November 1930 as "CARTRIDGE, S A, BALL, REVOLVER, .380 inch, MARK I," but is always listed as the ".38 – 200." Quite soon after issue of the Mk I .380 cartridge began, it was found the revolvers chambered for commercial .38 cartridges, including the ubiquitous Smith & Wesson .38 Special cartridge, would not accept the Government-issue Mk I .380 cartridge. After December 1940, many revolvers were re-chambered to accept the Government .380 cartridge and those originally regulated for the Smith and Wesson .38 special cartridge are stamped on the barrel:

38/380

Unmodified weapons designed for the Smith & Wesson .38 Special had the rear end of the barrel painted with a red band and were additionally marked with a stencil, in black:

38 SPECL

Some early cartridges were loaded with 2.5 grains of nitrocelluolose, instead of the 3.7 grains of cordite of the conventional round, and these bear a "Z" in addition to their normal head stamp. It was declared obsolete for Land Service on 6 September 1957.

Mk II .380 revolver cartridge (.380/ 4/ 180): Introduced on 22 October 1937 as "CARTRIDGE, S A, BALL, REVOLVER, .380 inch, Mark II." Mk II cartridges were also loaded with three grains of nitrocellulose, and these cartridges had a head stamp:

MARK II. Z

It was declared obsolete by 1963, when the Browning Hi-Power was introduced as the British Army's government-issue handgun.

CHAPTER SEVEN

Accessories

Firearms accessories form a collecting field all their own, although the auction value of such items is usually much lower than weapons from the same period. There is also quite a lucrative, reputable market in reproduction items of this sort. Oil bottles, Dixon and Hawkesley powder flasks, bullet molds, and even case labels are all available from well known and entirely reputable retailers. Needless to say, these items have not escaped the attention of less scrupulous members of the gun collecting fraternity, and a particularly careful inspection of any such additions is recommended, especially if they seem out of place: for example, a particularly good label on a worn case, apparently containing a rare gun.

BULLET MOLDS

Bullet molds are usually found included with sets of cased pistols and revolvers. They were essential for very early weapons, as calibers tended to be variable and bullets usually had to be cast by the owner to ensure they would fit a particular weapon.

Molds were produced in a number of patterns. Most common are those made in two halves, in a form similar to a pair of pliers or pincers. In operation, the mold is closed and molten lead is poured through an orifice at the top. Excess lead is removed by operation of a flat plate called the sprue cutter, attached to the top of the mold. When cool, the bullet or ball is simply tipped or knocked out. Revolver molds are often made to cast either a round ball or shaped bullet, while other types were designed to allow multiple castings, usually two or four balls at a time. Modern versions of most molds are available and have been found included in cased sets in place of the original.

Molds are sometimes offered for sale separately or as part of a collection of accessories.

GUN CASES

Made to contain a particular type of weapon and of characteristic construction, these items were sold with a set of accessories for use with a particular pistol and constructed in polished hardwood, often fitted with brass reinforcing.

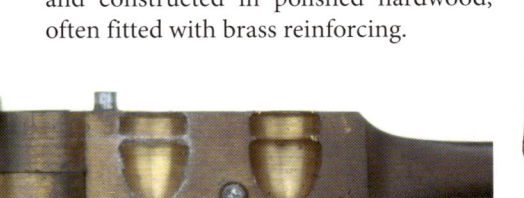

Cased Daw revolver showing compartments and a complete set of accessories. Such cases are characteristic of those made for revolvers, being divided into compartments, rather than molded for the weapon, as was the case with earlier flintlock and percussion arms. Both the barrel and butt of the weapon reach completely to the end of its compartment, showing the case was originally made for either this revolver or the same model.

Exterior of the Daw case, showing a brass plate or escutcheon inset in the lid.

Bullet mold. This one was sold with an Adams revolver and makes two conical bullets, rather than the more usual ball.

A leather carrying case frequently supplied with Webley revolvers. This one is marked "H.C. NOEL 17th LANCERS"; the mark has clearly been applied by the owner. *Courtesy of James D. Julia Auctioneers, Fairfield, Maine (www.jamesdjulia.com).*

A case label from an Adams-Tranter, Kerr revolver. Robert Garden is listed in Blackmore's "Guide" at this address from 1862-1877, providing good evidence for the date of manufacture of this revolver. *Courtesy of James D. Julia Auctioneers, Fairfield, Maine (www.jamesdjulia.com).*

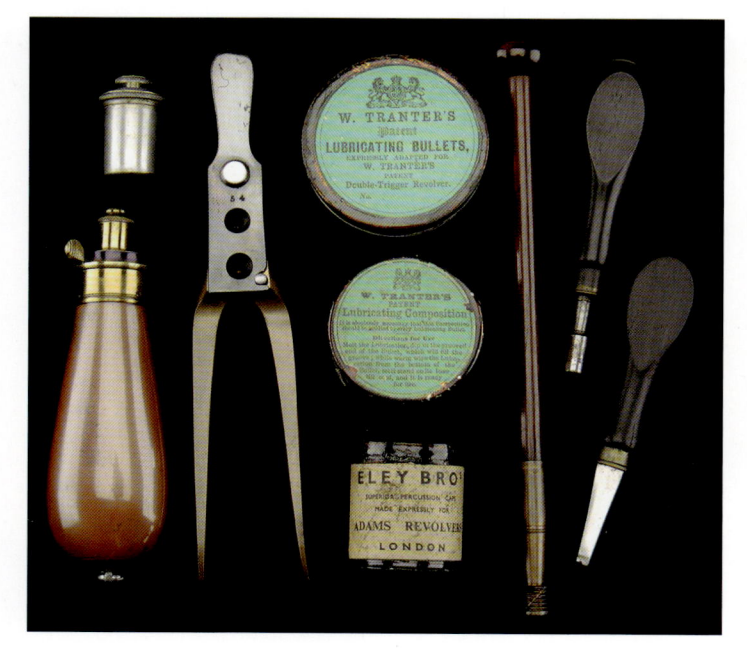

Accessories from a cased Adams-Tranter, Kerr revolver, shown left to right: a powder flask, an oil bottle (above), bullet mold, various tins, a cleaning rod, a nipple key, and a screwdriver. The tins and their labels are in particularly good condition. *Courtesy of James D. Julia Auctioneers, Fairfield, Maine (www.jamesdjulia.com).*

ACCESSORIES

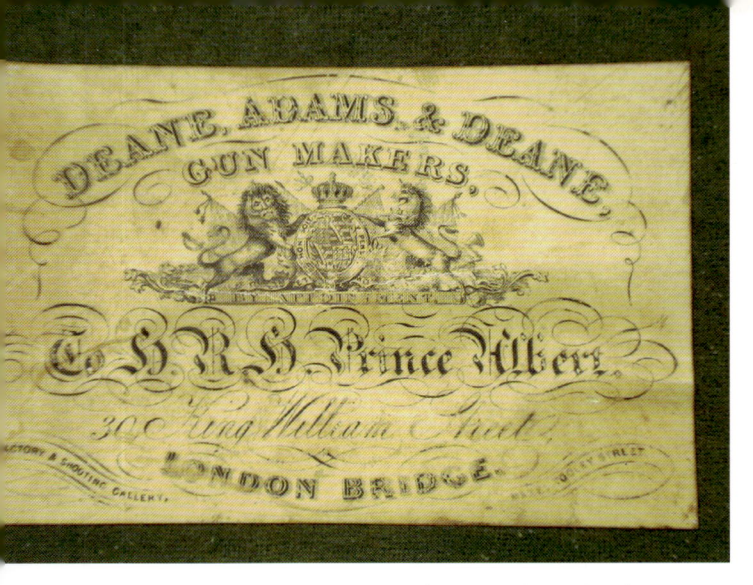

Case label of a Deane, Adams & Deane; this example is taken from a cased Deane-Harding revolver.

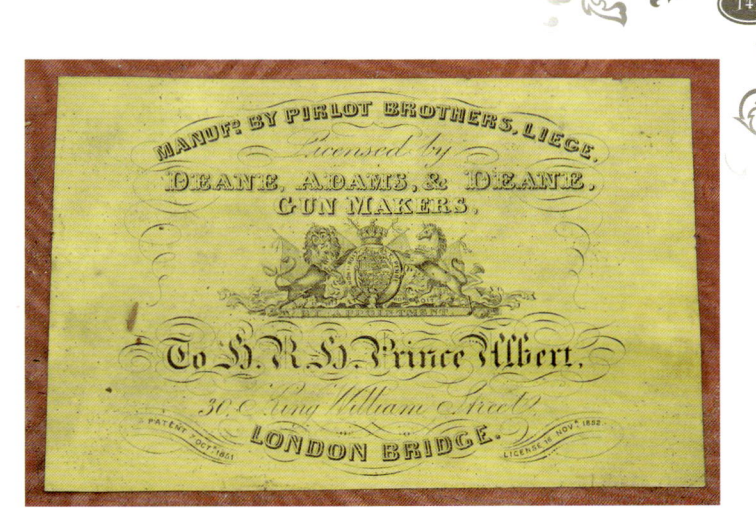

Case label from an Adams revolver of Belgian manufacture, "PIRLOT BROTHERS, LIEGE." *Courtesy of James D. Julia Auctioneers, Fairfield, Maine (www.jamesdjulia.com).*

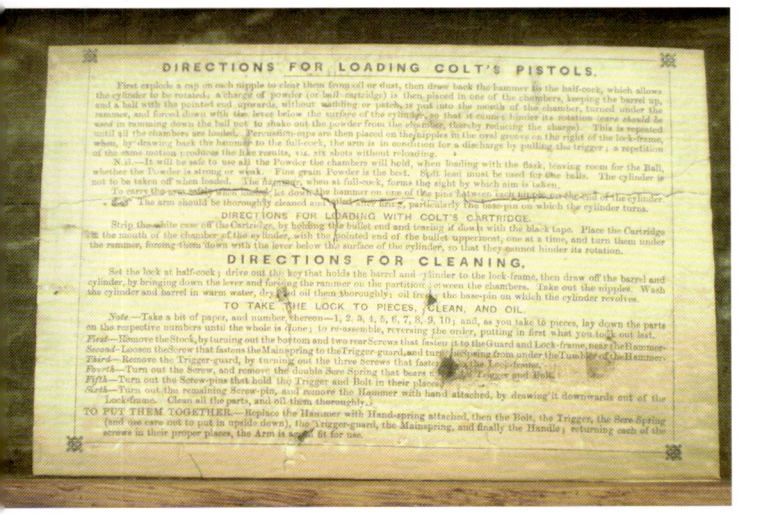

Label frequently included in a case with a Colt percussion revolver, giving directions for loading and cleaning the weapon.

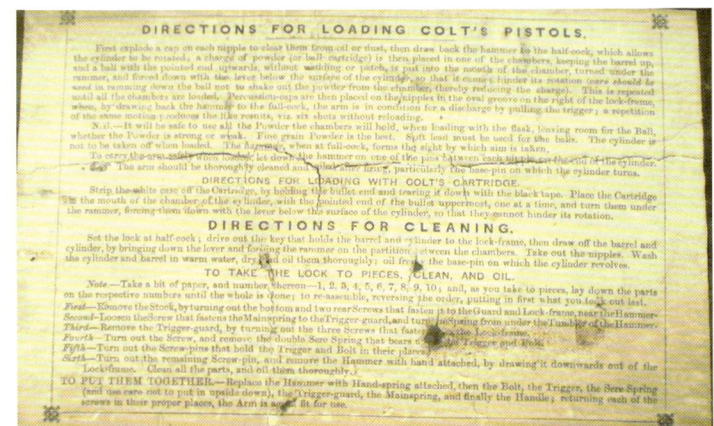

Colt cleaning label at high magnification.

Maker's label for "E. M. REILLY & CO. Gun Manufacturers, 502, NEW OXFORD STREET, LONDON" from a case containing a Webley 3rd Model Longspur. *Courtesy of James D. Julia Auctioneers, Fairfield, Maine (www.jamesdjulia.com).*

Maker's label for Wilkinson & Son from a case containing an Adams revolver. *Courtesy of James D. Julia Auctioneers, Fairfield, Maine (www.jamesdjulia.com).*

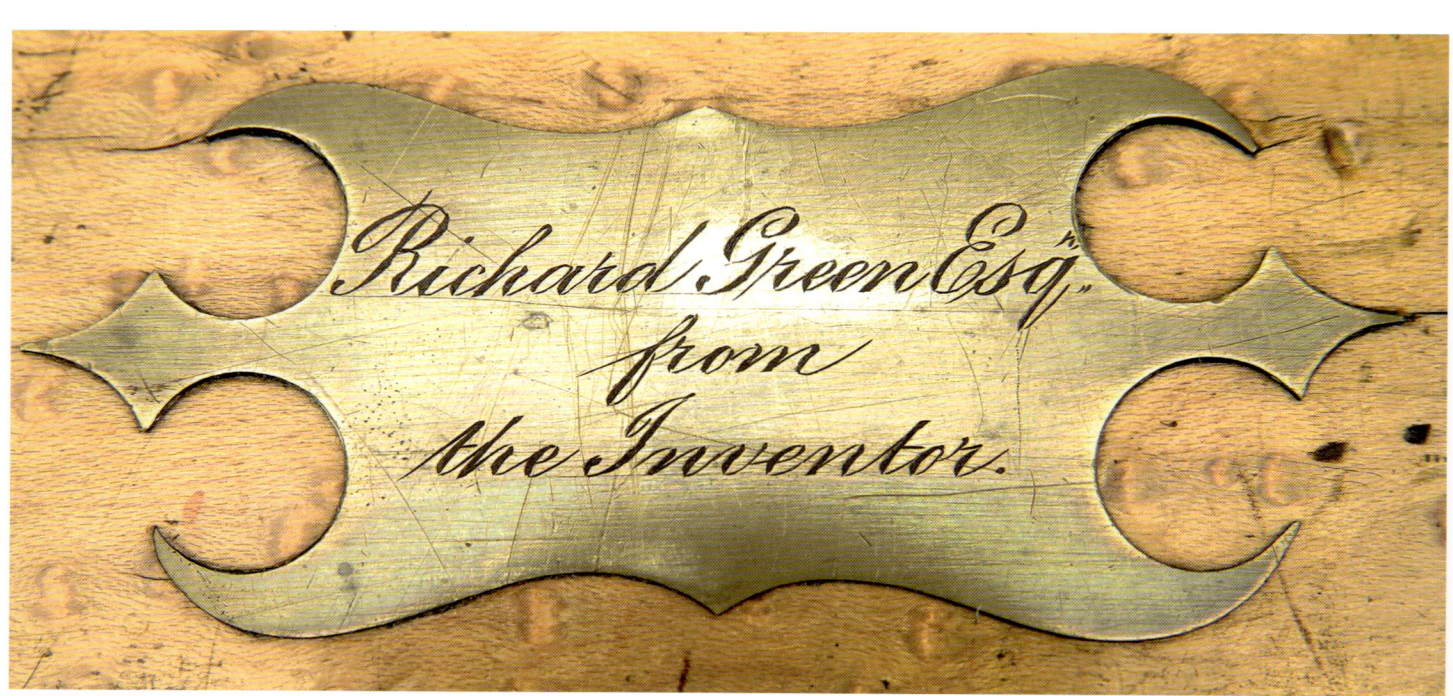

The brass plate or escutcheon from the lid of a presentation Colt revolver. *Courtesy of James D. Julia Auctioneers, Fairfield, Maine (www.jamesdjulia.com).*

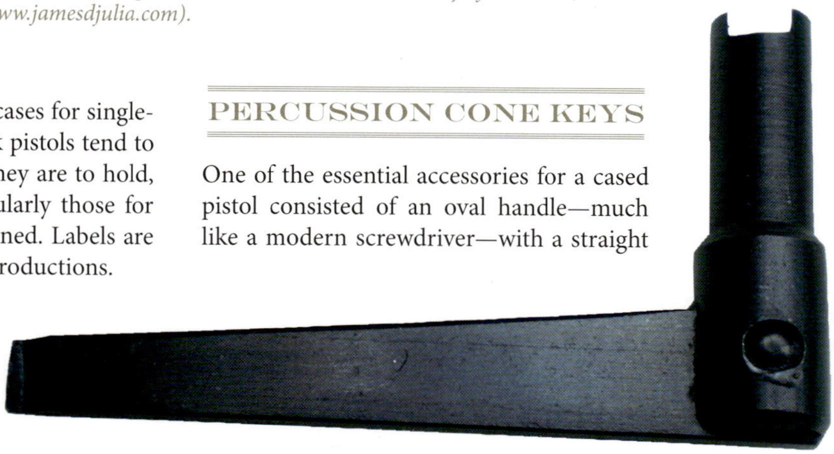

The key for removing the cones from a percussion revolver, in this case a Colt.

As a general rule, early cases for single-shot percussion and flintlock pistols tend to be molded for the weapon they are to hold, while later examples, particularly those for revolvers, are simply partitioned. Labels are available as very accurate reproductions.

PERCUSSION CONE KEYS

One of the essential accessories for a cased pistol consisted of an oval handle—much like a modern screwdriver—with a straight

ACCESSORIES

shaft ending in a socket of appropriate shape to fit the percussion cone supplied with the gun. Revolvers were also often supplied with a small collection of tools, such as a screwdriver, cleaning rod, and other more (or less) useful items. They are not usually considered very collectible, except where a single item may be required to complete the accessories of a cased revolver.

OIL BOTTLES

Supplied by a number of makers, as usually indicated by a stamp or inscription on the body of the bottle. Produced in a variety of shapes, but mostly square or round, they have a tight-fitting screw cap. In a cased set, the compartment for the oil bottle was designed to accept a specific shape and modern manufacturers offer a variety of replacements for this component. Originals appear to be rare and, apart

Modern copy of an English "Dog and Partridge" powder flask from a design by Hawkesley.

from their condition, new and original bottles are difficult to differentiate.

In reality, whether the oil bottle in a cased set is of original or modern manufacture probably will not affect its value very much. However, if a seller does try and pass off a modern bottle as original, the question then arises: what else has not been made clear? Small details can sometimes add up to a significant problem and the rule is or should be, if something is not original, the buyer should be told.

POWDER FLASKS

Produced in a huge variety of patterns, powder flasks form a significant collecting field of their own. Early patterns may be found in metal, wood, and, most frequently, cow horn, and they are usually fitted with some form of powder measure.

The lid of a box originally containing percussion caps produced by Eley & Co.

The spout of the Hawkesley flask, showing its spring-loaded operation.

A powder flask made by James Dixon & Co. This is a standard accessory sold with a cased English percussion revolver. The spout may be adjusted to give powder measures of 5, 10, and 15 grains.

Cased pistols, revolvers, and sometimes rifles were sold with a flask, and some of these had a nozzle that could be adjusted to give the correct load for the firearm being charged. These later flasks were die-stamped from a variety of metals and produced by a number of companies, the most commonly found being those made by Thomas Sykes, James Dixon & Sons, G & J Hawkesley, and Peter Frith & Sons. Hawkesley powder flasks are available as modern reproductions.

CARTRIDGES AND CARTRIDGE BOXES

Cartridges and cartridge boxes are another collecting field that is becoming increasingly popular. In many ways, some of the earlier ammunition, such as Williamson's "Teat-fire" (made for Moore's revolver), Pond's "cup-fire," and Crispin's phenomenally dangerous "belted" cartridges are as interesting as the weapons they were designed for. A good Internet site for the beginning collector is www.oldammo.com.

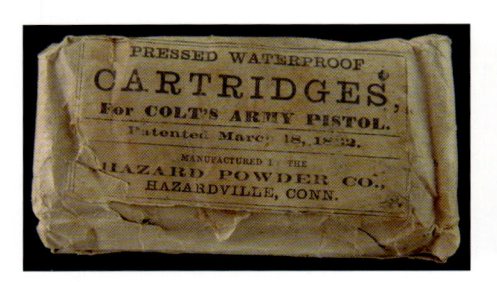

Cartridge box containing supposedly waterproof cartridges for a Colt percussion revolver. *Courtesy of James D. Julia Auctioneers, Fairfield, Maine (www.jamesdjulia.com).*

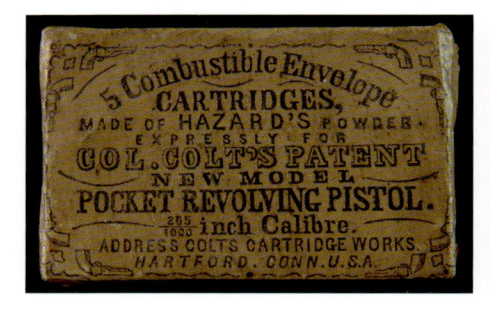

Cartridge box containing five foil cartridges for a Colt Pocket Model percussion revolver showing the "265/1000 inch Caliber" label. *Courtesy of James D. Julia Auctioneers, Fairfield, Maine (www.jamesdjulia.com).*

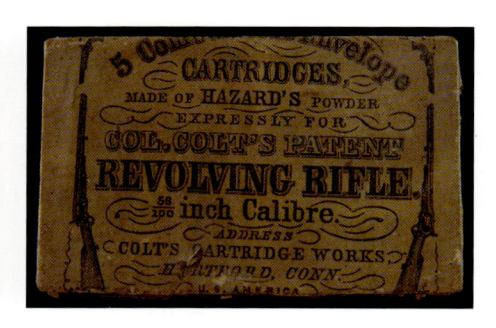

A cartridge box containing five foil cartridges for a Colt percussion revolver. *Courtesy of James D. Julia Auctioneers, Fairfield, Maine (www.jamesdjulia.com).*

Cartridge box containing five foil cartridges for a Colt revolving rifle showing the "56/100 inch caliber" label characteristic of these weapons. *Courtesy of James D. Julia Auctioneers, Fairfield, Maine (www.jamesdjulia.com).*

Cartridge box containing 50 center-fire cartridges for a Bull Dog revolver. *Courtesy of James D. Julia Auctioneers, Fairfield, Maine (www.jamesdjulia.com).*

Powder, percussion cap, and ball—vital ingredients for revolver shooting.

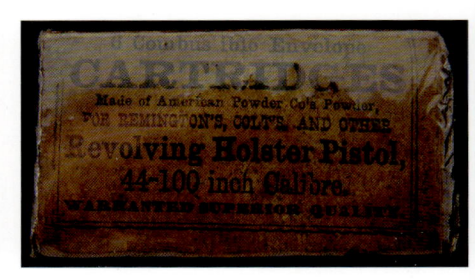

Cartridge box containing six foil cartridges for a .44 caliber revolver showing the "44-100 inch Caliber" label characteristic of these weapons. *Courtesy of James D. Julia Auctioneers, Fairfield, Maine (www.jamesdjulia.com).*

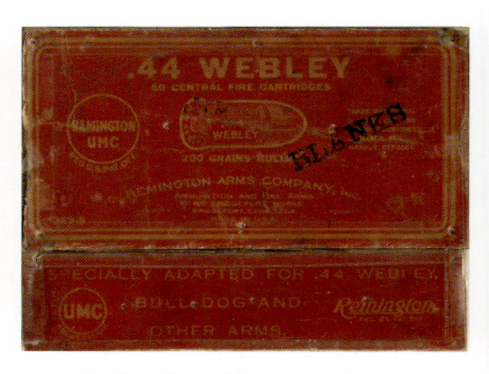

Cartridge box for Webley center-fire cartridges.

POWDER TESTER

This is a device for testing the quality of powder before it was used in a gun. They take a variety of forms, most having the appearance of a small, barrel-less pistol, but all worked essentially the same way.

A specified quantity of powder was placed in a receptacle, then fired. The force with which the lid of the container was blown off was measured against the pressure of a spring attached to a pointer. Different powders could only be compared using the same tester, as there was no method for calibrating one such device against another.

Only the more commonly encountered accessories for revolvers are described here. Full details of less common pieces are included elsewhere in Pollard.[1]

Powder tester. *Courtesy of Thomas Del Mar, Ltd.*

ACCESSORIES

CHAPTER EIGHT

Collecting Antique Revolvers

Since 1998, there have been changes to UK law which have made it increasingly difficult for British collectors to own revolvers of significant historic interest. It is therefore recommended that the most scrupulous care be exercised when buying revolvers, especially if the seller is not a recognized dealer.

WHAT IS AN ANTIQUE FIREARM?

What follows is only intended for guidance; it would be advisable to begin any collection with purchases from a reputable dealer who specializes in antique firearms.

In Britain, owning an antique firearm does not require a firearms certificate [FAC], so long as that gun is kept as an antique or curio, no ammunition is held for it, and it is not of "modern manufacture," which means made after 1939 (Section 58(2) of the Firearms Act 1968).

Such an antique firearm is not defined in law, but guidelines from the Home Office suggest the following may be considered antique:[1]

- A muzzle-loading firearm of original manufacture.
- A breech-loading firearm using a rim-fire cartridge exceeding .23 caliber (although there are some exceptions).
- A breech-loading firearm of original manufacture, using an ignition system other than rim-fire or center-fire.
- A breech-loading center-fire firearm originally chambered for cartridges that are now obsolete and retaining that original chambering. If modern cartridges may be easily obtained for it, then the gun may not be considered an antique. In this case, however, such a weapon may be held if it is deactivated and the subject of a deactivation certificate supplied by a reputable gunsmith.

Certain antique weapons may be fired legally, but they must then be shown on the user's FAC.

If there is any uncertainty about the status of a firearm, it is advisable to check with the local Police Firearms Licensing Unit or the Home Office before purchasing that weapon, whatever the owner's purpose for owning it.

In America, any gun made before 1898 is considered antique and does not require a Federal Firearms license. Most replica muzzle-loading guns are also exempt from federal jurisdiction, although antique exemptions are also the subject of state regulations and may vary depending on the state the owner of an antique resides in. Weapons over 50 years old may also be held by an individual holding a Curios and Relics License (Type 03 Federal Firearms Licence). Once again, the best advice for a collector is to check with the local police or federal authority if one is unsure about the status of a particular weapon.

IDENTIFICATION AND THAT INITIAL EXAMINATION

Preliminary identification of a firearm is reasonably straightforward, in that it will be fairly obvious if the firearm being examined is a rifle or pistol, flintlock, percussion, or metal cartridge, and either single or multiple shot.

When making this initial examination, there are a few simple rules—just plain courtesy, really—which may save a lot of trouble and expense:

1) Never pick up a gun without first obtaining the owner's permission and ensuring that it is not loaded.
2) Never point a gun at anyone, even if it is an antique.
3) Never "dry fire" or similarly abuse any firearm, especially an antique. Having obtained the owner's consent, test the action by bringing it to full cock and then, with a thumb over the hammer spur, ease back the trigger and lower the hammer carefully to rest. Better still, get the owner to demonstrate the action first, especially if you are unfamiliar with that type of weapon.
4) Handle a gun only by the stock or butt, and if it is necessary to touch the metal parts, do so as lightly and as little as possible. If available, a pair of light cotton or thin rubber gloves are useful to prevent the residue from fingers being deposited on the metal, where they are a potential source of rust.

Having made a preliminary examination and identified the type of weapon, it is the next stage—that of determining the maker and possibly the model, along with its authenticity—where most difficulty arises, particularly with an older piece. For the beginner, the following examination procedure may be helpful, but it is only a guide and should be treated as such. When first starting to buy and collect firearms, there is no substitute for advice from a more experienced friend. Points to observe include:

Look for any form of maker's or retailer's marks. These may be on the barrel, frame, or top-strap of a revolver, or occasionally some other area. For example, Webley cartridge revolvers are readily identifiable by the company's famous "Flying Bullet" trademark. Care needs to be exercised, however, because such marks are often faint and covered by rust or surface pitting.

Check for proof marks. These may be from the London or Birmingham house and are discussed more fully in the appropriate Appendix. Although not as good an indicator as a maker's name, they can help in deciding the origin of a gun, as well as dating it.

Look at the overall appearance. This takes a bit of experience, but ask yourself, to begin with, simply does it look right? For example, is the wood work worn in the right way? Has a coat of new varnish been applied over worn wood work? Does the metal work similarly look properly aged? Is the finish original, or are there areas of wear on the metal—especially around any engraving—where the finish is new, but the metal underneath is worn, indicating that a new coating has been applied?

Is the condition of both metal and wood work consistent? For example, if the wood work is clean and crisp and the metalwork looks distinctly tired, or vice-versa, why is that?

What is the appearance of any numbers, letters, etc.? Are they all in similar condition, and do all the letters of any engraving match? Are they appropriate, e.g., does what is claimed to be a military gun have private markings? Are there any marks or scuffing around such engraving, indicating they may have been altered?

Is there any feature that is out of place, indicating a repair or worse, a change to increase the piece's value?

Do not be put off by this list. Most guns that a collector looks at will be exactly what they seem, especially if the weapon is in the hands of a dealer, but there are no guarantees, and so never buy without making a thorough examination.

CONDITION AND VALUATION

Assessing the condition and, therefore, ultimately, the value of an an antique firearm is a very subjective process. In order to make it less so, America's National Rifle Association (NRA) organized a number of collecting committees that formulated a set of guidelines termed "Condition Standards" which are summarized here. Detailed discussion of these Condition Standards and other factors affecting price are included in Flayderman's excellent "Guide." The condition standards are as follows:

Factory new (sometimes referred to as "mint"): Parts are all original, with 100% original finish; condition is perfect in all areas.
Excellent: Parts are all original, with approximately 80% of original finish; all marking on both wood and metal is crisp and clear; wood is without marks and the bore is clean and sound.
Fine: Parts are all original, with approximately 30% original finish; all markings on both wood and metal are crisp and clear; minor marks on wood, bore is clean and sound, but may have minor wear to the rifling.
Very Good: Parts are all original, with 30% original finish; all markings on both wood and metal are crisp and clear; wood may be worn or slightly damaged; the bore is clean and sound, but with signs of reasonable use.
Good: Various replacement parts; external metal and wood showing signs of use, which may include rusting, pitting, or some form of refinishing. All markings still legible. The weapon still has a working mechanism (although it is not necessarily safe to shoot).
NB: "Good condition" is a term often found imprecisely applied to guns, particularly by sellers who do not regularly deal in such items.

Fair: Some important parts may have already been replaced and there may be minor parts missing. Wood and metal parts may be in need of minor renovation, with markings only barely legible. The mechanism still works and any repair work is simple for an experienced collector.
Poor: The replacement of many important parts is required. Both metal and wood work are in need of significant replacement. Marks are not visible, and the mechanism does not operate. This is one for the amateur gunsmith.

PRICE AND VALUATION

Price, like condition, is a subjective process with firearms, and in the final analysis, a weapon is worth what the buyer is willing to pay for it.

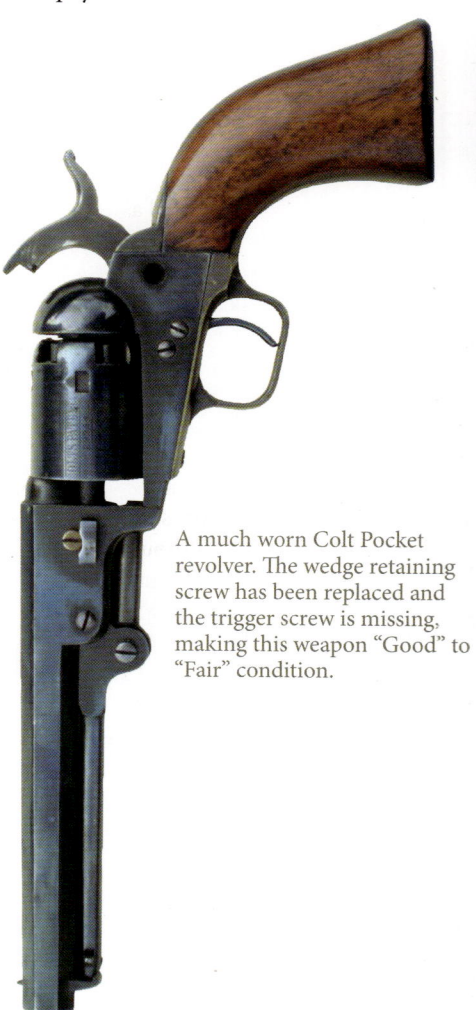

A much worn Colt Pocket revolver. The wedge retaining screw has been replaced and the trigger screw is missing, making this weapon "Good" to "Fair" condition.

The position of the serial number on a modern reproduction Colt Navy. Antique weapons often have matching numbers on the trigger guard, as well.

FAKES...AND FAKING

This is a subject for a book in itself, but a brief discussion is in order here.

RESTORATION...OR FAKE?

This is the most important question that should concern anybody buying an antique gun. What is legitimate restoration and what is a fake?

What follows is a personal assessment of a very difficult area, but it is offered here for what it may be worth.

If a weapon has suffered deterioration, from whatever cause and to whatever extent, and the owner subjects it to a process or a number of processes, including the manufacture of new parts, which is designed to restore it to its original condition, that is restoration. A restored weapon should always be sold as such, at least by the restorer, although a seller cannot be blamed if they unknowingly buy and subsequently sell a restored weapon. Depending on the weapon, a restored weapon is usually worth less than an original, untouched weapon in the same condition.

When a weapon is not returned to its original condition, but is enhanced or changed in some other way for the purpose of increasing its value, that weapon is a fake. Such processes can be as simple as inscribing a new, different serial number on a revolver cylinder so it matches the number on the frame, or stamping military markings on a weapon without such provenance.

Away from what may or may not be the restoration or faking of antique weapons is the field of replica arms. These are becoming increasingly common, and many are extremely good weapons. However, they cost significantly less than an antique example of the same gun and are potentially a good field for the antique swindler.

Reproduction revolvers that have been made to appear antique can be difficult to spot, although they all have serial numbers in places the originals do not, usually on the butt or barrel. Removal will usually leave a mark, most typically a dishing of the metal and scratches where the number has been removed. Also, they "feel" new: edges are sharp, brass furniture is not worn, and wood is crisper than it should be. In the last extremity, analysis of the metal from which a gun is made can be used to identify a reproduction revolver.

FAKING TECHNIQUES

Although this list is by no means exhaustive, some common devices to watch out for include:

- Changing a modern replica firearm to pass it as an original.
- Changing a common model so that it appears to be a less common model (for example, privately owned percussion Colts altered so as to appear to be a gun issued by the Confederate government).
- Adding engraving or frame marks to a gun. This also includes altering the serial number on a cylinder to match that on the frame (or vice-versa).
- Creating false historical documentation or adding engraving, e.g., a maker or owner's name, to create a false history.

Clearly, it is the intention of the owner that determines whether a weapon is a restoration project or a fake and, in this context, the relevant section in Flayderman's "Guide" is well worth reading.

APPENDIX ONE

Proof Marks

Weapons are "proved" in order to ensure that they have been properly made and are safe to fire. Every country has its own system of proof and individual marks to show that a particular weapon has passed the tests imposed by their Proof House. Weapons that have successfully undergone this process are said to have "passed Proof."

Proof of antique black powder weapons in nineteenth century England consisted of two processes. Barrels were first submitted to the relevant Proof House in an unfinished condition for "provisional" proof. They were inspected, and if the barrel passed this first "viewing" procedure, it was fired with a double or treble charge of powder and ball. Another inspection followed, and if the barrel was considered to have "passed proof," it was stamped with the "Provisional" Proof mark, although not all gunsmiths bothered with the expense of this initial procedure.

After finishing and before "setting up," barrels and cylinders were re-submitted for "definitive" proof. They were inspected or "viewed" once again to observe any obvious defects, and those that passed this second inspection were stamped with the House's "View" mark. After passing this stage, barrels and cylinders were fired with a lighter charge than that used for definitive Proof, usually double the normal load. They were then inspected, and if found to be satisfactory, were stamped with the House's definitive "Proof" mark.

LONDON'S PROOF HOUSE

In London, weapons made before 1638 were proofed either by the Honourable Blacksmith's or the Honourable Armourer's Company. Barrels seem to have been subjected to a single proof, since both companies had only one mark: that for the Blacksmith being a crowned anvil, while the Armourers used a crowned "A."

This situation became simplified in 1638, with the formation of the Gunmaker's Company, although records show that their first Charter of Incorporation did not confer sufficient powers to make gun barrel proving mandatory. This was rectified in 1672 by a second Charter, with proof testing now being the sole responsibility of the Gunmakers. Their first View mark was a "V" surmounted by a four-looped crown, while the definitive

Detail of the Royal cipher mark (GR) from a Ketland pistol.

Ketland pistol showing the position of the Cipher mark, visible below the pan.

London Gunmakers Company definitive Proof mark on the cylinder of a Beaumont-Adams revolver.

Gunmakers Company View mark on the cylinder of a Colt Navy Model revolver. Courtesy of James D. Julia Auctioneers, Fairfield, Maine (www.jamesdjulia.com).

Diagram of the London Gunmakers Company definitive Proof and View marks.

PROOF MARKS

Proof mark had a similar format: a "G P" also surmounted by a similar four-looped crown. By 1702, both marks had been modified, with the view mark being a "V" surmounted by a two-looped crown and the definitive proof mark taking the form of the conjoined letters "GP," also similarly crowned. In addition, both marks may be found stamped in oval recesses from this date. The Gunmakers' provisional proof mark for the whole period was the letters "G P" interlaced below a rampant lion, although this mark is not as commonly seen on revolvers as the other two.

GOVERNMENT PROOF MARKS

The Tower Armories conducted their own proof tests on weapons purchased for the government, so such marks are only encountered on military weapons. A proof house was erected at the Tower in 1682 and the royal C.R. cipher (for Charles, Regina), crowned, was adopted as the official service Proof mark. The Tower View mark for this period was a rose and crown.

After 1702, their View mark consisted of a crowned Royal Cipher (G.R. or V.R., depending upon the monarch) above a broad arrow, while the Proof mark was crowned, crossed scepters. The broad arrow, incidentally, was not actually part of the view mark, but rather denoted that the arm in question was government

Gunmakers Company View and definitive Proof mark on the breech of a Manhattan revolver. Courtesy of Mike Meulewy.

Breech of a Martini-Henry rifle showing the Royal cypher mark, a crowned "V.R." (Queen Victoria). Courtesy of Stewart Chamberlain.

Gunmakers Company definitive Proof mark on the cylinder of a Colt Navy Model revolver. Courtesy of James D. Julia Auctioneers, Fairfield, Maine (www.jamesdjulia.com).

Tower private View and Proof marks.

Birmingham definitive Proof mark on a Cooper's pepperbox. A crown and scepters may just be made out; the quality of this stamp is usual for weapons of this period.

property. Occasionally, private arms were also proofed by the Tower. Both View and Proof marks on these weapons were the same as the military Proof mark; that is, crowned, crossed scepters. Confusion may arise, however, because this stamp was also used by some Birmingham gunmakers—notably Ketland's private Proof House—prior to 1813. In these cases, a barrel address or maker's name may indicate the origin of the weapon.

Many military weapons will also be found with marks from the government's Enfield Armoury, which began weapons production in 1818. Their View mark for this period was a crowned "TP" above a broad arrow (standing for "Tower Proof"), the Proof mark once again being crowned with crossed scepters, making it difficult to distinguish from the Tower mark. Ordnance proof marks in the period between Charles 1st's execution and Victoria's reign are a complex collection, and those interested are best advised to consult the relevant authority.[1]

As well as these official marks, London guns may be found with several other types of stamp. After 1741, barrels were sometimes marked with a crowned "F" between the View and Proof marks. This mark denotes a weapon made by a "foreigner"; that is, a gunmaker who was not a member of the Gunmakers Company. Barrels may also be found stamped with a gunmaker's initials, as well as the View and Proof marks, showing that the weapon had been proofed by that gunmaker as well as the Proof House.

BIRMINGHAM'S PROOF HOUSE

London's Gunmakers Company was not the only organization authorized to proof firearms. A Proof House was also established in Birmingham in 1813, and proof there was conducted in exactly the same way as the London house. The Birmingham house is sometimes referred to as the "Guardians."

Prior to 1904, a Birmingham view mark consisted of a crown above crossed scepters with a "V" beneath. The provisional proof was denoted by a crowned, interlaced "BP." The definitive proof mark was slightly more complex, with the crowned, crossed scepters being interspersed with the separate letters "B," "P," and "C." Stamping of this mark is sometimes poor, and it is easily confused with the Tower stamp,

Alternative appearance of Birmingham View and definitive proof marks. They are poorly struck and details are not clear.

PROOF MARKS

A diagram of Birmingham House's definitive Proof and View mark.

although the presence of the unambiguous Birmingham "View" mark should prevent any difficulties of interpretation.

After 1904, the View mark became a crowned "BV" and the Proof mark also changed to a crowned "BP," although the mark for provisional proof remained unchanged.

Breech of a Martini-Henry rifle showing (bottom to top) the Birmingham Proof House provisional Proof mark, View mark, and definitive Proof mark for the period after 1904. *Courtesy of Stewart Chamberlain.*

FOREIGN PROOF MARKS

Foreign proof marks are also encountered on British revolvers, in particular those of the Liege House. Adams revolvers produced under license by Continental gunmakers often bear these marks, which consist of an "E" above an "L G," with a star beneath and the whole device enclosed in an oval ring.

A Krider Le Mat showing the Liege Proof mark on its cylinder. This example has a more legible appearance than is usually the case with the stamps from this House. *Courtesy of James D. Julia Auctioneers, Fairfield, Maine (www.jamesdjulia.com).*

Diagram of Liege Proof mark

One area of confusion concerning proof marks is their frequent presence on firearms that cannot possibly have been manufactured in England, leading to some confusion over the origin of such weapons. Any firearm that is imported into the UK by law must be submitted for proof, even if the weapon in question is only in transit. Similarly, if the barrel, lockwork, or cylinder of a weapon was repaired by a reputable gunsmith, such an arm was also usually re-proofed as a precaution, so clearly, English proof marks do not necessarily indicate a gun made, or even sold, in the UK.

SHOOTING ANTIQUE GUNS

If an antique weapon is bought for shooting, it would be prudent to have it checked by a reputable gunsmith and then re-proofed by the relevant authority. The nature of the powder originally used in such weapons means they are particularly prone to levels of corrosion that can make them extremely dangerous to shoot. Even after they are checked and re-proofed, antique weapons are best fired with a powder charge of half or even a third of that for which they were originally designed.

Endnotes

CHAPTER 1: English Revolvers
1. Taylerson, AWF, RAN Andrews, & J Firth. *The Revolver 1816-1865*. (London, UK: Herbert Jenkins & Co 1968), pg s 24-25.
2. Blackmore, H L. *British Military firearms: 1650–1850*. (London, UK: Herbert Jenkins & Co, 1961).
3. Taylerson, AWF, RAN Andrews, & J Firth. *The Revolver 1816-1865*. (London, UK: Herbert Jenkins & Co 1968), pg s 60-61.
4. Taylerson, AWF, RAN Andrews, & J Firth. *The Revolver 1816-1865*. (London, UK: Herbert Jenkins & Co 1968), pg 64.
5. Taylerson, AWF, RAN Andrews, & J Firth. *The Revolver 1816-1865*. (London, UK: Herbert Jenkins & Co 1968), pg 239.
6. Taylerson, AWF, RAN Andrews, & J Firth. *The Revolver 1816-1865*. (London, UK: Herbert Jenkins & Co 1968), pg s 209-215.
7. Chamberlain W.H.J and A.W.F Taylerson. *Adams' Revolvers*. (London, UK: Barrie & Jenkins, 1976), pg 67.
8. Taylerson, AWF, RAN Andrews, & J Firth. *The Revolver 1816-1865*. (London, UK: Herbert Jenkins & Co 1968), 117–119.
9. Taylerson, AWF, RAN Andrews, & J Firth. *The Revolver 1816-1865*. (London, UK: Herbert Jenkins & Co 1968.)
10. Taylerson, AWF, RAN Andrews, & J Firth. *The Revolver 1816-1865*. (London, UK: Herbert Jenkins & Co 1968), Appendix, pg s 293–342.
11. Chamberlain W.H.J and A.W.F Taylerson. *Adams' Revolvers*. (London, UK: Barrie & Jenkins, 1976).
12. Taylerson, AWF, RAN Andrews, & J Firth. *The Revolver 1816-1865*. (London, UK: Herbert Jenkins & Co 1968), Appendix, pg s 293–342.

CHAPTER 2: Smaller English Revolver Manufacturers
1. Rosa, Joseph G. Colonel. *Colt London: The history of Colt's London firearms, 1851–1857*. (London, UK: Arms & Armour Press, 1976).
2. Flayderman, Norm. *Flayderman's Guide to Antique American Firearms …and their values*. (Iola, WI: Krause Publications), pg 87.
3. Rosa, Joseph G. Colonel. *Colt London: The history of Colt's London firearms, 1851–1857*. (London, UK: Arms & Armour Press, 1976).
4. Rosa, Joseph G. Colonel. *Colt London: The history of Colt's London firearms, 1851–1857*. (London, UK: Arms & Armour Press, 1976).
5. Taylerson, AWF, RAN Andrews, & J Firth. *The Revolver 1816-1865*. (London, UK: Herbert Jenkins & Co 1968), pg 188.
6. Taylerson, AWF, RAN Andrews, & J Firth. *The Revolver 1816-1865*. (London, UK: Herbert Jenkins & Co 1968.)
7. Taylerson, AWF. *The Revolver: 1865-1888*. (London, UK: Herbert Jenkins & Co, 1966), pg 220, 236.
8. Taylerson, AWF. *The Revolver: 1865-1888*. (London, UK: Herbert Jenkins & Co, 1966), pg 236.
5. Blackmore, HL. *A dictionary of London Gunmakers*.(London: Christies, 1986), pg 180.
6. Sword, Wiley. *The Confederate Enfield and LeMat*. (Woonsocket, RI: Andrew Mowbray Incorporated, 1986).
7. Adams, Doug. *The Confederate LeMat revolver*. (Woonsocket, RI: Mowbray Publishing, 2005).
8. Taylerson, AWF, RAN Andrews, & J Firth. *The Revolver 1816-1865*. (London, UK: Herbert Jenkins & Co, 1968), pg 363.
9. Taylerson, AWF, RAN Andrews, & J Firth. *The Revolver 1816-1865*. (London, UK: Herbert Jenkins & Co, 1968.)
10. Albaugh III, W. A., H. Benet, and E. Simmons. *Confederate handguns: Concerning the guns, the men who made them and the times of their use*. (Philadelphia, PA: Riling & Lenz, 1963.)
11. Albaugh III, W. A., H. Benet, and E. Simmons. *Confederate handguns: Concerning the guns, the men who made them and the times of their use*. (Philadelphia, PA: Riling & Lenz, 1963).
12. Sword, Wiley. *The Confederate Enfield and LeMat*. (Woonsocket, RI: Andrew Mowbray Incorporated,1986).
13. Sword, Wiley. *The Confederate Enfield and LeMat*. (Woonsocket, RI: Andrew Mowbray Incorporated,1986).
14. Taylerson, AWF, RAN Andrews, & J Firth. *The Revolver 1816-1865*. (London, UK: Herbert Jenkins & Co 1968.)
15. Adams, Doug. *The Confederate LeMat revolver*. (Woonsocket, RI: Mowbray Publishing, 2005.)
16. Albaugh III, W. A., H. Benet, and E. Simmons. *Confederate handguns: Concerning the guns, the men who made them and the times of their use*. (Philadelphia, PA: Riling & Lenz, 1963).

17. Albaugh III, W. A., H. Benet, and E. Simmons. *Confederate handguns: Concerning the guns, the men who made them and the times of their use.* (Philadelphia, PA: Riling & Lenz, 1963).
18. Taylerson, AWF, RAN Andrews, & J Firth. *The Revolver 1816-1865.* (London, UK: Herbert Jenkins & Co 1968.)
19. Taylerson, AWF, RAN Andrews, & J Firth. *The Revolver 1816-1865.* (London, UK: Herbert Jenkins & Co 1968.)
20. Albaugh III, W. A., H. Benet, and E. Simmons. *Confederate handguns: Concerning the guns, the men who made them and the times of their use.* (Philadelphia, PA: Riling & Lenz, 1963).
21. Albaugh III, W. A., H. Benet, and E. Simmons. *Confederate handguns: Concerning the guns, the men who made them and the times of their use.* (Philadelphia, PA: Riling & Lenz, 1963).
22. Adams, Doug. *The Confederate LeMat revolver.* (Woonsocket, RI: Mowbray Publishing, 2005)
23. Blackmore, HL. *A dictionary of London Gunmakers.*(London: Christies,1986), pg 120.
24. Chamberlain W.H.J and A.W.F Taylerson. *Adams' Revolvers.* (London, UK: Barrie & Jenkins, 1976), pg 201.
25. Adams, Doug. *The Confederate LeMat revolver.* (Woonsocket, RI: Mowbray Publishing, 2005)
26. Taylerson, AWF. *The Revolver: 1865-1888.* (London, UK: Herbert Jenkins & Co, 1966), pg 77.
27. Taylerson, AWF. *The Revolver: 1865-1888.* (London, UK: Herbert Jenkins & Co, 1966), pg 325.
28. Taylerson, AWF, RAN Andrews, & J Firth. *The Revolver 1816-1865.* (London, UK: Herbert Jenkins & Co 1968.)

CHAPTER 3: Adams and Beaumont-Adams Revolvers
1. Chamberlain W.H.J and A.W.F Taylerson. *Adams' Revolvers.* (London, UK: Barrie & Jenkins, 1976), pg 55.
2. Chamberlain W.H.J and A.W.F Taylerson. *Adams' Revolvers.* (London, UK: Barrie & Jenkins, 1976).
3. Taken from the original London Armoury Company (Limited) trade circular, included in Chamberlain W.H.J and A.W.F Taylerson. *Adams' Revolvers.* (London, UK: Barrie & Jenkins, 1976), pg 78.
4. Chamberlain W.H.J and A.W.F Taylerson. *Adams' Revolvers.* (London, UK: Barrie & Jenkins, 1976), pg 92.
5. Chamberlain W.H.J and A.W.F Taylerson. *Adams' Revolvers.* (London, UK: Barrie & Jenkins, 1976), pg 70.
6. Chamberlain W.H.J and A.W.F Taylerson. *Adams' Revolvers.* (London, UK: Barrie & Jenkins, 1976), pg 62.
7. Chamberlain W.H.J and A.W.F Taylerson. *Adams' Revolvers.* (London, UK: Barrie & Jenkins, 1976), pg 53.
8. Chamberlain W.H.J and A.W.F Taylerson. *Adams' Revolvers.* (London, UK: Barrie & Jenkins, 1976), pg 74.
9. Chamberlain W.H.J and A.W.F Taylerson. *Adams' Revolvers.* (London, UK: Barrie & Jenkins, 1976), pg 108.

CHAPTER 4: Tranter Revolvers
1. Taylerson, AWF, RAN Andrews, & J Firth. *The Revolver 1816-1865.* (London, UK: Herbert Jenkins & Co 1968), pg 272.
2. George, J.N. *English Pistols and Revolvers.* (Whitefish, MN: Kessinger Publishing, reprint 2010).
3. Taylerson, AWF, RAN Andrews, & J Firth. *The Revolver 1816-1865.* (London, UK: Herbert Jenkins & Co 1968), pg 278.
4. Taylerson, AWF, RAN Andrews, & J Firth. *The Revolver 1816-1865.* (London, UK: Herbert Jenkins & Co 1968), pg 286.
5. The Firearms Technology Museum (www.firearmsmuseum.org.au).
6. The Firearms Technology Museum (www.firearmsmuseum.org.au).
7. The Firearms Technology Museum (www.firearmsmuseum.org.au).
8. The Firearms Technology Museum (www.firearmsmuseum.org.au).

CHAPTER 5: Webley Revolvers
1. Bruce, G., and C. Reinhart. *Webley revolvers: Revised from William Chipchase Dowell's the Webley Story.* (Verlag Stocker-Schmidt AG, 1988), pg 19.
2. Bruce, G., and C. Reinhart. *Webley revolvers: Revised from William Chipchase Dowell's the Webley Story.* (Verlag Stocker-Schmidt AG, 1988), pg 31.
3. Taylerson, AWF, RAN Andrews, & J Firth. *The Revolver 1816-1865.* (London, UK: Herbert Jenkins & Co 1968), pg 263.
4. Taylerson, AWF, RAN Andrews, & J Firth. *The Revolver 1816-1865.* (London, UK: Herbert Jenkins & Co 1968), pg 265.
5. Taylerson, AWF, RAN Andrews, & J Firth. *The Revolver 1816-1865.* (London, UK: Herbert Jenkins & Co 1968), pg 265.
6. Taylerson, AWF, RAN Andrews, & J Firth. *The Revolver 1816-1865.* (London, UK: Herbert Jenkins & Co 1968), pg 324.
7. Taylerson, AWF, RAN Andrews, & J Firth. *The Revolver 1816-1865.* (London, UK: Herbert Jenkins & Co 1968), pg 265.
8. Taylerson, AWF, RAN Andrews, & J Firth. *The Revolver 1816-1865.* (London, UK: Herbert Jenkins & Co 1968), pg 270.
9. Bruce, G., and C. Reinhart. *Webley revolvers: Revised from William Chipchase Dowell's the Webley Story.* (Verlag Stocker-Schmidt AG, 1988).
10. Bruce, G., and C. Reinhart. *Webley revolvers: Revised from William Chipchase Dowell's the Webley Story.* (Verlag Stocker-Schmidt AG, 1988), pg 74.
11. Bruce, G., and C. Reinhart. *Webley revolvers: Revised from William Chipchase Dowell's the Webley Story.* (Verlag Stocker-Schmidt AG, 1988) pg s 80– 81.
12. Black, J., H. Ficken, and F. Michaels. *Webley Solid Frame Revolvers: Nos. 1, 1 ½, 2, BullDogs, and Pugs* (Atglen, PA: Schiffer Publishing (Dec. 2008)
13. Bruce, G., and C. Reinhart. *Webley revolvers: Revised from William Chipchase Dowell's the Webley Story.* (Verlag Stocker-Schmidt AG, 1988), pg 89.

14. Bruce, G., and C. Reinhart. *Webley revolvers: Revised from William Chipchase Dowell's the Webley Story.* (Verlag Stocker-Schmidt AG, 1988), pg 116–117.
15. Bruce, G., and C. Reinhart. *Webley revolvers: Revised from William Chipchase Dowell's the Webley Story.* (Verlag Stocker-Schmidt AG, 1988), pg 102.

CHAPTER 6: English Military Pistols and Revolvers
1. Blackmore, H L. *British Military firearms: 1650–1850.* (London, UK: Herbert Jenkins & Co, 1961) Appendices E and D.
2. Chamberlain W.H.J and A.W.F Taylerson. *Adams' Revolvers.* (London, UK: Barrie & Jenkins, 1976), pg 29.
3. Chamberlain W.H.J and A.W.F Taylerson. *Adams' Revolvers.* (London, UK: Barrie & Jenkins, 1976), pg 36, pg 81.
4. Flayderman, Norm. *Flayderman's Guide to Antique American Firearms ...and their values*: (Iola, WI: Krause Publications), pg 76.
5. Chamberlain W.H.J and A.W.F Taylerson. *Adams' Revolvers.* (London, UK: Barrie & Jenkins, 1976), pg 133.
6. Chamberlain W.H.J and A.W.F Taylerson. *Adams' Revolvers.* (London, UK: Barrie & Jenkins, 1976), pg 81–84.
7. Chamberlain W.H.J and A.W.F Taylerson. *Adams' Revolvers.* (London, UK: Barrie & Jenkins, 1976), pg 149–153.
8. Chamberlain W.H.J and A.W.F Taylerson. *Adams' Revolvers.* (London, UK: Barrie & Jenkins, 1976), pg 147-148.
9. Chamberlain W.H.J and A.W.F Taylerson. *Adams' Revolvers.* (London, UK: Barrie & Jenkins, 1976), pg 101.
10. Chamberlain W.H.J and A.W.F Taylerson. *Adams' Revolvers.* (London, UK: Barrie & Jenkins, 1976), pg 154–158.
11. Bruce, G., and C. Reinhart. *Webley revolvers: Revised from William Chipchase Dowell's the Webley Story.* (Verlag Stocker-Schmidt AG, 1988).
12. Bruce, G., and C. Reinhart. *Webley revolvers: Revised from William Chipchase Dowell's the Webley Story.* (Verlag Stocker-Schmidt AG, 1988), pg 247.

CHAPTER 7: Accessories
1. Pollard, HBC(later editions edited by Claude Blair). Pollard's History of Firearms: (UK: Countryside books, 1983).

CHAPTER 8: Collecting Antique Revolvers
1. Home Office website. www. Homeoffice.gov.uk

APPENDIX 1: Proof Marks
1. Blackmore, H L. *British Military firearms: 1650–1850.* (London, UK: Herbert Jenkins & Co, 1961), Appendix D.

Bibliography

GENERAL

Blackmore, H.L. *A dictionary of London Gunmakers*. (London, UK: Christies, 1986). Just what it says, a complete list of every London gun maker from the days of the Guilds. Includes a section on gunmakers' marks and a discussion of the development of the trade, including the London revolver makers.

Brown, Nigel. *British Gunmakers: Volume 1 ; London, Volume 2 ; Birmingham, Volume 3 : Index , appendices and additional information*. (Shrewsbury,UK: Quiller, 2008). Complete information about the early British gun trade, including makers.

Flayderman, Norm. *Flayderman's Guide to Antique American Firearms ...and their values*. (Iola, WI: Krause Publications). An excellent book for the beginning collector. The author discusses fakes, buying, and selling; in fact, much that a newcomer to the arms collecting hobby needs to know. A good buy and a good read, even for those not mainly interested in American arms.

Pollard, HBC (later editions edited by Claude Blair). *Pollard's History of Firearms*. (UK: Countryside Books, 1983). Still one of the best and most thorough accounts of firearms history.

REVOLVERS

Blackmore, H.L. *British Military Firearms: 1650–1850*. (London, UK: Herbert Jenkins & Co, 1961).

George, JN. *English Pistols and Revolvers*. (Whitefish, MN: Kessinger Publishing, reprint 2010).

Taylerson, AWF, RAN Andrews, & J Firth. *The Revolver 1816-1865*. (London, UK: Herbert Jenkins & Co 1968).

Taylerson, AWF. *The Revolver: 1865-1888*. (London, UK: Herbert Jenkins & Co, 1966)

Taylerson, AWF. *The Revolver: 1889-1914*. (London, UK: Barrie & Jenkins: Clements Inn, London, 1970)

SPECIFIC MAKERS AND MANUFACTURERS

Adams D. A. Le Mat & Co.: P.G.T. *Beauregard and the American Le Mat Revolver*. (American Society of Arms Collectors Bulletin, 1995).

Adams, Doug. *The Confederate LeMat Revolver*. (Woonsocket, RI: Mowbray Publishing, 2005)

Albaugh III, W. A., H. Benet, and E. Simmons. *Confederate handguns: Concerning the guns, the men who made them and the times of their use*. (Philadelphia, PA: Riling & Lenz, 1963)

Berk, Wolfgang. *William Tranter, Birmingham*. (Devon, UK: Prospect Books, 2009)

Black, J., H. Ficken, and F. Michaels. *Webley Solid-frame Revolvers: Nos. 1, 1 ½, 2, Bull Dogs, and Pugs*. (Atglen, PA: Schiffer Publishing, December 2008)

Black, J, J.L. Davis and R.G. Michaud. *Webley Solid-frame Revolvers: Models RIC, MP, and No 5*. (Atglen, PA: Schiffer Publishing, 2008)

Bruce, G., C. Reinhart. *Webley Revolvers: Revised from William Chipchase Dowell's the Webley Story*. (Verlag Stocker-Schmidt AG, 1988). Unfortunately out of print and so extremely difficult to obtain.

Chamberlain W.H.J and A.W.F Taylerson. *Adams' Revolvers*. (London, UK: Barrie & Jenkins, 1976)

Dowell, W. C. *The Webley Story: A history of Webley pistols and revolvers, and the development of the pistol cartridge*. (London, UK: Armory Publications, 1987). An excellent book, although expensive and sometimes difficult to obtain. The British Library has several copies available in the UK through most local libraries. It is also available as a revised edition by Gordon Bruce and Christian Reinhart.

Edwards, William B. *The Story of Colt's Revolver: The Biography of Col. Samuel Colt*. (Mechanicsburg, PA: The Stackpole Company.)

Layman, George. *The British Bulldog Revolver: The Forgotten Gun that Really Won the West*. (Woonsocket, RI: Mowbray Publishing, 1978)

Rosa, Joseph G. Colonel. *Colt London: The History of Colt's London firearms, 1851-1857*. (London, UK: Arms & Armour Press, 1976).

Sword, Wiley. *The Confederate Enfield and LeMat.*. (Woonsocket, RI: Andrew Mowbray Incorporated,1986).

MODERN FIREARMS

Gander, T. *Jane's Guns Recognition Guide*. (London, UK: Collins-Janes, 2005)

Hogg, I. *Pistols of the World*. (Krause Publications, 4th Edition, 2004)

WEBSITES;

The Firearms Technology Museum (www.firearmsmuseum.org.au). An excellent collection of Tranter revolvers, both percussion and metal cartridge.

The Cartridge Collector Exchange (www.old ammo.com.). An excellent, well presented site and easy to use, even for the absolute beginner.

Index

Accessories	
Bullet moulds	139
Cases and cased guns	139
Percussion cone keys	142
Oil bottles	143
Powder flasks	143
Cartridges and cartridge boxes	144
Powder testers	144
Adams military revolvers	
Adams 1867 A	122
Adams 1867 B	123
Adams 1872	125
Adams MkI cartridge revolver	121
Adams MkII cartridge revolver	123
Adams Mk III cartridge revolver	125
Adams revolvers	
In use	50
Makers	53
Models	52
Safety bolt	51
Arbor catch	51
Rifling	51
Retailers	52
Adams, John	
Model 1857 revolver.	18
Model 1866 revolver.	19
Revolver making	13
Adams, Robert	
Revolver making	12
Antique firearms	
Classification in the United Kingdom	145
Home Office guidelines	145
Bailey Model 1858 revolver	19
Ball Model 1857 revolver	19
Beattie pepperbox revolver	20
Beaumont-Adams revolver	
Makers	56
Models	58
American-made revolvers	62
Cochran Model 1837 revolver	20
Collier Model 1818 flintlock revolver	21
Colt military revolvers	120
Colt, Sam	
Great Exhibition	14
Patent infringement: court case.	9
Revolver making	14
Revolvers	23
Cooper pepperbox revolver	29
Daw Model 1855 (see also: Pryse and Cashmore)	29
Deane, Adams & Deane	
Revolver making	13
Deanne-Harding Model 1858 revolver	31
Dodds Model 1835 revolver	34
Enfield revolver No 2	
Mk I	136
Mk I *	136
Mk I **	136
Enfield revolvers	
Mk I	126
Mk II	126
Faking	147
Flintlock and percussion military pistols	119
Harvey revolvers	
Model 1853	35
Model 1854	35
Kerr Model 1858/ 1859 revolver	36
Lang revolvers	38
Le Mat revolvers	
Krider revolvers	39
Continental Le Mats	40
1st Model revolvers	40
Transitional types	42
2nd Model revolvers	41
Barrel addresses and frame numbering	41
Moore & Harris Model 1852 revolver	45
Nock, Samuel	8
NRA condition standards	146
Pennel Model 1853 revolver	45
Pepperbox revolvers	11
Proof marks	
London House	148
Provisional proof mark	149
View mark	149
Definitive proof mark	149
Tower	149

Birmingham (Guardians)	150	Dual-Ignition model	71	"British Bull dog" revolver	99
Pryse and Cashmore (see also: Daw revolver)	29	Confederate revolvers	71	Copies	101
		Cartridge revolvers	72	.577 center-fire revolver	93
Reeves Model 1857/ 1858 Model revolver	46	No 1 revolvers	72	Pryse "No 4" revolver	104
		No 2 revolvers	73	Webley-Kaufmann	108
Restoration	147	House Defence revolvers	74	Pocket hammerless	117
Revolver characteristics	13	Model 1863	74	Webley-Fosbery Automatic revolver	116
Revolver making		Model 1868	75	Mk I – Mk VI revolvers	127
Hand-made	11	.577 revolver	75	Mk IV .38/200 revolver	135
Machine-made	12	Model 1868 "Extracting tip" revolver	76	Webley percussion revolvers	78
Robert Adams	12	Model 1868 "Pivoted rod extractor" revolver	76	1st Model Longspur	79
John Adams	13			2nd Model Longspur	81
Philip Webley	13	Model 1878	76	3rd Model Longspur	83
Sam Colt	13	RIC revolver	77	4th Model Longspur	85
		Kynoch revolvers	77	Philip Webley's Model 1853 revolver.	85
Transition revolvers	11				
Tranter revolvers		Wallis Model 1863 revolver	47	Bentley revolvers	86
Percussion revolvers	65	Webley metal cartridge revolvers	92	Webley-Bentley revolvers	87
1st Model	65	R.I.C. Model 1868, No 1	94	Double action revolvers	88
2nd Model	66	R.I.C. "New Model," No 1 RIC	96	Westley – Richards	
3rd Model	67	R.I.C. No 2	97	Pepperbox revolvers	48
4th Model	68	R.I.C. No 3	97	Model 1852 revolver	48
Triple-action Model	70	R.I.C. Model 83	98	Model 1855 revolver.	48
Adams, Tranter, Kerr Model	70	Metropolitan Police revolver	98		

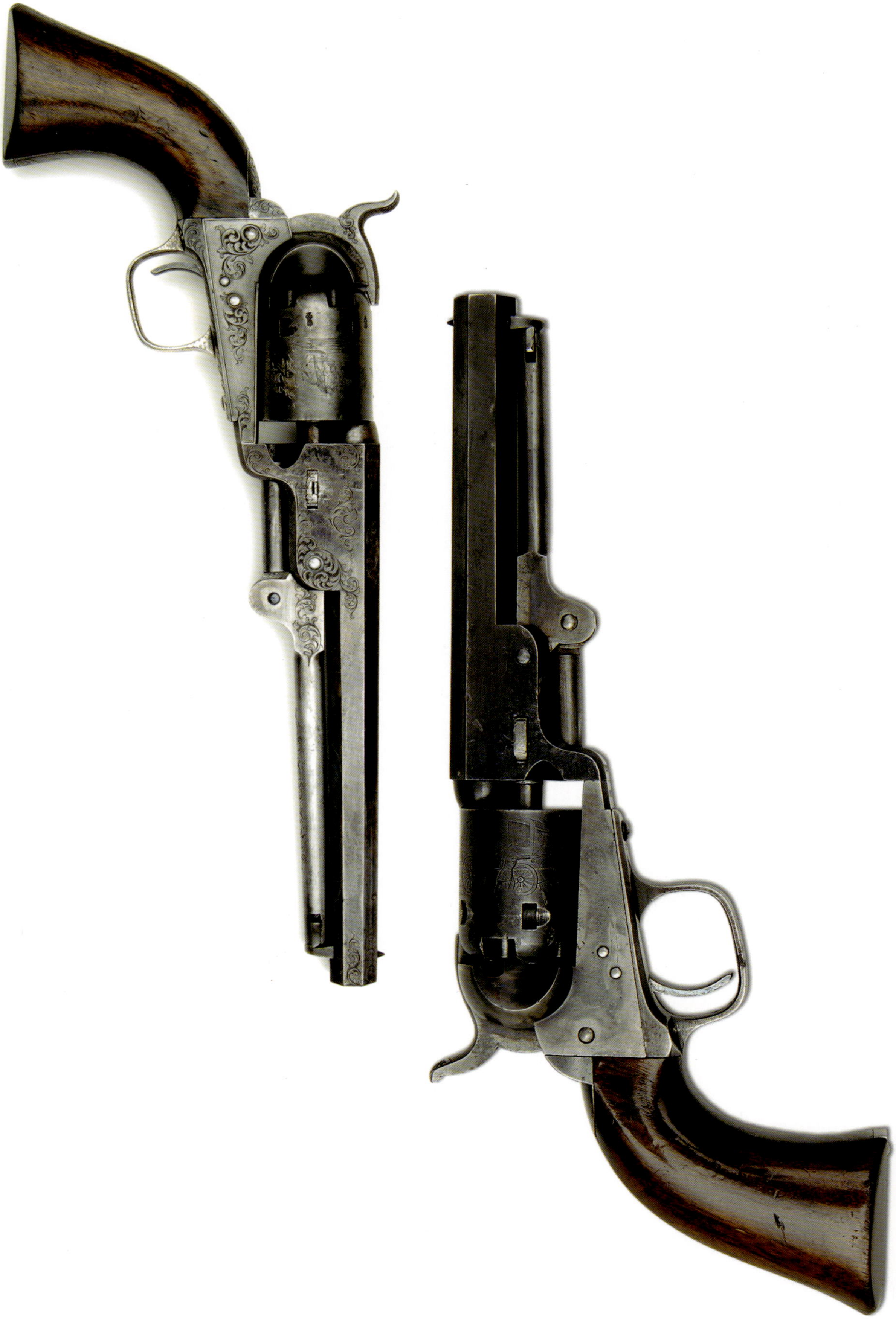

LR